READING THE LINES

READING THE LINES

A Fresh Look at the Hebrew Bible

PAMELA TAMARKIN REIS

HENDRICKSON PUBLISHERS

First Printing — June 2002

The chapters of the present work appeared in a different version in the following publications, and are used with permission: "The Bridegroom of Blood: A New Reading," *Judaism* 40, no. 3 (1991); "Dead Men Tell No Tales: On the Motivation of Joseph's Brothers," *Conservative Judaism* 44, no. 2 (1992); "Take My Wife, Please: On the Utility of the Wife/Sister Motif," *Judaism* 41, no. 4 (1992); "Collusion at Nob: A New Reading of 1 Samuel 21–22," *Journal for the Study of the Old Testament* 61, no. 1 (1994); "Vindicating God: Another Look at 1 Kings XIII," *Vetus Testamentum* 44, no. 3 (1994); "Eating the Blood: Saul and the Witch of Endor," *Journal for the Study of the Old Testament* 73, no. 1 (1997); "Spoiled Child: A Fresh Look at Jephthah's Daughter," *Prooftexts* 17, no. 2 (1997); "Cupidity and Stupidity: Woman's Agency and the 'Rape' of Tamar," *The Journal of the Ancient Near Eastern Society* 25 (1998); "Hagar Requited," *Journal for the Study of the Old Testament* 87, no. 1 (2000); "Rashomon and the Creation Narratives," *Bible Review* 17, no. 3 (2001); "What Cain Said: A Note on Genesis 4:8," *Journal for the Study of the Old Testament* 98, no. 4 (2002).

Cover art © The Jewish Museum, N.Y. / Art Resource, N.Y. Torah scroll, Germany, ca. 1840–50, 13 cm. high. Parchment with silver rollers.

Library of Congress Cataloging-in-Publication Data

Reis, Pamela Tamarkin, 1935–
    Reading the lines : a fresh look at the Hebrew Bible /
Pamela Tamarkin Reis.
        p. cm.
    Includes bibliographical references and index.
    ISBN 1-56563-696-1 (hardcover : alk. paper)
    1. Bible. O.T.—Criticism, interpretation, etc. I. Title.
    BS1188 .R45 2002
    221.6—dc21
                                                    2002003504

To my father, Joseph B. Tamarkin
May his memory be for a blessing

Table of Contents

Abbreviations

4QGen[b]	Qumran scroll of Genesis from Cave 4
AB	Anchor Bible
ASV	American Standard Version of the Bible
AThR	*Anglican Theological Review*
BDB	Brown, Driver, and Briggs, *A Hebrew and English Lexicon of the Old Testament*
Bib	*Biblica*
BZAW	Beihefte zur Zeitschrift für die alttestamentliche Wissenschaft
CamB	Cambridge Bible
CBC	Cambridge Bible Commentary
CBQ	*Catholic Biblical Quarterly*
HSM	Harvard Semitic Monographs
HUCA	*Hebrew Union College Annual*
IOSOT	International Organization for the Study of the Old Testament
JANESCU	*Journal of the Ancient Near Eastern Society of Columbia University*
JBL	*Journal of Biblical Literature*
JNES	*Journal of Near Eastern Studies*
JPS	Jewish Publication Society
JQR	*Jewish Quarterly Review*
JQRSup	Jewish Quarterly Review Supplements
JSJ	*Journal for the Study of Judaism in the Persian, Hellenistic, and Roman Periods*
JSOT	*Journal for the Study of the Old Testament*
JSOTSup	Journal for the Study of the Old Testament: Supplement Series
JSS	*Journal of Semitic Studies*
JTS	*Journal of Theological Studies*
KJV	King James Version of the Bible
LXX	Septuagint, the Greek translation of the Hebrew Bible/ Old Testament
MT	Masoretic Text, the traditional or received text of the Hebrew Bible/Old Testament
NICOT	New International Commentary on the Old Testament
NJPS	*Tanakh: The Holy Scriptures: The New JPS Translation according to the Traditional Hebrew Text*
NRSV	New Revised Standard Version of the Bible

OT	Old Testament
REB	Revised English Bible
RSV	Revised Standard Version of the Bible
SBLSP	*Society of Biblical Literature Seminar Papers*
SJOT	*Scandinavian Journal of the Old Testament*
USQR	*Union Seminary Quarterly Review*
VE	*Vox evangelica*
VT	*Vetus Testamentum*
VTSup	Vetus Testamentum Supplements
WBC	Word Biblical Commentary
ZAW	*Zeitschrift für die alttestamentliche Wissenschaft*

Introduction

In my sophomore year in college I read an article by Edmund Wilson, "On First Reading Genesis" (*The New Yorker,* May 15, 1954). In those days, when I bought a magazine, I felt compelled to read every article. I thought that was what grown-ups did. As a regular reader of *The New Yorker* from the age of twelve, I paid for enjoyment of the Profiles section and the fiction by plowing through every factual article, often despite little understanding and no interest—the race track news, the shopping advice, the political analyses—but I read Wilson's article with eagerness and attention.

Two aspects engaged me: one, that Wilson wrote as though he enjoyed reading the Bible, and two, that he had learned Hebrew at the advanced age of fifty or so and was able to read it in the original. I admired Edmund Wilson. I thought he was smart. He was the book reviewer for *The New Yorker,* after all, and he seemed to have read everything, to know several languages, and to be familiar with the literature of many periods and peoples. Just in this article on Genesis, he referred to Homer, Henry James, a recent issue of the German magazine *Der Monat,* John Burroughs, the tenses of Russian verbs, Anton Chekhov, and André Malraux. What did he see in the Bible—in Genesis, a book that I had started to read half a dozen times—that eluded me?

Although I kept returning to the Bible, it baffled and bored me. It was not its subtlety and sophistication that confounded me; on the contrary, I was blind to nuance, as I sped through the verses at my usual reading rate. What perplexed me was the fact that the Bible was the most read book in the Western world, that it was every year's best-seller, that college courses in "The Bible as Literature" were offered, that informal Bible study groups were advertised at my college and, I supposed, others as well. What was so good about it? What made people want to study it? I could understand its appeal to pious people who derived their beliefs from it, but why did it attract the non-religious like Wilson and me?

I had never attended Hebrew School or Sunday School, and so the only formal Bible study I had experienced was a week in a college summer school course called "Masterpieces of Literature." Along with other "masterpieces," the class read the book of Job. I knew the central idea of the book and was glad to think that I would be learning one explanation for the suffering of the innocent, for the evil in the world. It may not be an answer that contented me, I thought, but at least it would be a serious and time-honored response to a pervasive philosophical problem.

After conscientiously working through pages and pages of Job's scalding anguish and his friends' cold comfort, I was considerably disappointed to find that no answer is given at all. As Ring Lardner might have put it: "Shut up," God explained. Why was this book considered a "masterpiece of literature"? What was literary about it and about the rest of the Bible, I asked my professor. His reply had to do with universal themes, the same answer he gave to explain *Don Quixote*'s inclusion in our syllabus, but there were no *Don Quixote* study groups that I knew of, nor was it a yearly best-seller.

Edmund Wilson's article pointed out a few of the delights of Genesis; for example, he wrote of an instance of "telling" and "homely" dialogue when a visitor, God, informs Abraham that his elderly wife, Sarah, will have a son. Sarah, listening at the tent door, laughs to herself.

> "Why did Sarah laugh?" asks the visitor. "Does she think that God cannot do it?"

> "I didn't laugh," says Sarah, frightened. "No, but you did laugh," says God.

Well, O.K., that dialogue sounded homely to me; it sounded like an argument I might have with my brothers or sister: "Yes, you did." "No, I didn't." "Yes, you did." I could not see anything "telling" about it or masterful. To depict God bickering on a childlike level was certainly not elevating or instructive, as I assumed the Bible must be.

Mostly, however, Wilson stated without example that biblical situations were presented with a "sure stroke," that the personalities of the main characters "remain so convincing and interesting" that the narrative was "remarkable," and the stories had a "human truth" that has "caused them to haunt our imaginations." The verses were alive for Wilson, but not for me, and I attributed my failure to "get it" to the fact that I could not read the Hebrew Bible in the original (henceforth, whenever I refer to the Bible, I mean the Hebrew Bible—known to most non-Jews as the Old Testament), for the majority of his article concerned the nature of Hebrew. Tantalizingly, he praised non-translatable plays on words, jingles, vigorous expressiveness, and onomatopoeic effects. The allusions, the jokes and the puns, the emphases created by verb forms and syntax, apparent to him, were lost on me.

That a person in his dotage could learn a new language was the second aspect of Wilson's essay that had amazed me. By some means of calculation or another, I had figured out that Wilson had to have been at least fifty when he learned Hebrew. I was a preternaturally sophomoric nineteen; to me, college seniors represented the acme of adult wisdom and suavity. A man or woman of fifty appeared to me so wrinkled in mind and body, so slowed, so mentally dulled by the weight of years, that I could not imagine them capable of learning anything—much less anything so complex and difficult as a new language. Even my parents were not yet fifty. To be fifty was to be well on the way to the grave—with end-of-life concerns and debilitating aches and pains.

Because Edmund Wilson's mind was still agile despite his great age, I made a promise to myself. I resolved to learn Hebrew when I became fifty. It seemed unlikely to me that I could ever get that old, but if I did, what better way to steady a sputtering brain and to forestall senility than to learn something difficult and new? Wilson admitted that he may have been piqued by the fact that his grandfather, a Presbyterian minister, could read something that he, himself, could not. A similar incentive for me may have been that my three brothers, having become bar-mitzvahed, could read Hebrew, and I could not. But I do not remember any motivation other than the desire to deter decay.

And then the years passed, and fifty inexplicably neared. I remembered that I was supposed to learn Hebrew, but it seemed so hard to do—a whole new alphabet, and when would I fit instruction in, and besides, I felt as sprightly and alert as ever: not old at all. I had a daughter-in-law-to-be by this time, and she remarked one day that she wanted to learn Hebrew. I told her that I also wanted to learn Hebrew and had indeed vowed in my youth to do so right about now. "Why don't you then?" she ingenuously asked. My desire to look good to my future daughter-in-law trumped my laziness and inertia, and I enrolled in a synagogue class in biblical Hebrew for beginners.

My Hebrew progressed beyond the beginner's class but not much beyond. Once the class, was over, I worked my own way through *The First Hebrew Primer for Adults,* written by Nanette Stahl and others, a workbook of biblical and prayerbook Hebrew. My studies ended with this text. Edmund Wilson had said that he was able to read the Bible with the constant aid of a translation and a dictionary. I could do that.

Friends, proficient in Hebrew, say that I miss much, and I know that I do. But still, I catch something. The essays, collected here, have all been published previously in academic journals where they have been subjected to blind peer review. That is, the editors have no idea who wrote the articles they are evaluating. The authors could be, and usually are, fellow academics or perhaps an occasional advanced graduate student.

Strait is the gate and narrow the way that leads to publication in the world of biblical criticism. The select academic journals that address literary interpretation (or exegesis, which I learned is the preferred term in this discipline) of the Hebrew Bible publish quarterly or half-yearly, and some of these maintain a rigid critical position that precludes publication of contributions, however original and well-supported, written from an unconventional analytical perspective. Scholars the world over are eager to present their ideas; professors must publish or be denied promotion and even employment. Competition, therefore, for the few available avenues of publication is formidable. The refusal rate for submissions averages eighty-five percent. With no mastery of Hebrew, no background in biblical studies, and no ticket stamped Ph.D., I nevertheless had the *chutzpah* to venture into the ambitious world of literary criticism and to think that I could make a contribution to biblical scholarship because of three influences.

PERSPECTIVE

My first influence was my father. One day when I was about nine or ten, apropos of no previous conversation, he mentioned offhandedly to me that there were no mistakes in the Torah. I knew that the word, Torah, wasn't English, and I knew it referred to an important book of the Jews, but I did not know what book. I had already found the Bible boring, and if he had said Bible, I would have understood. But, as I learned many years later, he did not mean the entire Bible; he meant only the first five books, the Pentateuch, which to observant Jews are the words of God as recorded by the hand of Moses. The rest of the Bible could possibly have mistakes but not the Torah.

Although, as the joke goes, the synagogue that our family did not attend was of the Orthodox branch of Judaism, our home was non-observant. We did not keep the Sabbath, and we ate non-kosher food. My father had had a religious education (a religious education that extended from dawn to dusk six days a week—on the Sabbath, you studied for fun) growing up in Russia, but when he came to the United States in his teens, he worked six days a week and attended public high school at night. Once in a great while he would mention a talmudic dictum that he had learned in his youth. For example, if one of his five children sat in his accustomed chair, he would gently shoo the child away saying, "You're not supposed to do that." We might say, "Who says?" and he would reply, "The Talmud."

I confused the Talmud with the Torah for more years than I care to admit. They were both two-syllable words, beginning with "T," referring to Jewish writings. Nevertheless, despite my ignorance of what my father was talking about when he told me there were no mistakes in the Torah, I was not shy to sass and did not hesitate to rebut, "Oh, there probably *are* mistakes." "No," my father said patiently, "If you think there's a mistake, it's because you're too dumb to figure it out."

My father was speaking generally when he said "you"; he certainly did not literally mean me, as he thought I was smart enough to figure anything out. I thought so too, and the notion that there was a book with opaque passages, penetrable only to the bright, captivated me. I did not know if I would ever tackle the Torah, whatever it was, but I rehearsed my father's words to myself many times and contemplated solving the mysteries that others could not.

When I grew up and read about the Bible (reading the Bible itself was still too tedious), I found to my distaste and annoyance that the majority of biblical scholars since the nineteenth century has adhered to the source-critical or documentary hypothesis school of biblical criticism.

This persuasion scrutinizes the origins of the Bible and holds that all of it, in particular the first five books—the Torah that my father so respected—was compiled from disparate sources, written by diverse authors in different time periods and edited (or, to use the more stylish term, redacted) by a person or persons whose only mandate was to include every scrap of legend, myth, genealogy, political propaganda, and old wives' tale at hand no matter how contradictory or repetitive. Source critics study the entire Bible but particularly endeavor to demonstrate the composite nature of the Pentateuch, since everyone, however religious, agrees that the remaining books of the Bible were written by several authors.

The preponderance of biblical commentators believe the Torah was composed by four authors, or schools of authors, whom they label J, E, P, and D. J is the first letter of the name, Jehovah. In the chapters or verses credited to J, God's name is spelled יהוה in Hebrew. Initially, the dominant documentary hypothesists were German-speakers who considered the Hebrew ' similar to a J. Jehovah was their transliteration of יהוה. Jews make no attempt to enunciate these four letters, consider it disrespectful to do so, and in reading aloud, substitute another word, usually *adonai,* which means Lord. The letters in the Hebrew alphabet are consonants; vowels are indicated by little dots, dashes, and symbols written above and below the consonants. The vowels assigned to יהוה are those for adonai to remind the speaker to substitute this appellation. The Germans used these vowels in formulating their pronunciation. In subsequent years, recognizing the inaccuracy of their vowel use, Jehovah was replaced with Jahweh or Yahweh—an attempt to pronounce just the four consonants.

The E author is named for *Elohim,* the first letter in the transliteration of the Hebrew word for God or gods. This word can refer to the solitary God of the Hebrews, to a pagan god, or to an entire pantheon of divinities. According to the source critics, the E author uses this generic name for God in the parts of the Bible assigned to him. The P writer, or writers, are the priests, and D is the Deuteronomist—responsible for most of Deuteronomy. There are subsets of these schools, and, further complicating attribution, some verses are credited to boundary-crossing combinations of these originators.

"There goes the fun," I thought when I learned of the nearly universal multiple-author doctrine. What interest or amusement could there be in resolving a problem passage when it would be easier and perhaps more accurate to decree that the troublesome verses were written by authors with divergent agendas and were slapped together willy-nilly by inattentive or obsessive redactors? This critical bandwagon was not for me, no matter how many learned scholars were on it. I did not know whether my father and his orthodox teachers were right or if the source critics were right, but I chose to be biased in favor of my father's opinion—partly to honor his memory (he had died when I was twenty-five) but mostly because I resented the kill-joy convictions of the documentary hypothesists. I decided, should I ever get around to reading it, to proceed under the assumption that every word in the Torah was there for a reason. I did not believe that the first five books of the Bible were dictated to Moses by God, but I did not find that ideology necessary in order to enjoy the prospect of the Torah's intellectual challenge. Indeed, I elected to assume that everything in the entire Bible was written purposefully by some author or another or redacted brilliantly by a super-attentive literary genius or geniuses and not assembled by hazard or compulsion. I *am* from Missouri, as it happens (born in St. Louis), and the source critics would have to show me.

Having taken a position of scepticism toward popular biblical scholarship, I found that the more I learned about it, the more strained and arbitrary it seemed. Among the criteria documentary hypothesists use to establish multiple authorship of the Torah are the propositions that an author does not contradict or repeat himself, change style in the middle of a composition, or digress. Without giving these qualifications a whole minute's thought, I could readily call to mind a short story by the Irish writer, James Stephens, the force of which depends wholly on the techniques of contradiction and repetition. The first part of the story tells of an impoverished widow's only son who swerves his bicycle to avoid hitting a chicken, falls, and dies. The widow bewails his death, and cries something like: "Why did he have to swerve; what's a chicken?" The story then starts over again, repeating every detail, except that in the second part, the boy runs the chicken down. In this second version the mother berates her son, deplores his carelessness, asks if he realizes the value of a chicken to a poor woman, and so embarrasses him before the neighbors that he goes to America never to see her again. The power of chance in determining the alternate realities of the widow's loss of her son is thus flashed before the reader. Were Stephens's short story to fall under the gaze of the source critics, their own standards of seemly narrative would compel them to stipulate two authors. For these critics, Stephens's story would be a proof text signaling two original sources and a redactor unwilling to privilege one variation of the tale over the other.

As for digression and changes of style, how would these critics assess T. S. Eliot's poem, *The Waste Land,* if they thought it were anonymously authored centuries ago? The first two lines: "April is the cruelest month, breeding lilacs out of the dead land," would surely be emended to "April is the coolest month [for] breeding lilacs out of the dead land." "Cruel" would be considered a scribal error for "cool" as months cannot have human characteristics, and April is the coolest month of the year during which lilacs will bloom in England. Line 12 of the poem: "Bin gar keine Russin, stamm' aus Litauen, echt deutsch," digresses completely from the weather report of the earlier verses and, to make its independent authorship even more obvious to the source critics, is in German rather than English. The blatant style change in lines 170–172, wherein current British working class vernacular segues into a quotation from *Hamlet:* "Goonight Bill. Goonight Lou. Goonight May. Goonight. Ta ta. Goonight. Goonight. Goodnight, ladies, good night, sweet ladies, goodnight, goodnight," would flag a temporal and authorial inconsistency according to the literary conventions of the source critics. To them the awkward juxtaposition would expose that, led astray by the similarity in expression, the redactor spliced the quotidian to the Shakespearian, thus creating a clumsy and anachronistic suture in the narrative.

It seemed to me that these critics would allow any device of literary art to modern writers simply because they were contemporary, au courant, and therefore able to implement complex, sophisticated, elaborate techniques in their compositions; whereas they deny these same techniques, and others even more inventive, to ancient writers because they judged them bumpkins, too uncultivated and ignorant for such artifice. The ancients wrote so long ago, how could they employ the polished intricacies of today's artists? Even where the documentary hypothesists admit the artfulness of a particular passage—the more recent the scholarship, the more craft is discerned—when a difficulty arises, a mistake is called. If it is not the author's mistake, it is the redactor's; nowadays, when the redactor has begun to receive somewhat more respect from this school of interpretation, perceived mistakes are often imputed to the scribe. Source critics have to find someone at fault for their failure to grasp a perplexing patch, and it is never the reader. Because of my father's influence, if I do not understand a passage, I blame only my own obtuseness.

TECHNIQUE

My father gave me a bias; my next influence gave me a technique. In my senior year of college I registered for a course called "Understanding Modern Poetry." There were a few books of poetry around our house when I was growing up: Francis Palgrave's anthology, *The Golden Treasury,* A. E. Housman's *A Shropshire Lad,* and, the anthology that gave me trouble, Oscar Williams's *A Little Treasury of Modern Poetry.* The latter had some "easy" poems in it but also many incomprehensible ones. Learning to appreciate the poetry I found so obscure was the sort of opportunity I had hoped to find at college, and I could hardly wait for the first day of class.

When I walked into the classroom that first day, I saw that the professor had copied the following two-stanza A. E. Housman poem onto the blackboard.

With rue my heart is laden
For golden friends I had,
For many a rose-lipt maiden
And many a lightfoot lad.

By brooks too broad for leaping
The lightfoot boys are laid.
The rose-lipt girls are sleeping
In fields where roses fade.

"Oh, for pity's sake!" I thought to myself, "such an easy poem"; not only did I understand every word—the poet once had young friends; now they're dead—but I had learned it by heart years ago. If the class were going to be taught on the level of the thickest student, which it looked as though it were, I was going to slip away and register for something else.

The professor entered the room before I could make my get-away, gave the class a couple of minutes to read the poem, and asked: "Why does the poet use 'rue' in the first line?" Already slumping in my chair, I raised my hand and said wearily, "He needed a one-syllable word for sorrow." The professor (George Nitchie, himself a poet) did not suffer sass so patiently as my father and snapped: "Then he could have used 'grief.'" I sat up straight. "Yeah," I thought, "why didn't he use 'grief'?" Galvanized now by the surprise that the poet choose "rue," that very word and no synonym, for a reason, I paid attention.

Having elicited no other answer from the class with his first question, the teacher moved on to "laden"; why was that particular word chosen? I thought to myself that, had I been the poet, I would have said "With woe my heart is weighted" and gotten a little alliteration with the opening "With" going for me, but I was not about to stick my neck out again. Gradually, and by dint of much effort, the professor got the class to notice that "rue" and "laden" were old-fashioned words that heightened the romantic tenor of the first stanza with its golden maidens and lads. In the second stanza, he finally made us see, the romance comes crashing down; the alliterative description "lightfoot lads" is abdicated for the unromantic "boys." The "rose-lipt maidens" are similarly brought to earth with the designation "girls."

When the professor had said all there was to say about the contrast created by vocabulary between the sentimental nostalgia of the first verse and the flat realism of the second verse, he started on the meter, the cadence, the word order, the alliteration or lack thereof, and explained how these features of the poem added to the meaning. By the end of the period, there was nothing left of the deceptively simple poem I had memorized, and I had learned a technique that is now called "close reading." I knew no special name for it then. It was just the way one read a dense text like a poem or the Bible, a text that packs the greatest possible meaning in the fewest possible words. We did go on that semester to consider the works of poets I had deemed more difficult—Eliot, Yeats, Pound—and their poems provided practice in using the technique that had been imparted to me in that revelatory first fifty minutes.

The Bible has had no dearth of close readers who pondered its every word and labeled none as written in error. Religious interpreters, both Jews and Christians, have generally taken a reverent attitude toward the author or authors of the Bible, since they consider their writing to be divinely inspired. About fifteen hundred years ago, the Jews developed a literature called midrash (derived from the Hebrew verb "to seek") whose raison d'être was solving problems in the sacred books, supplementing the author's spare style, smoothing rough patches, and harmonizing contradictions. Although, since they believed there were no mistakes in the Torah, their approach is more to my taste than the condescending fault-finding of the source critics, I do not find the midrashic exegeses completely satisfactory either.

Midrash is more interested in the religious implications of the text than in its literary style. It will sermonize on the stimulus of a perceived gap or redundancy, an unusual spelling or syntax, and find in it concealed legal significance rather than artistic design. The midrashists also often become extremely creative, even fanciful, in their explication of a verse, and I prefer to stick to the words of the Bible, to rely not on imagination but on textual support, to read the lines, not between the lines.

My father related to me a well-known midrash that I thought for years was actually in the Bible. He said that when Abraham was a child, anxious to convert his idol-maker father to monotheism, he destroyed all but the largest idol in his father's inventory. When taxed to say what had happened, Abraham said that the large idol remaining had demolished the others. Not quite George Washington and the cherry tree, but Abraham's righteous purpose was to make his father recognize the powerlessness of man-made gods.

This story is not in the Bible; it was invented to solve a problem the midrashists found in the text. The problem lies in Genesis 12:1 in which God says to Abraham: "Get thee out of thy country and from thy kindred, and from thy father's house." The midrashists, who are comfortable with no redundancy, must have asked: "Why does the Torah say 'kindred' *and* 'father's house'; does not a man's 'kindred' include his father?" One midrashic answer to this question produced the ingeniously embroidered story of Abraham's boyhood. If Abraham's father were an idol-maker, a man with a vested interest in paganism, he had been and would continue to be a bad influence on his son. God is not telling Abraham to physically leave his father—that instruction is encompassed by 'kindred' in the preceding clause; God is giving Abraham a spiritual direction—to desert the example of his father and his idolatrous ways, and that is why it was necessary for the author to specify "his father's house."

Though my perspective is literary rather than religious, I, like the midrashists, also try to notice and account for every gap, redundancy, or seeming non-essential in the text. I am mindful that the Bible is a faith document and reflects a particular theology, but its artistry dazzles and absorbs me irrespective of its underlying philosophy. When I am seized by an idea and study the passage in question, I read and reread it over and over again. I try to sensitize myself to every word that is there and to whatever is not there but should be. I look at midrash on the passage to see if they have noticed a problem that I have missed, but I do not try to read "in" to the book; I try to read "out" of it, to see what the writer, by the exercise of his craft, intended the close reader to see.

The Bible demands reader participation. We must bring our own empathic sensibility to the text, for the author, in telling the story in the fewest possible words, leaves room for us. He rarely tells us what anyone feels or thinks; we must intuit that. He does not pass judgment on behavior; we must judge. He does not set the tone of a scene with description or guide us with adjectives and adverbs; he recounts sparely, and that is all. We must be more attentive than the modern reader is wont to be in order to see both what is and is not there.

I once heard a lecture by Bible scholar, Uriel Simon, on Genesis 22, the binding of Isaac. Professor Simon told of Abraham taking the wood, the fire, and the knife and going up the mountain to sacrifice his son, Isaac. Isaac asks his father: "Behold the fire and the wood, but where is the lamb for the burnt-offering?" (v. 7). Professor Simon asked the audience what was left out, what was missing in Isaac's question. There was a long pause before someone noted that Isaac omitted to mention the knife. This omission, Professor Simon said, indicates that Isaac is already apprehensive and cannot, in his fear, bring himself to say the word "knife." Once the subtle effect has been pointed out, it seems unarguable that when the author lists three items and only two are repeated, the reader is supposed to notice the missing third and to reflect on it. The pathos and terror of the scene become excruciating once the reader realizes that Isaac knows what is to befall him, and, from the word missing in his question, that his father knows he knows—and yet the two continue in silence together up the hill. Their silence and the author's silence is far more affective and chilling than any amount of piled-on adjectives describing Isaac's dread and Abraham's torment.

I remember a nonsense rhyme from my childhood:

When I was walking on the stair,
I met a man that wasn't there.
He wasn't there again today,
Oh how I wish he'd stay away.

How is one to know when words are purposefully omitted, left out by chance, or not left out at all? My perspective does not allow for the possibility of chance or accident in this brilliant author's work; what wordsmith uses, or fails to use, a word by mistake? But to preclude my inventing a verbal "man that wasn't there," I look for substantiation. Does it make logical sense to expect to read the missing word or words? Is meaning added by positing something missing? Does the rest of the story support that interpretation? The example above, the list of three items repeated with an item omitted, fulfills my criteria.

In the Joseph story, we are told that he is imprisoned in Egypt on a false charge of attempted rape. During his years of incarceration, he establishes a reputation as an interpreter of dreams, and when the Pharaoh has disturbing recurrent dreams, Joseph is summoned. The Bible says, "Then Pharaoh sent and called Joseph, and they brought him hastily out of the dungeon: and he shaved, and changed his garments, and came in unto Pharaoh" (Genesis 41:14). Although he was brought "hastily," the author slows the action to tell us that Joseph shaved and changed clothes. The Bible is terse; there is no filler. The close reader wonders why the author finds it important to include these details of Joseph's grooming. How is the story advanced by the knowledge that Joseph shaved and changed?

I think the need for this information is revealed by that which is missing from the account. Would not one expect Joseph to wash? The sanitary facilities of Egyptian prisons thousands of years ago were probably not up to AAA standards; had they been, it would not have been necessary for Joseph to shave and change clothing. Were we meant to assume that Joseph bathed, then why should we not assume the other preparations as well? If the author wanted to retard the story in order to hold the reader in suspense a little longer, he would have had all the more reason to include Joseph's ablutions. Yet he troubles to tell us that Joseph shaved and changed and does not mention that he bathed.

The issue, I believe, is not hygiene. The author did not tell us that Joseph bathed because he was not informing us of Joseph's toilette; he was imparting the fact that Joseph shaved and changed clothing in an attempt to look Egyptian—not to pass as an Egyptian, for the Pharaoh knew Joseph was a Hebrew, but in order, perhaps, to look more acceptable and familiar to the Pharaoh. We learn from the last chapter of Genesis that after his kindred came to Egypt they followed his lead in assimilation: not only are the excessive, and later proscribed, funerary practices of the Egyptians emulated, "And Joseph commanded his servants the physicians to embalm his father: and the physicians embalmed Israel. And forty days were fulfilled for him; for so are fulfilled the days of those which are embalmed" (50:2–3). But when Joseph and his brothers go to Canaan to bury their father, they are observed by the Canaanites who mistake them for Egyptians: "And when the inhabitants of the land, the Canaanites, saw the mourning in the floor of Atad, they said, 'This is a grievous mourning to the Egyptians'" (v. 11).

It makes logical sense to expect to read that Joseph bathed once we are told about shaving and changing. It advances the story, therefore, to posit that this word was missing in order to disclose that Joseph's motivation was identification with the Egyptians and not tidiness. The rest of the narrative confirms this interpretation, and the irony of the first chapter of Exodus is augmented: the Hebrews are considered strangers by the Egyptians and are enslaved by them. The integration attempts are unavailing;

bearded or shaven, dressed as Hebrews or clothed as Egyptians, mourning by Hebrew custom or by Egyptian rite, the Hebrews remain outsiders.

PERMISSION

My third influence was a verse in Deuteronomy, the fifth book of the Torah itself. When I was learning my smattering of Hebrew, I went to services so that I could fortify my studies by hearing Hebrew pronounced. As the Torah was read, I would try to follow along. Sometimes I noticed peculiarities in the narrative, and I wondered why the author told the story as he did, why he used a particular word, why he introduced but did not continue a plot line, why he omitted information I thought essential and included details that seemed insignificant. I wondered, but I did not pursue. I did not try to read the passage in question closely and to form my own conclusions because I did not think I knew enough.

The smug, unhesitating confidence of my childhood had been overtaken by the mature realization of my deficiencies. Once I learned how much I did not know, I was inhibited by a sense of futility; I was too far behind. People who had studied Hebrew from childhood or for whom it was their first language, professors who had spent their lives studying the Bible, authorities on narrative, experts on philology, religious sages, all had poured over the passages that caught my mind, and everything there was to say about them had probably been said. I had the point of view and the technique, but I no longer had the vanity to think that I could inform the waiting world of solutions to biblical cruxes.

One day in synagogue the rabbi read about the Israelites accepting the Torah. Moses says to them: "Not with you only do I make this covenant and this oath; but with him that standeth here with us this day before the Lord our God, and also with him that is not here with us this day" (Deuteronomy 29:13–14).[1] During the refreshment time after services, I asked the rabbi who were those who were not there. He said, "You." "Do you mean," I said, "that, according to the Bible, I received the Torah on the same day as everybody else?" He said "Yes," and I felt a heady rush of entitlement. The Bible was mine too; I got it when the experts did. No matter that Bible scholars had spent their lives learning and studying; no matter that they knew Hebrew, Akkadian, Ugaritic, and all the other cognate languages; no matter that they had pored over literary theory and were familiar with the works of other Bible scholars over the ages. I was no longer hopelessly far behind; we had all received the Torah on exactly the same day. I could go to the library and see if someone had already

---

[1] The verses in the Hebrew Bible are sometimes numbered slightly differently from those in Christian Bibles. In Christian Bibles these particular verses are vv. 14–15. In this book I cite the Hebrew Bible, but I shall not henceforth note the few discrepancies when they occur, as the Bibles are never more than a verse apart in the citations I use.

come up with my idea; if they had not, my opinion, provided I could back it up, was as good as anyone else's. The playing field had become level.

I did go to the library to make sure no one else had already written about the ideas I had. I was fortunate in that I was able to use the Yale University Library as well as its Divinity School Library. There were so many books on the Bible, so many commentaries; at first, I did not know where to start. I learned that I did not have to read or even skim every single book to see if they mentioned the passage I wanted to write about (or had already written about), as most books about the Bible have a convenient index to Scripture in the back. Just standing in the stacks, I could quickly see if there was mention of the passage that interested me. A librarian told me about computerized indexes of journal articles about the Bible in which I could locate the citations for published articles either by key word or by chapter and verse.

Many analysts had commented on the passages I wanted to write about, but I found none who had anticipated my ideas. Indeed, the interpretations of both ancient and modern commentators differed from mine not incrementally but almost diametrically. The first three articles I wrote have no footnotes, no citations of other authors, or so few that I could give credit in the body of my essay. My daughter and son-in-law, both college professors, wanted me to cite the authors whose conclusions corroborated mine as well as those whose comments I opposed. No one agreed with me, however, and the explications counter to mine were so familiar and so universal that I did not think it necessary to present them. My readers would be cognizant of the usual exegeses; my job was to convince them of my interpretation.

As a neophyte, I flinched from engaging in what appeared to be contentious dissension among Bible scholars. There was polite address of the "My esteemed colleague" variety; nevertheless, many of the footnotes I encountered were intimidatingly pugnacious. Since nearly all of the commentors were men, I ascribed the combative tone of these footnotes to testosterone. I had my idea, and I could defend it without attacking the ideas of others. Or so I thought, in the beginning. But my reluctance to use all the technical apparatus available to biblical scholars turned out to be a combination of diffidence and laziness. I was awed by academe, plus I wanted to write an essay not a term paper. The acceptance of my first three articles encouraged me, and the more works of established Bible scholars I read, the less awe I felt.

Certain critics excited my admiration and respect. I read Robert Alter's *The Art of Biblical Narrative* more than once, impressed each time with its clarity, brilliance, and originality. But there were other writers I became eager to contest. The source critics, it seemed to me, were avid to label any verses that did not fit into their explanations mislocated or maladroit. Far from maladroit, I found the verses in question apt, lucid, and aesthetically pleasing precisely where they were—provided that my interpretations and not those of the source critics were followed. I wanted to show these exegetes that it was condescending and presumptive to chop, change, and reorder the Bible to make it suit their theories.

Even those few writers who did not rely on the documentary hypothesis to prop their exegeses sometimes used faulty reasoning or employed unique translations, the only justification for which was that the novel rendering fit their explication; their translation was proof for the interpretation, and their interpretation confirmed the translation. But I had learned in college that "begging the question" was a logical fallacy. Logical fallacies, I found, abounded in biblical interpretation. There were even cases of false statement proffered to bolster an argument. I grew combative; testosterone, apparently, has nothing to do with it. There were things I wanted to say to my readers about the arguments of my esteemed colleagues. Footnotes no longer reminded me of term papers; they were tools of the trade, battle gear.

Beginning each chapter in this book, I explain how the idea for the interpretation occurred to me. I wish I knew the source of inspiration or how to stimulate insight. Creativity, I once read, favors the prepared mind, and so it must help to take a course in the Bible or to attend an informal Bible study class. I have done both, and it is true that they have forced me to focus on the passages studied. Sometimes contemplation becomes brooding, and brooding, with a heart-leap that historian A. L. Rowse has compared to the feeling that you have just sat on the cat, becomes vision. The beginning of each chapter describes my approach to and moment of heart-leap when I saw that I was on to something. Some of these prefaces also list, for those who may be skipping the footnotes, those notes I think particularly weighty, or feisty, or funny.

The Bible has been studied and written about for hundreds of years, and yet it remains a well of freshness that never stales or runs dry. Miraculously (if one believes in miracles), there is always something more or something different to say about it, and one does not need to be a teacher, minister, priest, rabbi, or professor to have an original interpretation. An amateur is, perhaps, more likely than an expert to take a fresh slant, for the professionals all initially learned what to think about the Bible from their teachers and may be predisposed to their conclusions by habit and tradition.

The Bible is distant chronologically, culturally, linguistically. We do not always know the meaning of the Hebrew words, and we never know their full range of nuance. If what you think about a passage follows the Hebrew text and conforms to the societal context gleaned from the rest of Scripture, then your explanation, your exegesis, is as valid as the opinion of the experts. What makes an interpretation tenable is not the erudition and reputation of its author but the quality and convincingness of its supporting evidence. An exegesis is authoritative to the extent that its evidence is compelling. I hope that you are persuaded, or at least provoked, by the arguments I present here.

CHAPTER ONE

Rashomon and the Biblical Creation Narratives

The Yale Catalogue listed a semester course that I wanted to audit. It was titled "*Imago Dei:* The Image of God in Jewish Thought" and was to be taught by a visiting professor from Israel. The catalogue said "limited enrollment." This meant that the class would not be a lecture, meeting in an auditorium with plenty of seats for all who wished to attend, but would be a seminar, meeting in a room with a large table around which fifteen or so students could sit and participate in discussion. If the class were over-subscribed, the auditors would be asked to leave, followed by freshmen, then sophomores, and so forth, until the number of students had been re-duced to a class size appropriate for a seminar.

I was the first to arrive, and sure enough the specified classroom con-tained a large seminar table and about fifteen chairs. The chairs filled up quickly, but the students kept coming. They sat in the window wells, on the radiators, and, finally, on the floor. When all the floor space was cov-ered by either students or their luggage (all students nowadays, even first graders, carry book bags the size of weekend carryalls), the Yalies began to range themselves against the walls, just standing and leaning. I tried to count them and gave up after I reached fifty. This will be my first and last day in the class, I thought, unless the professor decides to give a lecture course instead of a seminar and is able to locate an unoccupied lecture room.

When the professor came in, he seemed a little taken aback by the size of the turnout. He introduced himself and handed out a syllabus. There were not enough syllabi for everyone, and so he told us to pass around those he had so that everyone could get an idea of the course content. He then went on to explain that, as much of the assigned reading was in He-brew, those who took the course would have to be able to read books and articles in Hebrew. He said that those who could not do so should leave. Four or five students got up and left the room. I could not read modern Hebrew, but I stayed in my seat. After all, I decided, I was only auditing and would not take part in discussion. The students were to be graded on their participation; the floor had to be left to them. The class would be taught in English; I would read the English assignments, and, if I were al-lowed to remain in the class, that would have to suffice.

When the syllabus got around to me, I could not believe how much reading was expected, and I was looking at only the English assignments. I was a conscientious adult who *wanted* to do all the reading, who was taking no other classes that semester, who was not trying out for the school newspaper or track team, and whose idea of a fun evening was staying home; yet, though I read fast, I could not imagine myself being able to read all the assignments.

As the syllabi were circulating, the professor lectured. In the course of the semester, the class would cover the concept of humanity's creation in the image of God as that doctrine appears in the Bible, in Jewish literature, in philosophy, and in law—especially in its relation to capital punishment. Initially, we would have to understand the abstraction conveyed by the word "image," and so the professor began by talking about Plato's Allegory of the Cave. He assumed that all Yale students would be familiar with this amount of classical philosophy, but, alerted by the perplexed looks he was receiving, he notched back his expectations and lectured as though none of them had heard of Plato's famous allegory, which they had not. I, fortunately, had gone to college in the days of distribution requirements and so had been compelled to take a year of what my university called "Classics." I did not retain much, but I remembered studying Plato's Allegory of the Cave, and some of the themes the teacher outlined resonated faintly.

After class, I asked the professor if I ought to leave or if he were planning a lecture course in view of the large class size. He told me to come back the following week and see how things fell out. The class met only once a week, and he understood that Yale students have a try-out period of two to three weeks before they must absolutely commit to a course. It might be, he said, that fewer students would return the following week. The professor was right. Only two students returned for the next class, myself and a freshman pre-med student with good Hebrew skills.

Either the professor's syllabus or his level of discourse had frightened the students away, to their great loss. I got along fine reading about two-thirds of the English assignments, and from what I could see, the pre-med student had time to read even less. The professor's exhilarating lectures filled in any lack. After the first few weeks we were together, the three of us met cozily in a lounge next to the teacher's office, and my classmate and I agreed that these two hours were the intellectual highlight of our week. I was especially happy that I was able to continue with the course because, on that crowded first day, I saw that the professor, a young man in his early forties, wore a yarmulke. An observant Jew, who shows his respect for God by covering his head, must believe in the Bible's divine inspiration. I had faith in the biblical author's literary genius rather than in divine inspiration, but my reverence for the former was so ardent it almost constituted a religion. I thought this devout professor would not exasperate me, as did other scholars, by championing the documentary hypothesis.

I was wrong. The professor was observant and may have believed in the divine inspiration of Genesis, but if he did, he must have believed that

God inspired a number of writers, for he was a convinced source critic. I had no inhibition about speaking up in this class, as there was ample opportunity for my classmate's participation, but I argued against the professor's creed only once. He was talking about the two creation accounts in Genesis. In chapter 1, we are told that "God created man in his image, in the image of God created he him; male and female created he them." I liked the author's position that when God created man (i.e., humankind), he created men and women simultaneously. In chapter 2, however, the Bible says, "And the rib, which the Lord God had taken from man, made he a woman, and brought her unto the man." This report did not please me so much as the first. The two stories differ, the professor said, because they were culled from two distinct sources. Chapter 1 of Genesis was written by the P source, and chapter 2 was written by J. Disparate authors resulted in contradictions, in dissimilar writing styles, and in idiosyncratic appellatives for the deity—the first chapter uses God, and the second uses Lord God.

I could not think of a defense for my position that the two creation stories had but one brilliant author who made no mistakes, but I could remember an explanation for the disparity between the two chapters that I had heard at my Shabbos Group:[1] the first chapter was a general outline and the second chapter dealt with specifics. I proffered that rationale, but it was quickly dismissed by both my teacher and my classmate. It did not account for the contradictions—in chapter 1, for instance, flora precedes fauna, but in chapter 2, man, or rather, *a* man, is formed before any vegetation sprouts—nor did it justify the noticeable stylistic incongruity between the lofty, rhythmic, rolling periods of chapter 1 and the ordinary workaday exposition of chapter 2.

"Fine," I said, "I'll grant you discrepancies of fact and of style, but don't you think there's a reason for these inconsistencies? The author or, if you insist, the redactor surely read these chapters over before he said, 'This stuff's good, and it's ready for a wider audience.' The two chapters must have satisfied his aesthetic vision, discrepancies and all, and we just don't grasp his literary subtlety."

I do not remember the professor's exact words, but his rejoinder ran like this: the redactor's task was not to fit all his sources together in an artful design; it was to preserve traditional folklore, earlier legends, myths, and theological expressions lest they get lost. He could connect them and work them into a narrative montage, and he could be quite clever, but the religious and historical aspects of these composite and fragmentary materials were paramount, not the redactor's aesthetic. These chapters were

---

[1] The New Haven Shabbos (Sabbath) Group, which I describe more fully in the introduction to Chapter Eleven, is a group of friends who meet at one another's houses on Saturday afternoons to study the Bible. There is no teacher; responsibility for leading the discussion is shared by the participants.

written by different authors, centuries apart, and had been stitched together, despite discrepancies, without consideration for their artistic coherence.

My professor's answer made me want to imitate the vaudevillian who popularized the catch phrase "Vas you dere, Cholly?" Whatever his partner's unlikely assertion, the comedian would ask, "Vas you dere, Cholly?" to substantiate or refute it. I would not quote that question to my teacher of course, as it would be fresh and as he, being Israeli, would not have understood the reference, but those words ran through my mind. I was not there when the Bible was written or redacted or compiled, but neither was the teacher. I stopped arguing because I had no ammunition, but from past evidence of the Bible's virtuosity, I was convinced the teacher was wrong.

The day after this class, I went to the library to see how earlier commentators, religious commentators who did not believe in the documentary hypothesis, had resolved these contradictions. Their solutions did not convince me. Some exegetes denied any disagreement; addressing the example above, they said that plants were indeed created on the third day in seed form and remained under the soil until after the sixth day when man was created and the Lord God caused rain. Once there was a man to till the soil, verdure grew.

These explanations were not satisfying to me because they did not attend to the obvious stylistic difference between the two chapters and because they seemed awkward and forced. It was possible to defend each and every inconsistency between the two chapters, and the medieval commentators did so, but at the cost of lengthy rationalization. The biblical author I admired wrote with precision and simplicity. The explanatory addenda required to harmonize chapter 1 with chapter 2 littered the Bible's elegant prose.

Some analysts said that chapter 1 was a poetic prelude and not a creation story at all. It had elements of the later creation story to come in chapter 2, but as an overture, it took poetic license in introducing these themes. Saying that the problem did not exist was not a solution, as far as I was concerned. Nor did I want chapter 1 denied as a creation story, for I much preferred its account to that of chapter 2. Not only was the language more elevated, but men and women were created simultaneously, suiting my preference for gender equality.

And so I began sleepless nights of mulling the two creation stories, fastening on the contradictions, seeking the simple key both to their resolution and to the stylistic variation, trying to see what the first reader readily saw. I did not believe that the first reader just naturally assumed all of the discursive complexities of the medieval commentators. I believed that there must be one plain, naked, sensible explanation consistent with the author's style of literary economy. In my mind I pictured the often-reproduced optical illusion that appears to the eye either as the black silhouettes of two women's profiles facing one another or as a white goblet. If one is shown the picture and told, "This is a goblet," it is hard to see the two women in profile. If one is told, "This is a picture of two women in profile facing one another," one cannot at first visualize the goblet. Only by application can one eventually switch back and forth mentally between the two images. I had been told that I was looking at two contradictory stories by two separate authors. Somehow, by some angle of view, these two chapters were a single entity, but the goblet eluded me.

One Saturday, my professor came to the Shabbos Group. I thought I would take advantage of the pre-session socializing to point out the deficiencies of the documentary hypothesis. I keep beating my little drum; though I can get no source critic to march to its tattoo, at least, at Shabbos Group, I would not be squandering class time. I asked him if he had ever seen the Japanese movie, *Rashomon*. He said that he had. I said that since the movie was based on older legends and since it repeated the same story again and again with contradictions and in different narrative styles, true believers in the documentary hypothesis would be forced by their criteria to conclude that the movie was spliced together from earlier film clips by a redactor and that therefore the movie did not have a single artistic director. My teacher laughed, but before he could respond to me, his attention was diverted by someone who wanted to meet him. We never did get back to my statement, but it did not matter to me since, even as the words left my mouth, I realized that I had just framed the answer to the divergent creation stories question. I saw the goblet.

Like *Rashomon*, the two creation stories depict different points of view. The first story, chapter 1, gives an account of creation from God's viewpoint, and chapter 2, starting with the latter half of v. 4 and continuing through the last verse in chapter 4, describes the beginning of all things from man's perspective. In the author's portrayal, God, of course, knows how he created the world. Man can only surmise how the world began from the evidence he sees around him and from his own predilections. Man's negativity, egotism, misogyny, materialism, and self-pity are highlighted and underscored by the contrast to God's optimism, gender impartiality, beneficence, and might. The styles of the two chapters necessarily differ. The rhetoric in which God's version is related is appropriately exalted; the expression of man's story is suitably prosaic.

Even though *Rashomon*'s format was unique in its genre, movie buffs had no difficulty recognizing that the movie was the work of one artist and did not result from the random splicing of a compulsive redactor. Similarly, the Bible's first readers, noticing contradiction and change of style, as well as cues that now screamed at me from the text, had no problem apprehending that a single dazzling author was capable of depicting discordant points of view in divergent styles of discourse, and, in so doing, of revealing his perception of the characteristics of both God and man.

Rashomon, the Japanese movie directed by Akira Kurosawa, won the Venice Film Festival grand prize for best film in 1951 and the American Oscar for best foreign movie in 1952. The picture is based loosely on two short stories published in 1921. One of these stories was itself based on tenth century Japanese narratives.[2] The movie was considered a complete departure from the conventions of cinematography and received much acclaim in the United States. It was widely reviewed and analyzed and continues, almost fifty years after its debut, to be studied and critiqued by film aficionados.

Beyond commenting on the film's format and cinematographic technique, many movie reviewers deliberated its philosophical and moral implications. Kurosawa, impatient with what he considered over-analysis, wanted his movie to be regarded as a mystery story.[3] Annoyed though he may have been with the dissection his movie received, Kurosawa did not also have to contend with advocates of the documentary hypothesis—source critics, who, using the same criteria with which they prove that the Hebrew Bible is the work of multiple authors, could demonstrate that his film was the product of disparate directors.

This chapter argues that just as Kurosawa's film is an integrated, intelligible, cohesive work of one master's art so also are the two creation stories of Genesis 1 and 2—despite their repetitions, contradictions, and changes of vocabulary and style. I shall show that the discrepancies between the creation accounts in chapters 1 and 2 reflect not separate authors, as the source critics insist, but rather separate points of view.[4] In Genesis 1:1–2:4a the narrator tells the story of creation from God's perspective, and in 2:4b the narrator begins man's view of creation and continues through 4:26 with man's rationalization for his world's lack of perfection. By considering the disagreements and comparing the distinct viewpoints presented in each chapter, the reader gains his initial insight into the author's conception of God and assessment of man.

Kurosawa's movie has four main characters—a wood-cutter, a patrician, the patrician's beautiful young wife, and a bandit—each of whom relates an encounter in the woods. Their accounts are depicted as they speak and, depending upon the speaker, describe a murder or a suicide and a rape or a seduction. The stories are at once contradictory and overlapping, and the viewer is hard-pressed to sort out the truth. Part of the artistry of the

---

[2] Tadao Sato, "*Rashomon*," in *Focus on* Rashomon (ed. Donald Richie; Englewood Cliffs: Prentice-Hall, 1972), 96.

[3] Richie, "Introduction," in *Focus on* Rashomon, 1.

[4] Chapter 1 of Genesis is commonly attributed to the P source and chapter 2, supposedly written centuries earlier, to the J source. In recent years it has been proposed that the J author was a woman.

film is the dissimilarity not only of the versions but also of each witness's vocabulary and style of exposition. The wood-cutter eyewitness is simple and uneducated, the bandit jumpy and jittery, the patrician dignified, and the damsel hysterical.

To the source critics, the unconventionality of Kurosawa's opus would speak against him; he uses neither the idiom nor the technique appropriate for coherent, comprehensible Japanese cinematography. Also, the fact that his achievement is based on earlier stories, some from centuries earlier, would make these critics suspect that *Rashomon* is not an original work of art but is a compilation and a splicing together of these earlier tales and that Kurosawa is, at best, the editor, or as they prefer, the redactor of these popular fictions. One tenet of the documentary hypothesis is that a good author is not repetitious. Nor, according to the source critics, does an author contradict himself, vary his style, or use different vocabulary from one scene to the next. Kurosawa is in trouble. The "Higher Criticism," applied to *Rashomon,* might be able to separate and distinguish at least four different directors. Perhaps these would be labeled J, P, E, and D—J for the director who dramatizes the story of the jumpy, jittery bandit, P for the framer of the patrician's account, E for the person responsible for the wood-cutter's eyewitness story, and D for the architect of the damsel's tale. There might also be some critics who propose that this last director was a woman because of the segment's perceptive portrayal of a woman's sensibilities.

Traditionalist commentators, who believe the Bible is the inspired word of God, defend as I do the single authorship of Genesis, but they explain that the second creation story is an expansion and clarification of the first. They assert that Genesis 1 provides the general outline of creation and Genesis 2 supplies the specifics. Chapter 1 states that God creates vegetation, beasts, and humankind; chapter 2 tells how he did it. This interpretation, however, does not explain the inconsistences between the two accounts. To give but one example, in the first account man is created last, and in the second he is formed before the other animals. Nor does this explanation elucidate the change in style from the majestic balanced cadences of the first chapter to the pedestrian, and even choppy, dissymmetries of the second.

Some scholars, among the minority who do not adhere to the documentary hypothesis, seek to harmonize the two chapters by denying that chapter 2 is a creation story at all. To these interpreters, chapter 2 confirms chapter 1, and they reconcile the differences by proposing that chapter 1 is a poetic prologue, with all the license poetry is permitted, and chapter 2 is a prosaic etiology. I agree that, besides its profound moral and theological precepts, 2:4b through 4:26 affords a homespun etiology describing how the animals got their names, how death and evil entered a "very good" world, why man has to labor for a living, why woman has to labor in childbirth, why man is the only animal who wears clothes and feels shame, why the snake has no legs, why women are subservient to men (in patriarchal times, at least), why men cling to their wives and forsake their parents, why there is animosity between brothers (which all men basically are), where the population who drowned in the flood came from, and from whence sprang cities and occupations other than agriculture. Nevertheless, to deny that chapter 2 is a creation account blinds one to the portraits of God and man that the author delineates by way of the differences between the two accounts.

In Genesis 1 we learn of God's power: he can create with a word; of his unselfishness: he creates in his own image and grants man earthly dominion; of his magnanimity: his first words to man and beast are a blessing; and of his optimism: everything created is "good" and "very good." Nothing is lacking; nothing is "not good." The words "no" and "not" do not appear; there is no discouraging word on God's range.

In the first full verse of man's version, however, we see man's innate negativity and egocentrism: there is no shrub, no herb, no rain, and, deficiency most dire, no man (2:5). In his overweening self-importance, man sees himself as needed by the Lord God; he is required to till the earth. On the plus side for man, he hardly needs the Lord God: in v. 10 we are told the Garden of Eden is well watered; man will not depend upon the Lord God for rain.

Man's materialism and acquisitiveness are exposed in vv. 11–12: in the land of Havilah, the narrator reports, there is gold "and the gold of that land is good." The only things seen as "good" in man's creation story are food (v. 9) and the gold in a land not his. If the reader were unsure of the second creation vignette's viewpoint, the uncertainty is now dispelled. In whose value system is gold good? Certainly not God's. Gold is not valuable to God; what would he buy with it, and from whom? Man is a corporeal being and must eat; his assessment of food as good is natural and predictable; his appreciation of trees as being pleasant to the sight displays aesthetic sensibilities, but his conviction that gold found elsewhere is good bodes ill for the future peace of mankind.

All direct speech in the Hebrew Bible is revealing, and a character's first address bears extra freight. The reader constructs personality from the observation of appearance, deeds, and words. We do not discern God's appearance, but we do learn some of his deeds in chapter 1, and his first speech to man is a blessing. There is talmudic disagreement as to whether "Be fruitful and multiply" is a commandment to be obeyed or a blessing to be enjoyed, but v. 28 clearly labels these words a blessing. God's second speech to man tells of a gift—man and beast are given all green plants for food (v. 29). In chapter 1, the reader's first impression of God is of primacy, might, order, beneficence, and plenty.

In the second creation narrative, the Lord God's first words to man are not a blessing but a commandment. The inclusive dietary "all" of 1:29 is restated and immediately contravened by a negative "Thou shalt not" that threatens death (2:16). Benevolence transmutes to oppression. Man does not view the Lord God as a source of blessing and abundance but as a fearsome dictator who deals in death and restricts freedom. The commandment excluding the fruit of the tree of knowledge is all the more egregious because it is the only instance of God directly commanding man in all of the Hebrew Bible. The reader is told that God commanded Moses and others, and individuals report that God has commanded them; the phrases "As God commanded" and "According to all God commanded" are ubiquitous, but only here in the second chapter of Genesis do we see God expressly command man.

The Lord God's second utterance to man in chapter 2 is to declare a "not good." The world declines from universal goodness in the first chapter to a perceived deficit here: the Lord God's earth is not complete and sufficient; man is a social being and needs a mate. Unlike the Darwinian progression in chapter 1 of less highly evolved species preceding the more highly evolved—sea creatures preceding land animals, and men and women appearing concurrently—man gives himself pride of place and deprecates the Lord God in the process; in man's view he was formed first and, due to the Lord God's error, alone.

Now, in this second creation version, the Lord God forms all the animals, species by species, and trots them before man to be named. Man competently gives names to all the beasts, but the Lord God, in man's perspective, fails again and again to provide a suitable mate; man is attracted to none of the animals. Unsuccessful at numberless attempts, the Lord God builds a woman from man's rib. Man is so in love with himself, the author amusingly implies, he cannot but be charmed by bone of his bone, flesh of his flesh.

Man does accept the Lord God's handiwork as his mate but not with open arms. After one more poke at the deity, man names the new creature with a generic name "woman" (as he named the other animals), acknowledges that this one is of the same substance as he, yet seems to regard her with disdain. Let us examine the first words of the first man in the world. "This time!" he exclaims, as if to commend condescendingly, "Now finally, Lord God, you've got it right!" He continues (I translate literally), "Bone of my bone and flesh of my flesh. To this I name woman, for from man she was taken, this."[5] Man uses the demonstrative pronoun "this" three times; three is the number for emphasis in the Hebrew Bible. Most translations leave out one or two of the demonstrative pronouns and obscure the supercilious articulation with the warmer, more polite, "she."

---

[5] Ronald Hendel, in his recent rigorous textual study, omits the final "this" from his critical edition of the Hebrew text. To Hendel it is "plausible" that the final "this" is not original but is an explicating addition by a scribe. I do not agree that a scribe might have found explication necessary, as there is no possibility for confusion about the creature man is naming (*The Text of Genesis 1–11* [New York: Oxford University Press, 1998], 44).

The author, however, stresses man's patronizing attitude toward woman, this second comer, by the repeated use of the disparaging and distancing pronoun. Hebrew is a gendered language; the verb "taken" requires the feminine suffix, which translates as "she." Had the author said "from man *it* was taken," the first man's scornful point would have been more obvious to English-speakers, but "it" is not possible in Hebrew. In the Hebrew Bible, however, the demonstrative pronoun "this," in both its feminine and masculine genders, is frequently used to distance and malign.[6] With the insistent repetition of the alienating pronoun, we see that man espouses woman at arm's length. The denigratory "this" is the first word of man's first speech, the last word of his speech, and precisely the middle word of his speech (in Hebrew). In view of the word's number and regularity, it is difficult to imagine that its chilling effect was not calculated.

The coda following man's aloof reception of woman, "Therefore shall a man leave his father and his mother and cleave to his wife and they shall be one flesh" (Genesis 2:24), is generally thought to be a conclusion of the narrator's; the first man is ignorant of parents. According to my analysis, he has also not yet begun to cleave to his wife. We do not see him warming to his wife until he gives her a personal name in 3:20 immediately following the Lord God's cursing of the pair. Man bonds with woman at this point, at the height of their grief, for they now share the same burden. Earlier in v. 12, as has often been noted, he was quick to defend himself at her expense and at God's: "The woman that *you* gave to be with me, she gave me of the tree, and I ate."

Just as the author of Genesis accentuates the derisive "this" in man's initial speech by a threefold repetition, so too does he use repeated triplets in chapter 1 to pre-emptively counter man's treatment of events in chapter 2. In 1:29 God says "Behold" (so that man and reader pay attention) and then states that man has been given *all* herbs bearing seed on the face of *all* the earth and *all* trees that have fruit-bearing seed for food. God permits man the fruit of every tree; the prohibition in chapter 2 is a figment of man's explicating etiology. In 1:27 God creates humanity in his image, male and female simultaneously; "created" is used an emphasizing three times in this one verse. The word "image" is also repeated three times in chapter 1. God's creation narrative stresses that woman is not an afterthought fashioned from man's rib; she is created together with man in the eminence and exaltation of the image and likeness of God.

The summing up in 2:4a: "These are the generations of the heaven and of the earth when they were created," concludes God's version of cre-

---

[6] To give but two examples: in an effort to minimize the difference between his two daughters, Laban, speaking to the deceived Jacob, diminishes both Leah and Rachel by referring to them only as "this." "Fulfill the week of *this,* and we will give you *this* also" (Genesis 29:27, emphasis added). Pharaoh's servants, referring contemptuously to Moses, ask Pharaoh, "How long will *this* be a snare to us?" (Exodus 10:7).

ation. The Hebrew verb "created" will not appear again until 5:1 when, I will argue, the narrator has finished man's etiology and resumes from where he changed perspective at the end of 2:4a.

Man's perspective on creation begins in the second half of 2:4 with the words, "In the day that the Lord God made earth and heaven." From man's point of view, the Lord God "makes" earth and heaven. The Hebrew verb "create" is not used in the second creation story, nor is it ever used throughout the Hebrew Bible to characterize an act of any entity other than God. Only God creates. Man cannot even imagine the process by which God engenders, and so "create" is not used in man's version of the world's inception. From 2:4b through 4:26, the Lord God makes, forms, builds, plants, takes, puts, commands, walks, and sends—all acts conceivable and capable of accomplishment by man.

Another indication that a human account begins in 2:4b is that the phrase "heaven(s) and earth" occurs three times prior to v. 4b. Each time, "heaven(s)" precedes "earth"—God's perspective. In v. 4b, "earth" precedes "heaven"; man is more concerned with his own dwelling place than with the cosmos. Man's story of creation is literally "down to earth"; it skips the celestial.

The story from man's perspective ends with the last verse of chapter 4, and with the first verse of chapter 5, the narrator picks up where he left off at 2:4a. Henceforth there will be no chapter-long sequence devoted solely to God's perspective—sometimes the viewpoint will be God's; sometimes it will be man's. The first three verses of chapter 5 reprise the essence of God's creation vis-à-vis humans beings: we are again assured that humanity was created in God's likeness, that both man and woman were created (again repeated three times), not formed or built, that this creation was simultaneous, and that they were blessed, not cursed, and given the name "humankind." In the next verse, man, Adam, has a son in his own image and likeness, and the reader is assured thereby that the gift of at least some aspect of godliness inheres in man and is transmitted to his descendants.

The literary styles of the two creation accounts differ markedly. In Genesis 1 God moves in stately periods to create a world. Like the procession and recession of waves pounding against a shore, the echoing phrases of chapter 1 separate the acts of generation and establish a rhythm. Each "And God said" advances the development, and the recurring phrases, "And it was so," "And God saw that it was good," and "And there was evening and there was morning" recede from it. The ebb and flow of the action confer a decorous, unhurried, deliberate ceremoniousness. The construction job of creation is not messy; it is methodical.

The metrical resonance and cyclic intervals with which the narrator renders God's august and systematic expression in the first creation account subside at 2:4a. In its stead the narrator commences man's mundane and somewhat discontinuous articulation (the Lord God places man in the garden in v. 8 and again in v. 15). The dramatic stylistic divergence of the two chapters does not escape the discriminating eye of the source critics. To them, such radical rhetorical contrast advances our understanding of neither God nor man and must surely derive from a change of authorship. My interpretation of the disparity is that, like Kurosawa, the artist wishes to limn character by way of style.

An even more striking difference between the two versions, and the one that initially exercised the source critics, is the deity's name change from the Hebrew *Elohim,* God, in chapter 1 to *YHWH Elohim,* Lord God, in chapter 2. (The use of "Lord" for the Hebrew *YHWH* is a convention I share with most English translations of the Bible.) In the Bible, the word *Elohim* refers to pagan gods as well as to the God of Israel. Similarly in English, the same word, non-capitalized, designates pagan gods while, capitalized, it represents the God of Scripture. In English, God has no intimate name. *YHWH,* however, is considered by Jews to be the sacred, unpronounceable, personal name of God, and it always and only signifies the one God of the covenant and the universe.

To source critics, who can envisage no artistic or theological reason for such a transition, the shift in nomenclature from God, *Elohim,* in Genesis 1 to Lord God, *YHWH Elohim,* in 2:4b proves a change in the authorship of the first and second chapters. In my hypothesis of disparate points of view, as well as in the interpretations of those few scholars averse to source criticism, the name of the deity changes in chapter 2 because God is no longer depicted as the transcendent creator of every thing and every person, pagan and Israelite alike; he is shown by the use of his intimate name to be in an immanent relationship with the man who will be the ancestor of all humanity. Lest the reader fail to realize that the Supreme Being is one and the same in both chapters, the author pairs God's personal name, *YHWH,* with *Elohim,* the designation of the impersonal Creator of chapter 1.

As we have seen, it is not necessary to stipulate separate authors in order to explain the differences and deviations of the two creation stories. Indeed, positing independent authors detracts from the richness and wit of the narrative; it is not comically revealing for man to see the world as lacking his presence unless we are first given a more approving view of the universe. Rather than disclosing two authors, the variations between the first two chapters of Genesis distinguish God from man and manifest attributes of both. An author can speak in many voices, vary vocabulary, tell essentially the same story in conflicting ways, and keep his audience engaged for millennia. To the film experts, who credited Kurosawa with inventing a new approach, a new method to depict the relativity of truth and reality, I can say only: "What has been is what will be, and what has been done is what will be done, and there is nothing new under the sun" (Ecclesiastes 1:9).

CHAPTER TWO

What Cain Said: A Note on Genesis 4:8

Yale University's Hillel convened a weekend teach-in open to the public. Hillel is a Jewish students' organization, and the weekend was comprised of lectures and seminars on topics of Jewish interest—literature, history, current events. Scholars came from within the Yale community and from other institutions as well to lead the classes. I remember almost nothing from one of the classes I attended because the teacher lost me in the first two minutes of her presentation. She was teaching about the Torah, the first five books of the Bible, and each student in her class had been provided with a Pentateuch. Hillel had plenty of copies because Jewish worship services are held there throughout the year, and the Torah is read during services every Monday, Thursday, and Saturday morning. In the course of the year, at Hillel as in every Jewish congregation, the Pentateuch is read from beginning to end.

After the instructor invited us to question or comment freely during the class, she began her talk. She introduced her topic and then said, "As you know, contrary to fundamentalist belief, there are many mistakes in the Pentateuch." Although I am not a fundamentalist believer, these were, of course, fighting words to me on literary grounds, and I raised my hand and said, "Like what?"

The teacher put her topic aside and directed the class's attention to Genesis 4:8. Our English translations said: "And Cain spoke unto Abel his brother. And it came to pass, when they were in the field, that Cain rose up against Abel his brother, and slew him." This looked all right to me, but she explained that the English smooths what in Hebrew is not "spoke unto" but rather "said to." According to her, if translated literally, the verse would read: "And Cain said to Abel his brother: and it came to pass, when they were in the field, that Cain rose against Abel his brother, and slew him." She said that Cain's words, whatever it was that he had said to Abel, were missing.

Our copies of the Pentateuch contained both Hebrew and English. The teacher resumed her topic, and I looked at the Hebrew for the verse she had pointed out. Fortunately, the verse used simple, frequently seen words, and even with my elementary Hebrew I was able to read them without the aid of a dictionary. I saw that the teacher's translation was one possible alternative. Another alternative that seemed possible to me was, "Cain *spoke against* Abel, his brother." The Hebrew word, אמר, was usually translated as "said," but perhaps "talked" or "spoke" were legitimate, though less customary, renderings. I knew there was a common synonym for אמר that unquestionably means "spoke," but unlike אמר, this synonym does not also connote "thought." If אמר could be construed as "spoke," then the author kills two birds with one stone by using it: in a single word, he tells us that Cain both spoke and thought against Abel his brother. I liked that idea because, like a poet, the biblical author characteristically chooses the most loaded and pregnant word for his tightly packed prose.

The word the teacher translated as "to" in her phrase "Cain said to Abel" also means "against." Indeed, she rendered the very same word as "against" when she translated the last clause of the verse: "Cain rose against Abel, his brother and slew him." I reasoned that "to" should be construed as "against" in the first clause as well. If the preposition were read as "against" in both parts of the verse, the reader could not help but notice the parallelism of "Cain spoke against Abel, his brother" and "Cain rose against Abel, his brother." The author must have wanted the reader to recognize and consider the duplication, for otherwise he could have said, "Cain rose against *him*."

Glancing just a few verses further afield, I could see that the writer effects more than a graceful parallelism when he twice repeats "Abel, his brother" in our verse. Cain's birth is recorded in the first verse of the chapter. When Eve has a second child in v. 2, we are told she bore Abel, *his brother.* Readers know the boys are brothers before the author points it out. But, by the use of the redundant—and therefore, mind-catching—phrase, *his brother,* we are made to regard that second son relative to Cain. When Cain is born, the Bible could have said that Eve bore a son just as Seth is termed a son in 5:3, or as Leah, Bilhah, Zilpah, and Rachel bear sons in Genesis 29 and 30. When Cain enters the world in 4:1, however, he is called a "man"; he is an autonomous individual. Abel, too, could have been termed a son or a second son, but Abel, at birth, is labeled "his brother." This fraternal dependency could be indicative of Adam and Eve's perspective, or it could reveal Cain's point of view. Either way, close readers feel the tug of Abel on Cain. Is he a burden, or is he a friend? The end of the verse gives us a clue: Abel becomes a sheep herder and Cain a farmer. The boys go their separate ways.

In the story of Amnon and Tamar, the author repeats the terms "brother" and "sister" over and over, underscoring incest. In the story of Sarai, Abram, and Hagar, the words "husband" and "wife" are emphasized, highlighting the marital relationships and establishing that, though Hagar becomes Abram's wife, Abram is truly husband only to Sarai. In Genesis 4, not only does the belabored "brother" stress the fratricide, in v. 2 it prepares readers for the coming sibling disaffection, and in v. 8—the verse the teacher said evinces a mistake—the rhetorically pleasing symmetry of "Cain spoke against Abel, his brother" and "Cain rose against Abel, his brother" demonstrates, via the equilibrium, a cause and effect relationship. One magnificently aimed stone, many birds.

Translating the verse my way and not the teacher's way not only made sense, but one would not have to second-guess the author, decree that something was missing, and call an error. The Bible could be telling us that after Cain spoke/thought against his brother (or as Scripture expresses an interval, "It came to pass"), he worked himself into such a rage that he killed him. Like children of equal weight balanced on a seesaw, the first and last clauses of v. 8 are balanced by syntax and achieve equal moral weight. This conclusion fits well with later expressions of Jewish ethics, for the Talmud teaches that speaking ill (*lashon hara*, evil tongue) of anyone is equivalent to murder.

Danny Thomas was a television personality in the 1950s. Eventually he starred in a situation comedy of his own, but he appeared initially as a stand-up comedian on variety shows. He invariably told a signature joke that was my father's favorite. It would seem odd nowadays for a comedian to offer the same joke again and again, but I can remember another comedian, Henny Youngman, who always used the "Take my wife, please" line that I appropriated as a title for Chapter Three. Perhaps, in the early days of television, viewers did not demand so much novelty as they do today. Thomas told the joke well, and the self-induced passion upon which it turned was universally familiar to viewers. Even though my father knew the punch line, the joke's truth made him laugh every time.

The joke went like this: a motorist, driving on a back road in the small hours of the morning through sparsely settled farm land, gets a flat tire. In trying to change the tire, his jack comes apart in his hands. Thinking that no one might come by for hours, he starts walking down the road in the hope of eventually coming to a farmhouse. As he walks, he anticipates his conversation with the farmer:

"I'll ask him for the loan of his jack. He's got to have a car or a truck. He'll have a jack; why shouldn't he let me use it? Well, maybe, he'll let me use it for a price! Sure, why not? All these farmers think about is money. So, O.K., he *rents* me his jack. How much can he charge? Five bucks? Ten bucks? Whatever. What's my choice? I'll be here forever without it. I'll give the man his ten bucks, change the tire, and get out of this god-forsaken dump."

By now the sun is higher in the sky, and the motorist is getting hot. He removes his jacket and carries it over his shoulder. A farmhouse is in sight, and as he approaches it, he thinks:

"Ten bucks? What makes me think he'll loan me his jack for ten bucks? He may be a hick, but he's not blind. He sees the spot I'm in. He could charge me twenty, thirty, fifty bucks! He's got me right where he wants me."

The motorist now reaches the porch of the farmhouse. The farmer steps out of the house to meet the stranger, and the motorist punches the astonished man squarely in the nose, shouting: "And you can keep your lousy jack!"

My translation of the Cain and Abel verse reminded me of this joke. I could easily envisage how Cain, by talking and thinking against his brother over time, worked himself into a fury. Just as the motorist must have justified his assault on the blameless farmer, Cain could have justified his murderous attack against his innocent brother with the imagined conviction that his brother's inequity merited violence. The motorist stewed during his long walk, and Cain also was given time to brood by the author's interposition of the three word/phrases (in Hebrew), "And it was," "when they were," "in the field," between the cause part of the verse, "Cain spoke against Abel, his brother," and the effect part of the verse, "Cain rose against Abel, his brother, and slew him."

I lifted my head from the Bible and was about to raise my hand to share the fruits of my contemplation with the teacher and the class, when I thought better of it. The teacher was well launched into her topic, and I did not think it right to usurp her planned presentation with a defense of my personal perspective on the Bible's integrity. Also, much as I would have liked to articulate my alternate reading and set the teacher straight, I knew that those who believe there are mistakes in the Torah are stubborn in their opinion, just as I, who choose to believe there are no mistakes, am tenacious of mine. The teacher would not change her mind and say, "Hallelujah, the scales have fallen from my eyes. Not only is there no mistake in this verse, but, read your way, it imparts a moral, necessitates every word of the text, and models biblical style. You're right and I'm wrong." Nor, in this class of mostly undergraduates, would I displace the students' naive trust that a bonafide professor's interpretation was superior to an unknown stranger's. I hated to leave the young people with the impression that there were mistakes in the Pentateuch, but I held my tongue.

This time, sleepless nights did not drive me to the library. I went out of curiosity to see if there were precedents for reading אמר as "spoke" and to see how others had interpreted this verse. The source critics, I knew, would expeditiously determine that the author, or the redactor, or the scribe had made a mistake, but how had other exegetes, less prone to ascribe error to the Bible, read Genesis 4:8?

אמר *was* used as "spoke" elsewhere in the Bible, and there were quite a few scholars, medieval and modern, who had written commentaries on this verse, but none of their critiques suited me. Either their exegeses relied on unique translations of אמר, or they hinged on convoluted and esoteric assessments of human emotion. I thought my translation was simple and obvious and depended on ordinary, though intensified, personality traits. Perhaps it was too simple to engage the fancy of earlier commentators, as their psychological interpretations came from so deep between the lines that you had to be a trained psychoanalyst to excavate them. Where were these academics in the fifties while I was watching TV? Were they too young or too conscientious, hunched over their books in the stacks, to have watched Danny Thomas tell his joke?

Cain's murder of Abel is an object lesson in self-indoctrination. Despite the adversary's innocence and the absence of provocation, a person can become convinced by churning resentment over time that hatred is appropriate and aggression justified. This chapter proposes a new translation of the much-debated Genesis 4:8 that depends upon this scenario of vengeful brooding; Cain indulges his hostility toward Abel until rage results in murder. My rendering of the first clause of v. 8 is: "And Cain spoke [thought] against Abel, his brother." As we shall see, this interpretation explicates and extends the narrative, preserves the spare elegance of the unemended Hebrew text, and conforms to the poetics of biblical style.

The King James Version of Genesis 4:8 is: "And Cain talked with Abel his brother: and it came to pass, when they were in the field, that Cain rose up against Abel his brother, and slew him." The New Revised Standard Version is more extensive; it tells us what Cain said: "Cain said to Abel his brother, 'Let us go out to the field.' And when they were in the field, Cain rose up against his brother Abel, and killed him." The words "Let us go out to the field" are absent in the Masoretic Text, the Qumran 4QGen[b], and Targum Onqelos, but these or similar words are supplied in other ancient versions—the Septuagint, the Vulgate, the Samaritan Bible, and the Palestinian Targums—as well as in almost all contemporary English translations.[1]

Scholars differ as to the probable original text. Jouette Bassler says the recounting of Cain's words to Abel in the early versions above "suggests a common basis in a pre-Masoretic reading."[2] Ephraim Speiser boldly asserts: "The original must have contained Cain's statement, but the text was accidentally omitted in MT."[3] Abraham Habermann maintains that difficult passages are often diminished by emendation, and that translating v. 8 as "And Cain spoke," is sufficient to explain this verse as it stands. Though he believes that "something seems to be missing" and that the fuller text of the ancient versions is "clearer," he nevertheless holds that the additional words are "almost certainly incorrect. It is not to be

---

[1] Everett Fox, *The Five Books of Moses* (vol. 1; Schocken Bible; New York: Schocken, 1995) and W. Gunther Plaut, *The Torah: A Modern Commentary* (New York: Union of American Hebrew Congregations, 1981) employ an ellipsis to indicate what the former says "appears incomplete" (27) and the latter terms an "omission" (44).

[2] Jouette Bassler, "Cain and Abel in the Palestinian Targums," *JSJ* 17 (1986): 56.

[3] Ephraim A. Speiser, *Genesis* (AB 1; Garden City, New York: Doubleday, 1964), 30 n. 8.

supposed that the copyists omitted words which are so clear and so apparently necessary for the proper understanding of the text."[4]

In his impressive new textual critique of Genesis 1–11, Ronald Hendel uses the word "plausible" three times in accepting the inclusion of Cain's supposed statement, "Let us go to the field," as the archetype or original text (47). Though I concede that his inclusion is plausible, it rests on the fact that אמר is used as "said" the five other times it appears in the story of Cain and Abel. Since the usages of אמר as "spoke" are so scant compared to the myriad times it is used as "said" (see below and my note 13), I do not find this evidence compelling and prefer to adhere to Hendel's own methodological principle:

> Where the arguments for the primacy of one or another variant are of roughly equal weight, or where the critic has good reason to be skeptical of the various claims to primacy, I have chosen, as a default value, to adopt the reading of M [MT].[5]

I agree with Habermann that the correct understanding of אמר is "spoke" rather than "said." There are two instances other than Genesis 4:8 in which אמר, followed by no direct quote, denotes "spoke": 2 Samuel 21:2 and 2 Chronicles 1:2. Unless אמר is translated as "spoke" in 2 Samuel 21:2, the Bible stutters: "And the king . . . said to them" followed by no speech, a parenthetical phrase, and the needless repeat of אמר in v. 3, "And David said." By understanding the initial אמר as "spoke," the passage achieves fluency. In 2 Chronicles 1:2 אמר is clearly "spoke" and is so translated.[6] As neither of these proof texts entails hostile speech, there are no other examples of אמר אל as "spoke against," though דבר, the word that is commonly used as "spoke," provides many instances of דבר אל as "spoke against."[7] דבר is not so pregnant a term as אמר, however, for it does not signify both thought and speech.[8] The use of אמר in Genesis 4:8 denotes that Cain both spoke against his brother and thought against his brother.[9] I also agree with Habermann that the MT is emended to its loss, for I do not find Cain's words necessary for the proper understanding of the text;

---

[4] Abraham M. Habermann, "Bible and Concordance," introduction to *Thesaurus of the Language of the Bible* (vol. 1; ed. Samuel E. Loewenstamm; Jerusalem: Bible Concordance Press, 1957), xxx.

[5] Ronald Hendel, *The Text of Genesis 1–11* (New York: Oxford University Press, 1998), 8.

[6] An exception is the NRSV that rather freely renders this אמר as "summoned."

[7] See BDB, 181.

[8] דבר is used for supplicating God in Genesis 24:45 and 1 Samuel 1:13. These inaudible entreaties can hardly be termed "thought"; in 1 Samuel 1:13 we are even told that the petitioner's lips move.

[9] "Think" is the preferred understanding of אמר in Genesis 20:11; 26:9; Exodus 2:14; Numbers 24:11; Judges 15:2; Ruth 4:4; 1 Samuel 20:26; 2 Samuel 5:6; 12:22; 2 Kings 5:11; Malachi 1:7; and see BDB, 56.

indeed, their inclusion causes problems. Why would Cain need to invite or to entice his brother outside when both men pursued outdoor occupations? They must both have spent the majority of every day out of doors, and even though their domains differed, it should not have been difficult for Cain to apprehend his brother at work in the field.

More tellingly, if the invitation were intended to show that the murder was not an impulsive act but was premeditated and dependent upon Cain luring Abel outside, then Genesis 4:8 would better have read: "Cain said to Abel his brother, 'Let us go out to the field.' And Cain rose against his brother Abel, and killed him," omitting those three words (in Hebrew)— "and it was," "when they were," "in the field"—that separate the summons from the slaughter. Verbs of existence such as "was," used here in the phrase "And it was," are used far less frequently in Hebrew than in English. Often they serve to indicate a passage of time.[10] The use of the phrase in v. 8 implies an interval of some length between Cain's words and their supposed denouement. The succeeding phrase, "when they were," provides a second dispensable temporal intervening word, doubling the effect of the first. Both are deleterious to the thrust of the passage if the reader is to believe that the addition of "Let us go out to the field" is necessary to harmonize the commencement of v. 8 with its immediate culmination.

The Hebrew Bible is terse; it does not use three words where two or one or none will do. The inclusion of these three word/phrases so distances the proposal from its presumed consequence, both literally and rhetorically, as to convey that the manslaughter occurred a significant period of time after Cain spoke. A murder that takes place days, weeks, months, or even years after the victim is lured outdoors does not appear to be contingent upon this enticement. If the words "Let us go out to the field" were added in some ancient and modern versions to plug a perceived gap, the gap remains. Cain speaks, but the words ascribed to him fail to link the invitation to the murder; the triple sequence of Hebrew phrases following his proposal signals and stresses a length of time—a hiatus that interrupts the action and divorces the summons from the slaughter.

Previous exegetes have proffered ingenious hypotheses to explain the passage as it stands in the MT. The midrash stipulates that אמר refers to an argument (*Genesis Rabbah* 22:16). W. Gunther Plaut offers the same gloss in his translation of the passage.[11] There are two difficulties with

---

[10] For examples we need look no further than vv. 2–3 of our chapter: each infant propels from birth to breadwinner in the duration of a "was," and a "was" mediates the time span before sacrifice is offered. In the remainder of our chapter and in the four succeeding chapters, ויהי denotes a passage of time in each of its occurrences: 4:17; 5:23; 5:31; 5:32; 6:1; 7:10; 7:12; 7:17; 8:6; 8:13.

[11] W. Gunther Plaut, "Cain and Abel: Bible, Tradition, and Contemporary Reflection," in *Preaching Biblical Texts: Expositions by Jewish and Christian Scholars* (ed. Frederick C. Holmgren and Herman E. Schaalman; Grand Rapids, Mich.: Eerdmans, 1995), 12.

understanding אמר as "argued," however. One is the problem mentioned above: if the murder were precipitated by a quarrel, one would expect the assault to attend immediately upon that altercation. In v. 8, these events are separated by two time-extending word/phrases and one geographical word/phrase that all function to dissociate the controversy from the crime. The other objection is that, in Scripture, אמר is nowhere employed in the sense of "to argue."[12] Accepting it as "argued" in this one instance requires a unique translation for one of the most common words in the Hebrew Bible.[13]

Mitchell Dahood proposes a solution that solves the first problem. He renders אמר as "to see," and translates "Cain spoke to his brother" as "Cain was watching for his brother."[14] This interpretation has the virtue of accommodating the three time-stretching word/phrases. The Bible may be intimating that Cain was on the look-out for his brother over a considerable period. Unfortunately for Dahood's rendering, no word in the verse means "for." The preposition אל means "to," "toward," "against," or "on."

Dahood avoids the unique-translation issue by stating that the one other application of אמר as "see" is Genesis 20:11. Typically, אמר is construed here, as in many other verses in the Bible, as "think." Instead of the usual, "And Abraham said: 'Because I *thought* surely there is no fear of God in this place,'" he translates, "And Abraham replied, 'Indeed, I have *beheld* worthlessness: there is no fear of God in this place.'" The verb "beheld" requires a direct object. Dahood contends that the root of רק is not רקק as it is vocalized in the MT, and the word does not mean "surely" but stems from the root ריק and denotes "worthlessness." This understanding appeases the grammatical necessity for a direct object but confronts us with another exceptional translation: nowhere else is רק used to indicate worthlessness.

Ellen van Wolde believes that the omission of Cain's speech is meaningful, for it represents "the negation of the existence of the other as an equal, as a brother." According to her, God's mention of Cain's fallen face in v. 6, refers to Cain's refusal to lift his head and look forthrightly at his brother. Cain's not-looking and empty-speaking foreshadow his later mute bestial attack.[15]

Mayer Gruber terms the latter clause of v. 8 a non sequitur expressing the irrationality of Cain's act and believes the unemended text needs psy-

---

[12] BDB, 55–56.

[13] אמר is used 5,299 times in the MT according to David J. A. Clines, ed., *The Dictionary of Classical Hebrew* (vol. 1; Sheffield: Sheffield Academic Press, 1993), 68.

[14] Mitchell Dahood, "Abraham's Reply in Genesis 20:11," *Bib* 61 (1980): 90–91.

[15] Ellen van Wolde, "The Story of Cain and Abel: A Narrative Study," *JSOT* 52 (1991): 35.

choanalytic "embellishment" to connect Cain's depression with his violence. Rejected by God, Cain loses his self-esteem and becomes depressed because of aggressive impulses turned inward. He regains his self-esteem and dispels depression by releasing these aggressive impulses against his brother.[16]

My analysis of Genesis 4:8 is simpler and less theoretical than those above. Cain's denigratory speaking against Abel could have been directed to Adam and Eve or could have been silent. Parents know the "speaking against" that is brought to their ears by even the most attached siblings. In this case, Cain's parents may not have discouraged such calumny. Cain holds the prestigious position of firstborn; Eve distinguishes his birth with an exclamation. Unlike most male births in Genesis, Abel's nativity is recorded but unremarked.

Those three space-taking, time-stretching word/phrases placed between the "speaking against" and the killing complement my interpretation, for they give Cain an opportunity for his resentment to build. Cain's acrimonious speech and brooding thought intensify into furious savagery over time. The act of murder, unthinkable at one stage, becomes inevitable at another. God may be warning Cain of this potential in v. 7 when he cautions that sin lies לפתח, at the opening. "At the door" is the usual translation, but the word literally means "opening" and is frequently used to refer to opening a mouth.[17] God may be adjuring Cain that it is within his power to control his tongue and thoughts to avoid transgression.

The use of אל for "against" is well-attested in Scripture.[18] The most apt and proximate example is its use in the last clause of our verse: "And Cain rose against Abel his brother, and killed him."[19] My translation of the first clause of the verse is thus felicitous, for it aligns the two parts of the verse in aesthetic balance: Cain spoke against Abel his brother, and Cain rose against Abel his brother. The second clause of v. 8 is not the non sequitur Gruber terms it. By its almost word-for-word reiteration of my reading of the first clause, it confirms the inevitability of cause and effect—evil speech leads to murder.

This understanding of Cain's path to homicide requires neither conversance with psychoanalytic literature nor facility at imaging Cain as a glowering wild animal, for my interpretation of v. 8 hinges on ordinary failings

---

[16] Mayer Gruber, "The Tragedy of Cain and Abel: A Case of Depression," *JQR* 69 (1978): 95–97.

[17] Numbers 16:32; 22:28; 26:10; Isaiah 53:7; Ezekiel 3:2; 3:27; Psalms 38:14; 39:10; Job 3:1; 11:5; Proverbs 8:6; 24:7; 31:8; others.

[18] Exodus 14:5; Numbers 32:14; Joshua 10:6; Judges 1:10; 9:57; 20:30; 1 Samuel 2:34; 22:13; 24:8; others.

[19] Although almost every English rendering includes "up" in this verse, the adverb does not appear in the Hebrew, is unnecessary in English (one cannot rise "down"), and detracts from the elegant parallelism of the last clause to the first clause in this verse.

of human nature that are familiar to every reader. Further, it makes greater use of the text than does any previous explication. "And it was," "when they were," and "in the field" are not redundant and purposeless in my exegesis but are necessarily interposed between speech and act to establish an interval. God's words in v. 7 are also made more comprehensible by this new conception of v. 8. Rather than speaking in ambiguous metaphor, God may be quite literally locating the source of sin at the opening of man's lips. The translation has the additional recommendation of doing no violence to the MT; no words need to be added or subtracted or construed with unique meanings. And lastly, the measured sonority of repetition, so characteristic of biblical style, is here given prominence to the advantage of both the sound and the sense of the passage.

CHAPTER THREE

Take My Wife, Please: On the Utility of the Wife/Sister Motif

The New Haven Board of Jewish Education arranged for a once-weekly, lunch-hour, non-denominational Bible class to be held in the electric company's office building downtown. The twenty or so attendees were executives of the utility, lawyers and doctors from surrounding office buildings, a couple of Yale professors, congregants of the rabbi who taught the course, and me. The students were both Christian and Jewish, and the teacher concentrated on literary/historical aspects of the Hebrew Bible, not on theology—except to show how Israelite religious values shaped the narrative.

The class was ideal for me in its subject matter. We were to start with Genesis, the first book of the Bible, and read through it and the remaining books at the rate of a chapter a week as long as the class and the teacher were game. I had never read the Bible in this systematic fashion, following the story as it unfolded. I had only listened to the Bible reading those Saturdays I attended synagogue in order to improve my Hebrew. My acquaintance with the Bible was episodic and scant. At synagogue, the rabbi would say a few words about the day's reading or invite questions, but he did not have time to dwell on the text for an hour. The teacher of this class came prepared each week to talk about some aspect of the chapter under consideration. Often he brought hand-outs, essays written by Bible scholars about some issue in the chapter we were to read.

The class was not ideal for me in approach. The teacher, a Ph.D. in Bible, was proficient at ripping the author's delicate literary lacework into its J, E, P, and D strands. Many times I wanted to say, "Wait, wait, don't dismantle that. Don't you see the intricate pattern there?" I did not say it, however, because I did not see the intricate pattern myself; I just knew there had to be one. It seemed unlikely to me that the inconsistency or the contradiction or the repetition, upon which the teacher pounced, had escaped the notice of author, redactor, first readers, and centuries of later readers and was detectable only by the literati since the nineteenth century.

Although I did some noiseless gnashing of the teeth, I could not always maintain the respectful silence the teacher surely would have preferred. I spoke up in defense of the seamless unity of the text by pointing out that the so-called flaws must have been obvious to the author or redactor also. The teacher countered that the editor could sift but not winnow. He could refine the verses and insert them where he liked, but the redactor was required, according to the teacher's perspective, to include all the primal material and to make no selection among his sources. The reason we know the redactor was compelled to forego artistry and include segments that do not fit is that the Bible contains segments that do not fit. Does that argument seem circular to you? You can imagine my sighs and rolling of the eyes.

When the class reached the wife/sister stories, these became the instructor's proof texts for a patchwork composition of the Bible. Repeatedly in Genesis, a husband believes his life is endangered by the physical desirability of his wife. He tries therefore to pass her off as his sister to the ruler he perceives as libidinous and threatening. Since the sister is reputedly single, not a married woman with a husband standing between her and the monarch's lust, she is available. All the pharaoh or king need do is pay for her. It is not a pretty story, and it happens three times.

These three stories, the teacher maintained, had to have been folkloric traditions about an individual patriarch. One source named Abraham and the Egyptian pharaoh as the seller and buyer; another said the deal was between Abraham and the Philistine king, Abimelech; and still another identified Abraham's son, Isaac, and Abimelech. The redactor/editor, the teacher said, could privilege no particular source over another and so recorded and preserved all three versions of the one urtext (this word refers to the original, parent text).

Of course, I found this disparate-derivation hypothesis inimical, but I could not think of a hypothesis I preferred. Did the author expect us to believe that all three of these tawdry bargains were made, that Abraham did not learn caution from Sarah's first ordeal, that the son, Isaac, learned nothing from his parents' tribulations? How far can a reader's credulity stretch?

But maybe the author was not concerned with whether or not the reader believed that these perilous gambles actually took place. Maybe he gave the reader credit for being able to grasp and appreciate a complex, layered exposition of information. Maybe he created three variations on an original theme or put a well-known myth, folktale, scandal, or whatever it was, to triple use for an exquisite literary purpose. To a modern reader, accustomed to more prosaic literary fare, the author's presentation of these three wife/sister tales was as mystifying as a game of three-dimensional chess would be to a tic-tac-toe enthusiast, but perhaps the more skillful or practiced ancient reader had no difficulty conceptualizing on multiple levels.

I suggested these possibilities to the teacher, but he rejected them. His acceptance of the documentary hypothesis was so absolute, his conviction so adamant, I could not induce him to admit of other alternatives—especially since I had no counter theory. I decided I would ruminate over the three wife/sister stories until I had determined the writer's design to my satisfaction. My motivation was nothing more elevated or admirable than the aspiration to chip at my teacher's certainty.

I started by reading what others had written about these tales. "Take My Wife, Please" does not cite these authors, as it is only the third essay I wrote. I was not yet comfortable donning full scholarly armor, and nothing in my reading supported me anyway. Contemporary scholars ascribed two stories to one source and one story to another—no encouragement there for my assumption that all three stories were the work of one artist. The midrashists agreed with my lone-artist premise, but their explanations of the triumvirate were either too frilly or too legalistic to content me. They provided elaborate genealogies proving that Abraham was indeed Sarah's half-brother, for example, as though his veracity were the crux of the problem. To my surprise, none of the scholars I read, medieval or modern, showed any concern for the feelings of the disposable wives. Medieval scholars sympathized with Abraham and Isaac's predicament, but no one I read had a single thing to say about their wives' sensibilities.

The presumable dismay of the women was the first feature of the narrative to disturb me. Though we are explicitly told that Isaac loved Rebecca (Genesis 24:67), I had learned in school that marriage for love was a fairly late societal phenomenon, and so I could believe that biblical marriages had mores different from today's unions. But when a man and woman live together, sleep together, have children together (in Isaac and Rebecca's case), do not obligation, protectiveness, and possessiveness develop? No monarch has ever desired me, I must frankly admit, but *twice* while dining out with my husband I have had occasion to say, "Honey, there's a man at that table over there who's winking at me." I do not know what I expected my husband to do—scowl aggressively at the men, perhaps, and thereby assert his prior claim—but I do know that I did not expect him to go over to the men and say, "You want her; you can have her. How much will you give me for her?" Such a response would be unthinkably unloving and unmanly for him and heartbreaking for me. And so why did the commentators not pity Sarah and Rebecca for Abraham and Isaac's lack of virile defense? True, my husband did not believe winking men imperiled his life, and they both turned out to be old college buddies of his, but since the patriarchs believed Pharaoh and Abimelech were murderers as well as debauchees, were they not handing their wives over to mortal, as well as carnal, danger? Would not flight have been a better plan for the women's sake?

I believe the reason for exegetic indifference to the ostensibly misogynist nature of the stories is that modern analysts are more interested in sorting out and labeling the tales' sources than in contemplating portrayal of character, and traditional exegetes paid little attention to women's circumstances or sentiments. Nor does the biblical narrator express disapprobation of the men's craven selfishness. Rarely, if ever, throughout the Bible does the narrator evaluate or appraise behavior. The reader must deduce the wages of wrongdoing from the unwinding of the plot. As I continued in Genesis, mindful of the derelictions that troubled me, I saw that whether or not these two couples had enjoyed loving marriages before the wife/sister episodes, their unions could only be labeled dysfunctional after the incidents.

Abraham owed Sarah a debt for his treatment of her; both of them recognized his liability, and Sarah extracted her due. Just as he had twice placed her at risk, she twice took her compensation. Isaac too was under obligation to Rebecca, and she wrung his arrears from him without a qualm. There is a talmudic saying that each verse in the Torah has seventy faces. It means that the words of the Torah are many faceted and call forth many glosses. When I wrote the article, "Hagar Requited," years after I wrote about the wife/sister stories, I again assessed the discord between Abraham and Sarah. Since my Hebrew and familiarity with the rest of the Bible had improved in the interim, my lexical analyses became less conjectural and more corroborated. The thrust of some of the Hebrew words and phrases used to reveal Abraham and Sarah's marital friction differ in the more recent article from those in "Take My Wife, Please." Nevertheless, both interpretations can co-exist as separate sparks from the connubial conflagration.

As I continued to deliberate on the wife/sister stories, I could trace their reverberations in the political realm as well as in the familial, and I describe these international consequences in the chapter, but the breakthrough that had me leaping in the air with the "sat on the cat" sensation was the discovery that the wife/sister stories had equivalent counterparts in Exodus and in 1 and 2 Samuel. For all I know (and all anyone knows) Genesis and these other three books had the same author. I would not want to stipulate that, but I will nevertheless call whoever ingeniously correlated these six incidents the "author."

The first equivalency I discovered, and the only one I later learned that others had not previously noticed, is that between the account of Isaac and Rebecca and the clash between King David and his wife, Michal, in 2 Samuel 6:16, 20–23. I happened to skip ahead in the Bible and read about David and Michal because my son, David, married a young woman whose Hebrew name was Michal—the daughter-in-law mentioned earlier. (Fortunately, by the time I read about the biblical character for whom my daughter-in-law was named, she and my son were already parents, and so I did not take the biblical Michal's childlessness for a bad omen.) In Genesis 26:8, the third wife/sister story, a king looks out a window and becomes angry when he sees amorous "sporting" (from the Hebrew root צחק, laughter, play) between Isaac and Rebecca. In 2 Samuel, Michal, a king's daughter also looks out a window and becomes angry when she sees David "sporting" (the Hebrew word used in 2 Samuel 6:21 is שחק, an alternate form of צחק). The similarity is obvious; the significance of the parallel is not.

After more than a year, the lunch-hour class finished Genesis and started reading Exodus. Except for the resemblance noted above, I had received no illumination on the wife/sister stories, other than recognition of the wives' mistreatment, their eventual retaliation, and the national ramifications of Abraham and Isaac's thwarted pandering, but I continued to turn the stories this way and that in my mind. One of the hand-outs the teacher gave us about Exodus mentioned, in passing, that the first wife/sister story is similar to the story of the exodus. In both, Pharaoh holds captive something precious—Abraham's wife in the wife/sister story, the Israelite people in the exodus story. In order to force him to release his captives, God afflicts Pharaoh with great plagues, and the wife or slaves' release is accompanied with considerable Egyptian wealth. The correspondence between these two stories, I learned, was well-recognized, but the only inference drawn from it was that the first wife/sister story is just another of the many echoes of the exodus story throughout the Bible. I was gratified that I could now see two parts of the puzzle: the exodus analogy to the first wife/sister story and the Michal corollary to the third. But where was the missing piece between these two that must relate to the second wife/sister story, and what was the purport of these affinities?

While working my weekly way through Exodus with the lunch-hour class, I also attended another Bible study group—the New Haven Shabbos Group that I mentioned in note 1 of Chapter One. This group was studying 1 Samuel, and one week they reached the story of a Philistine battle with the Israelites in which the Philistines capture the holy ark (1 Samuel 5:1–6:13). The ark is a hot potato in Philistine hands, and they move it first to Ashdod, then to Gath, then to Ekron. Each of these cities suffers greatly while the ark is in its possession. Many die, and those that live are stricken with hemorrhoids (5:12). The priests and diviners of the Philistines liken their chiefs to the Egyptians and Pharaoh when they would not let the Israelites go (6:6), and advise these warlords to return the ark to the Israelites with costly gifts: golden replicas of hemorrhoids and golden mice.

The account of the Philistines nervously shuttling the ark from city to city as though it were radioactive is funny. Hemorrhoids are considered a funny ailment; this fact does not speak well for human empathy, but it is nevertheless true. Golden hemorrhoids are even funnier, and golden mice also have a ludicrous aspect. The Shabbos Group had fun with this story, though we all put on our straightest faces and agreed that hemorrhoids were no joking matter.

That night, I could not fall asleep. I counted sheep; I counted backwards from a hundred by sevens; I said the alphabet in reverse. No insomnia remedy was efficacious. What was keeping me up? Surely not sympathy for the Philistines, though my thoughts kept reverting to their troubles with the ark. "All right," I finally said to myself, close to 1:00 A.M., "If you want to think about Philistines, then think about them; you'll sleep tomorrow night." I rolled over on my back, opened my eyes, stared at the ceiling, and thought about the portion we had read that Saturday.

I could not shout "Eureka" and wake my husband, but I was so excited that I wanted to shout something. After pondering my inability to dismiss Philistinian distress from my mind, I saw that the capture and retention of the holy ark resembles the second wife/sister story. In both, the Philistines hold something invaluable—Sarah in one story, the ark containing the tablets of the law in the other. In order to force their release, God afflicts the Philistines with barrenness in one story, hemorrhoids in the other (both maladies, with wicked cleverness, concern the nether parts of the body), and the captive prize is returned to its rightful possessor with rich gifts. Not only was I now able to fit the missing piece into the puzzle, but I saw a rationale for the necessity of three wife/sister stories.

First, a little algebra: let us call the three wife/sister stories A, B, and C, and let us further say that $A=B=C$, since they are so much alike. Now let us suppose that there are three other stories, call them X, Y, and Z, so much like A, B, and C respectively, that one could say $A=X$, $B=Y$, and $C=Z$. This being so, then, *quod erat demonstrandum* (as my geometry teacher used to say), $X=Y=Z$. The algebraic notation helped me to understand the author's model and is the way I mentally configured my analysis, though the chapter deals with these equivalencies in non-algebraic terms.

The first wife/sister story, Sarah in the possession of Pharaoh, or A, equals the story of the Israelite slaves in Egypt, or X. B, the retention of Sarah by the Philistine king, equals the retention of the ark by the Philistines, or Y. And the third wife/sister story, or C, in which the precious object never leaves its proper domain, but a king looks out a window and sees, to his chagrin, "sporting" with a wife, equals Z—in which a king's daughter looks out window and sees, to her fury, "sporting" before the holy ark. The three wife/sister stories, $A=B=C$, have led us by algebraic comparison to see that $X=Y=Z$.

The equivalence established by the similarity of the wife/sister stories, A, B, and C to the three stories labeled X, Y, and Z has a theological significance. If the X story, the exodus, is like the first wife/sister tale A, then, by analogy, the Israelite people, may be considered the bride of God—his treasure. The word of God, contained in the captured ark, in story Y, may, by analogy to wife/sister narrative B, be considered Israel's bride, *its* inestimable treasure. When King David dances before the ark in Z, he sports with his metaphorical bride, his treasure, the word of God, just as in the equivalent wife/sister story, Isaac sports with his love, Rebecca. The wife/sister stories, I could now clearly see, were anything but misogynistic; indeed, the women in these stories are equated to God's chosen people as well as to his holy word, the Torah.

My son-in-law's mother, a woman who has reflected much on the Bible, once asked me why I thought King David gets such a free pass in life. He lies, cheats, steals, and even murders; yet God, though he chastises him, continues to hold him dear. The third wife/sister correlation may be her answer. Isaac "sports" with his wife; David "sports" with the word of God. We are meant to learn that the Torah is David's dearest love. He may not always live by it, but he values it over all else.

So which came first—the chickens or the eggs? Is the first wife/sister story an anticipation of the exodus, or is the exodus a representation of Israel's mystical marriage to God? Did the author of 1 Samuel place the second wife/sister story to bolster the ark/wife analogy, or did the Davidic faction of latter day spin-doctors position the second and third wife/sister stories in Genesis to eventually show by analogy what a devout fellow their king was? Maybe all three wife/sister tales are divinely inspired proleptic ("proleptic" and "prolepsis," favorite terms of literary theorists, refer to the representation of a future act, foreshadowing) metaphors of events that will transpire centuries hence. I do not know, but I do know that the three wife/sister stories are segments that fit; they are necessary plot elements on the domestic, the political, and the spiritual levels; they are not the unpremeditated and indiscriminate inclusion of an artless redactor.

Three times in the book of Genesis we are told of a husband passing his wife off as his sister lest he be killed by those who desire her. In Genesis 12:10–20, Abraham deceives the Egyptians about Sarah's status. (At this point in the Bible, Abraham and Sarah are still called Abram and Sarai. I shall, however, use their final names throughout.) In Genesis 20:1–18, Abraham deceives the Philistines, and, in Genesis 26:1–12, the Philistines are again deceived, but this time by Abraham's son, Isaac.

To advocates of the "Higher Criticism," the triple repetition presents little difficulty. To these exegetes it is obvious that two of these stories come from one source and the remaining story from another. According to the documentary theorists, the redactor preserved all three tales, unlikely as their multiple occurrence may have seemed, to fill space, as a sort of editorial stutter, or because he did not feel at liberty to give one folktale preference over the others.

Traditional interpreters find the proofs of these source analysts shallow and arbitrary. All of these stories, orthodoxy maintains, come from one source: the mouth of God by the hand of Moses. In this view, each version teaches us different ethical and theological principles. Repetition is necessary and beneficial because we may learn by comparing and contrasting the stories, and because it is only with the emphasis of repetition that these principles are impressed and inculcated.

My position is neither the linguistic and historiographic one of the source analysts nor the religious and didactic one of the traditionalists. As the Bible comes to us as a single text, I prefer to treat it as a unified entity and to focus on its literary and narrative qualities. At the supposed seams where source critics discover rough stitching together of disparate texts, I see, not fault lines, but gold mines of subtlety and allusion.

Accordingly, apparent anachronisms do not worry me. Source critics find it particularly telling to their case that in the second and third stories Philistines are placed in Gerar, although Philistines did not then exist. Orthodox apologists conclude from these stories that either there *was* a small colony of Philistines in Gerar at that time, or that the inhabitants of Gerar were the ethnic precursors of the Philistines and might just as well be called by that name. To me, the statement that Abraham and Isaac encountered Philistines is of great narrative significance, as will be shown, and it was brilliant of the author, anachronism or no.

Similarly, I am not troubled by a detail such as Sarah's age in the chronology of the first two stories. Documentary hypothesists argue the haphazard insertion of these stories by observing that Sarah is sixty-five the first time her honor is placed in jeopardy and ninety the second time. Since she could not have been the object of Egyptian and Philistine desire at these ages, the stories must be clumsy interpolations. Orthodoxy maintains Sarah's beauty was so sublime that even at ninety she retained her freshness and pulchritude. I find the threat to Sarah's virtue and, particularly, the temporary Egyptian and Philistine possession of Abraham's greatest treasure, his wife, a literary necessity, and so her years are not a critical factor. Besides, that she is a woman of a certain age serves the author's intention to make these stories amusing.

From my literary perspective I see coherence, integrity, and intent in this thrice-told tale. All three stories function to explain the subsequent motivations of the individuals and nations involved and to reveal the inner objectives of persons whose actions will be described centuries hence. Like an operatic overture the wife/sister narratives refer to melodies that we must wait to hear developed fully. Though the stories are comic, and repetition heightens their humor, each has serious ramifications. I shall argue that it is necessary for the author to tell three nearly identical stories, for each of them is analogous to events that will occur later in the text. The later stories shed light on one another, but the reader would not connect them without the clue provided by the obvious similarity of their corresponding wife/sister counterparts. The purpose of this chapter is to show how the wife/sister motif is utilized to further and to enhance the narrative on the political, the domestic, and the theological levels immediately as well as over a long time span.

THE JOKE

My title begins with an old joke. The wife/sister stories are even older jokes—dangerous, blameworthy, practical jokes. Abraham is a clever and successful strategist who manages, with his wit and considerable help from God, to turn the tables on his powerful adversaries and leave their respective towns with his life, his unsullied wife, and his host's bounty.

When Abraham asks his wife to pass herself off as his sister, he says, "Say, I pray thee, thou art my sister; that it may be well with me for thy sake, and that my soul may live because of thee" (Genesis 12:13). Traditional interpreters as well as non-religious readers recoil from the hint that Abraham plans to enrich himself from the bride-price he will get for his wife. They explain, "that it may be well with me for thy sake," does not refer to doing well in the financial sense but means only that Abraham needs to stay alive so that he can somehow protect Sarah from the depredations of the Egyptians. Therefore, the phrase, "that it may be well with me," is the exact equivalent of "that my soul may live."

Traditionalists, however, cannot supply a more scrupulous sounding equivalent for the repetition of the phrase in the description of the transaction Pharaoh and Abraham make, "and the woman was taken into Pharaoh's house. And he dealt well with Abram for her sake; and he had sheep, and oxen, and he-asses, and men-servants, and maidservants, and she-asses, and camels" (Genesis 12:15–16). To the ancient reader, I am convinced, this shady deal was funny. Pharaoh, more fool he, is paying all those livestock and servants for a woman who is not even a virgin. And no spring chicken into the bargain.

Another example of this order of humor may be found in Exodus 2:9, in which we are told that Pharaoh's daughter pays Moses' mother wages to nurse him. The Hebrews were slaves, after all; to require a slave to nurse without compensation would have seemed more appropriate. The reader derives ironic enjoyment from the fact that the mother is paid to nurse her own baby. The humor celebrates the minor victory of the victim over the oppressor. When the Hebrew slaves are finally expelled from Egypt there is a similarly "amusing" reversal of fortune (12:35–36), and the Israelites walk away rich from four hundred years of slavery, just as God foretold in Genesis 15:14.

Ancient readers reveled in stories of victim turned victor and had an earthy appreciation of the comedic element in Abraham's shrewd gambles. The humor is stressed even more in the second wife/sister tale. We see Abimelech, king of the Philistines, make the same bad deal as Pharaoh; we observe him trying to claim a little more innocence than God will allow (20:5–6), and we witness Abraham's embarrassed, untruthful, bumbling justifications for his deception. Inside of three sentences he catches himself in a lie: in the first sentence he says that he feared the people in *this* place, and in the third sentence he admits he had asked Sarah to lie about their relationship *every* place they should come. And he fields an excuse so beside the point that Abimelech's blood pressure must have sky-rocketed: Abraham says that Sarah is indeed his sister, his half-sister on his father's side (20:11–13). To Abimelech, whose entire household is barren because he has taken this man's wife, it does not matter if she is also his cousin, his aunt, and his grandmother. She is Abraham's wife, and God is wroth. Abimelech does not let the half-truth pass but says sarcastically to Sarah, "Behold, I have given your brother a thousand pieces of silver" (20:16). Abraham's defensive fumbling in response to Abimelech's anger sounds like an adolescent making inept excuses for a careless accident with the family car: "It wasn't me driving. And, anyway, it's not your car; it's registered in Mom's name. Besides, I was really driving slow."

Unpalatable as Abraham's tricks are to more modern tastes, they serve to illuminate his character. Some exegetes have said Abraham showed little faith in God by going down to Egypt in the face of the famine; he should have stayed in Canaan and relied upon God to feed his family, servants, and flocks. But Abraham shows great faith in God. He risks his life and his wife's honor on his trust that God would fulfill His promises in Genesis 12:2, 7. Before the sojourn in Egypt, God had promised Abraham offspring. Surely the Lord will not permit Pharaoh to retain Sarah, for, if he did, from whence would this offspring come? By the time of the second wife/sister story Abraham has a son by Hagar, but God has promised him a son by Sarah as well (17:19); therefore, somehow, God will preserve Sarah from the lust of Abimelech.

To be certain that the reader understands that Abraham is a trickster rather than a cowardly and rapacious man, the author tells us the story of Abraham's brave rescue of Lot soon after Abraham leaves Egypt. Abraham's physical courage is evidenced by his unhesitating campaign to retrieve his nephew from captivity. When Abraham is offered the spoils of victory by the king of Sodom, and refuses to take so much as a shoelace from him, we see that Abraham is not greedily ambitious for wealth (14:12–23). He will not be enriched by the likes of the king of Sodom simply because they happen to be on the same side of a just cause, but he is willing to enrich himself by defeating those who would tyrannize him— Pharaoh and Abimelech.

THE NATIONAL LEVEL

A practical joke does not seem funny to the butt of the joke nor to other participants who might be hurt by it. The Egyptians and the Philistines never forgive the Hebrews for what Abraham and Isaac did, and the political consequences of their acts reverberate across the centuries. The patriarchs engendered lasting enmities for doing "deeds . . . that ought not to be done" (20:9).

The events leading to the exodus are a paradigm of the first wife/sister tale. All of the salient circumstances of Abraham's prank on Pharaoh echo in the account of Joseph's descendants in Egypt. Just as Abraham and Sarah go to Egypt because of famine, so does Joseph's family. Pharaoh takes Sarah, Abraham's most precious possession, and a later Pharaoh enslaves and keeps Israel, a people precious to God. In both stories, the captives are not released until God smites Pharaoh with plagues. In both stories the Hebrews leave Egypt with Egyptian wealth. The tune we first hear in Genesis is repeated in Exodus.

When the Israelites escaped from Egypt, God did not lead them through "the land of the Philistines, although that was near, for God said: 'Lest peradventure the people repent when they see war, and they return to Egypt'" (Exodus 13:17). Once again, the mention of Philistines in this time and in this place raises the source critics' charge of anachronism. Traditional interpreters wonder, to which war does God refer? I believe the author names the Philistines here to pick up the melody and play out an old hatred. The Philistines would have attacked the Israelites in retaliation for Abraham and Isaac's centuries-old transgressions.

The Bible does not record God's opinion of Abraham and Isaac's ploy, but extrapolating from later evidence, we may assume some degree of silent sympathy for the Egyptians and the Philistines. Again and again in Scripture, God commands the Israelites to show no mercy and to utterly destroy the peoples with whom they contend. The Moabites and the Ammonites are spared this judgment; they are related to the Israelites, for they descend from the incestuous children of Lot (Genesis 19:37–38). The Israelites are told not to abhor the Edomites because they descend from their brother, Esau (Deuteronomy 23:8). The non-family Amalekites, Hittites, Amorites, Canaanites, Perizzites, Hivites, Jebusites, and Gergashites, however, are all sentenced to extermination (Exodus 23:23; Deuteronomy 7:1–2, 20:17; 1 Samuel 15:3). Only the Egyptians and the Philistines are not designated for obliteration, though neither are related to the Israelites and in spite of the fact that they had either oppressed Israel for four hundred years or warred with Israel for generations (the prophesy against Egypt in Ezekiel 29:2–16 portends stringent punishment over a period of forty years but not annihilation). They had been wronged by the Hebrews and have a right to their hereditary hatred.

THE DOMESTIC LEVEL

The wife/sister stories have domestic as well as national repercussions. Sarah and Rebecca are not the targets of the trick, but they too are hurt. Their chastity is not profaned, but their honor is certainly violated: they are forced to assent to a lie. In the first and third stories their silence implies their consent; in the second story Abimelech reports that Sarah told him, "He is my brother" (Genesis 20:5). Abraham's genealogical explanation, furious though it must have made Abimelech, serves to validate Sarah's assertion. Abraham's regard for Sarah is such that he will not let her be considered a bald-faced liar. Yet, neither Abraham's nor Isaac's regard for their wives extends to a real concern for their self-esteem.

How does a woman feel when her husband's survival plan is to sell her to the king? Even if Abraham and Isaac have perfect faith in the providence of God, surely their wives feel devalued, shamed, frightened, and angry. Doesn't he love me? Couldn't he have thought of something else? Why did we even have to come to Egypt/Gerar? Of course they want their husbands to live, but the men's lives must be bought with their wives' freedom and chastity. Each woman risks spending the rest of her life in the ruler's harem—in Rebecca's case, never to see her children again. They both agree to take the risk, but in the economy of marriage, in the *quid pro quo* of human relationships, their husbands owe them. And Sarah and Rebecca collect.

In Genesis 12:11–13, when Abraham asks Sarah to let him pass her off as his sister to the Egyptians, he uses a particular form of supplication. He says, "Behold, please," to point out the peril of her beauty and the Egyptians' lasciviousness and repeats the participle of entreaty (נא), "Please," in making his request. Sarah uses exactly the same formula in appealing to Abraham to father a child by her maid. She says "Behold, please" and points out that the Lord has not allowed her to bear children; then she says "please" again and makes her plea for Abraham to have sexual relations with Hagar (Genesis 16:2). The duplication in language signals the reciprocity to the reader; having granted a favor, Sarah now asks for a favor in return.

It is reasonable to assume that Sarah was not eager to accede to Abraham's demeaning request; neither is Abraham inclined toward Sarah's plan. The narrator intimates this in 16:3 by telling us that Hagar was Egyptian and interjecting the apparently irrelevant information that Abraham, by this time, had lived in Canaan ten years. Presumably, Hagar was one of the maidservants they had acquired from Pharaoh. Had Abraham wanted to get an heir by her, or by anyone other than Sarah, he would not have waited ten years to do so. God had promised progeny to Abraham, and he was content to rest on that promise.

The transaction with Pharaoh was profitable as far as Abraham was concerned, but it was disastrous to Sarah's scheme. As soon as Hagar was confident in her pregnancy, "her mistress was despised in her eyes" (16:4). The Hebrew root translated as "despised" means dishonored, held in contempt, and lightly esteemed. Why should not Hagar esteem Sarah lightly? Hagar saw Abraham hold her lightly, and Sarah can be taunted with that disgrace, derided for living a lie, and perhaps even smeared with the insinuation that Pharaoh had lain with her before the plagues effected her release. Abraham tells Sarah to do that which is good in her eyes. Often in the Bible, when one is told to do as one pleases, the speaker deplores what he knows will be done (Judges 17:6; 19:24; 21:25; 1 Samuel 14:40). The prospect of Sarah's harsh treatment of Hagar pains Abraham, but he knows that he has done Sarah an injury and that she is still being hurt by it.

Abraham again falls into moral debt to Sarah by the events in Gerar, the second wife/sister tale, and she again collects her due by banishing Hagar and her son, Ishmael. The Gerar experience is much worse for Sarah than was the Egyptian episode. That Abraham plays the same trick again, despite her remonstrance with him, must be wounding; that he does not bother to ask her compliance, but now takes her for granted, is belittling. This time there is more anxiety. She has already had the experience of being taken to Pharaoh's harem; she knows too well what is likely to happen. And in Gerar she does not get away with silent assent; she must voice her participation in the deceit (Genesis 20:5). Her anguish is greater the second time, and Abraham pays a higher price for it.

Sarah sees Ishmael "sporting" (see Chapter Four) and tells Abraham that his firstborn son and Hagar, Ishmael's mother, must be banished, but she does not tell Abraham the true reason why this must be so. Abraham loves Ishmael and might make excuses for him, saying he is only a boy and will grow out of his bad behavior. Sarah needs a subterfuge to get rid of these thorns, and so she says she does not want Ishmael to share in Isaac's inheritance. Of course it had not taken her years, from Isaac's birth to his weaning, to notice that Ishmael was also an heir.

In the third wife/sister story Isaac too becomes indebted to his wife Rebecca, for she, to her hazard, must accede to his guileful stratagem. Rebecca collects the debt when she devises the deception of switching her favorite son, Jacob, for Isaac's pet, Esau (27:6–13). A trick for a trick, a sister for a wife, a second born for a firstborn. Like Sarah, she proffers a plausible excuse when she tells Isaac why she wants Jacob to leave town (27:46). She could have told him the truth; he knew that he had given Esau's blessing to Jacob and that Esau was unhappy. She could have said, "Let Jacob leave town for a few days until Esau cools off." Maybe she feared that Isaac would say, "A good thrashing is just what Jacob needs." Or maybe we learn here that their husbands had taught both Sarah and Rebecca to lie.

THE THEOLOGICAL LEVEL

The marked congruity of the first wife/sister story and the Israelite liberation alerts the reader to expect similar agreement between the other wife/sister tales and later events in the Bible. The second wife/sister account has been compared to the capture of the holy ark by the Philistines in 1 Samuel 4–6. Umberto Cassuto, in *Commentary on Genesis* (vol. 2, 341), observes the striking parallels between the first wife/sister story and the narrative of the Hebrew bondage in Egypt. He mentions the agreement between the second wife/sister story and 1 Samuel 4–6 but, since he finds it less clear than the first association, does not ascribe any particular significance to it. I, however, find it significant in several respects. It reiterates the theme of animosity between the Philistines and the Hebrews, it repeats the leitmotif of comedy, and it introduces the metaphor of the holy ark as the bride of Israel.

In this passage of 1 Samuel, the Philistines capture the ark from the Israelites in battle and keep it until God afflicts them with, apparently, hemorrhoids. They then return the ark to the Israelites along with propitiatory gifts: images of hemorrhoids cast in gold and golden mice. To some interpreters, this combination suggests that the Philistines had bubonic plague and were sending symbols of their buboes and of the rodent carriers of the disease. I think the conjecture projects backward a greater scientific sophistication than the civilization possessed. Perhaps the author names mice as objects of the Philistines' veneration and specifies hemorrhoids as their disease to heighten the humor of the account and increase its resonance with the comedic second wife/sister tale. Certainly, as conciliatory gifts to *YHWH*-fearing Hebrews, these infidel symbols seem risibly inappropriate.

The concordance between 1 Samuel 4–6 and the story of Abraham in Genesis 20 is manifest. In each story the cherished object is taken by the Philistines—another reason for "anachronistically" placing the Philistines in Abraham's time. In each story, God afflicts the Philistines (with barrenness in Genesis 20, with hemorrhoids 1 Samuel), and in each the captive prize is returned with gifts. Just as Sarah is dear to Abraham, so is the word of God contained in the ark dear to Israel. The equivalency established here between Abraham's love for his wife and Israel's love for the word of God is critical to a third analogy that I find—that between the third wife/sister tale and 2 Samuel 6:16–23.

In this passage of 2 Samuel, King David joyfully accompanies the ark into Jerusalem. King Saul's daughter, David's wife, Michal, looks out a window and sees David "leaping and dancing before the Lord" (that is, before the word of God contained in the ark), and she "despised him in her heart" (6:16). She speaks sharply to David about his behavior, ostensibly angry at the improper, undignified exposure caused by his prancing about. David replies heatedly that he will make merry before the Lord (6:21).

The Hebrew word used for "make merry" is an alternate form of the verb "laugh" and of the root for Isaac's name. We have already noted its use earlier in the stories in which he figures. In this instance, I believe, it is specifically reminiscent of the use of the word in the third wife/sister tale in which Abimelech looks out a window and sees Isaac "sporting" or "making merry" with Rebecca (Genesis 26:8). In Genesis, a king looks out a window and sees "sporting" to his displeasure; in 2 Samuel a king's daughter looks out a window and sees "sporting" to hers.

The analogy Cassuto noted between the second wife/sister story and the theft of the ark by the Philistines leads the reader to consider that the word of God contained in the ark may be described metaphorically as the wife of Israel. The analogy between the third wife/sister tale and the

David story—in both a royal personage looks out a window and is displeased by a sight described by the same root word—further guides the reader to equate "sporting" with a wife and "making merry" before the Lord. David "sports" with the word of God; the connotation of conjugal sexuality that is so crucial to the Genesis story is important in 2 Samuel as well. It enables us to understand that Michal is jealous of David's love for the word of God. She is not indignant because he showed a bit too much thigh. Just as Sarah finds a plausible reason to banish Hagar and Ishmael, and Rebecca uses a pretext to separate Jacob and Esau, so does Michal use a specious justification for her anger with David. The function of the wife/sister stories here is to clarify the scene between Michal and David, expose their hearts, and explain God's disposition to both.

Romantic love is not stressed in the Bible as in modern Western literature, and yet we are explicitly told of the love nine different men have for individual women or a set of women. We are told that Isaac loved Rebecca (Genesis 24:67), Jacob loved Rachel (29:18, 20, 30), Shechem loved Dinah (34:3), Elkanah loved Hannah (1 Samuel 1:5), Amnon loved Tamar (2 Samuel 13:1), Rehoboam loved Maacah (2 Chronicles 11:21), Ahasuerus loved Esther (Esther 2:17), Samson loved Delilah (Judges 16:4), and Solomon loved his foreign wives (1 Kings 11:1–2). But only once in Scripture are we told of a woman loving a particular man. We are told Michal loved David, and we are told it twice (1 Samuel 18:20, 28). Her love for David is obviously remarkable in both senses of the word. And as it is doubly impressed upon us, we can also assume it is an extreme, possessive passion.

David has many wives and concubines. We are not told that Michal resents any of them. Perhaps she knows that they do not count in David's heart, that his greatest and only true love is for his bride, all Israel's bride, the word of God. Michal looks out a window and, obsessively, sees David embracing her only rival. We learn that she herself is not God-fearing, as she uses תרפים (small idols) to make a dummy in David's bed in order to fool her father's henchmen and save David's life (19:13). What is an Israelite woman doing with תרפים?

God, not Abimelech, causes Isaac to prosper at the end of the third wife/sister story (Genesis 26:12). Because of David's love for God he too is rewarded with military victory again and again, and his failings are forgiven. Because of Michal's jealousy of this love, she "had no child unto the day of her death" (2 Samuel 6:23). One might think she remained childless because David, offended by her outburst, would not live with her as husband and wife. If this were the case, Scripture would have had to say something like, "And David went in to her no longer." We would not be told simply that she was childless because childlessness, the Bible has shown us repeatedly, is caused not by man but by God. It is not clear whether Michal remained barren or died in childbirth, but either fate may be regarded as God's judgment.

CONCLUSION

The three wife/sister stories may all be historical fact. They may be a skillful inter-weaving of pre-existent stories, or they may be elaborated from a single, more primitive, folktale. Perhaps they are an ingenious creation of a redactor. However they come to us, each has its own function in the narrative and is inventively used to justify the ill-feeling between the Israelites, the Egyptians, and the Philistines; to explain why these enemies of the Hebrews are never consigned by God to oblivion as are other peoples; to warrant the seemingly cruel and devious actions of Sarah and Rebecca; and to make the theological point that the love of God is a surpassing virtue. The three stories are not repeated by mistake.

CHAPTER FOUR

Hagar Requited

I was at the American Academy of Religion/Society of Biblical Literature Conference in San Francisco to present "Spoiled Child," and because I am a woman I was invited to the yearly feminist breakfast. I usually do not attend such events, partly because of shyness—since I am not affiliated with a college or university and thus have no colleagues, I know no one at these academic conferences except by reputation—and mainly because the filtered viewpoint of feminists in the aggregate exasperates me. Although I bow to no one in my insistence on equal treatment and opportunity for all, in a gathering of other feminists I feel as I do when surrounded by Marxist or Freudian commentators: I want to wear sandwich boards stating that all progress is *not* a result of class struggle, and sometimes a cigar *is* just a cigar, and maybe, once, a man was *not* to blame.

The discussion topic for the breakfast, however, was Sarah and Hagar, and I wanted to learn about this pair. Two chapters in Genesis feature Hagar. Her story begins in chapter 16 when, after many years of a childless marriage, Sarah asks Abraham to have sexual intercourse with her maid, Hagar, so that Sarah can be "built up through her." Abraham complies, and Hagar conceives. Once pregnant, Hagar slights her mistress, and Sarah so afflicts her that she runs away into the desert. Hagar meets an angel who tells her to return to Sarah and Abraham.

In chapter 21, we are told that Sarah, in her old age, bears a son to Abraham whom they name Isaac. A few years later, Hagar's son, Ishmael, now in his teens, does something that alienates Sarah. Most translations say that he is mocking. The New Revised Standard Version says that he is playing with Isaac. Sarah tells Abraham that he must cast out the slave and the slave's son, as he will not inherit with her son, with Isaac. Abraham is distressed at the prospect of losing his son, Ishmael, but God tells him to listen to Sarah and assures him that Ishmael's line will become a great nation.

Abraham releases the slave woman and her son into the desert with only the bread and water Hagar can carry on her shoulder. They wander in the wilderness until their water runs out. Weeping and at the point of death, Hagar again hears the voice of an angel. God shows her a well, and her life and the life of her son are saved. The Bible says that God is with Ishmael, that he becomes an archer, and that Hagar finds him a wife.

When my daughter married, my husband and I met her in-laws-to-be for the first time a few days before the wedding. Like me, Jeanne Dennis, my daughter's prospective mother-in-law, studies the Bible, and she asked me if I had any thoughts on why Hagar is dealt with so cruelly. Why, the first time Hagar roams in the desert, does the angel of the Lord send her back to Sarah's harshness? She is going to be saved at the end of the story, and so why does God not free her at the first celestial encounter and spare her seventeen or so years of mistreatment? Why is Sarah not criticized or punished for her abuse of Hagar? Why does God encourage Abraham to send Hagar and Ishmael into the desert with scant rations? He assures Abraham that Ishmael, at least, will survive, but Hagar and Ishmael do not share that foreknowledge. They suffer all the fear and hopelessness of impending death. Are the first matriarch and patriarch of the Israelite faith merciless and their God uncaring?

I had studied the Hagar chapters in two different classes as well as read it with my Shabbos Group. In the electric company class, the teacher had pointed out the "mistakes" that indicated multiple authorship. The second class was led by a brilliant young woman named Ruth Fagen who taught Bible and Talmud in New Haven for a few bright years. Now she teaches teachers in New York City. It is good that her genius stretches to the maximum number of people, but her New Haven fans miss her. One of the classes I took with her was an eight-week look at the women in Genesis.

Though Ruth had been exposed to source criticism in her pursuit of a Ph.D., and may ascribe to it for all I know, she never relied on the pat patchwork explanation but tried to decipher each passage as it stood. In her class, we had been guided to see that Hagar does not have the vision to become the mother of the child whose seed, God had promised, would be as numerous as the stars. Ruth drew our attention to Sarah's ability to visualize the future. In chapter 21, for example, she is able to see that whatever Ishmael is doing disqualifies him from inheriting God's special blessing to Abraham; Hagar, though her life depends on it, is not able to see something so substantial as a well until it is pointed out to her.

Neither the classes nor the Shabbos Group had addressed the issues Jeanne raised. Were these questions embarrassing for the faithful, for Jews especially? Many parts of the Hebrew Bible do not bathe God in a kindly light. We see him order the Israelites to utterly destroy the Amalekites, man and woman, infant and suckling, ox and sheep, camel and ass (1 Samuel 15:3). By modern standards, the command seems a touch extreme; even present-day despots, bent on ethnic-cleansing, do not slay their enemy's animals. But I could defend the author's delineation of a vehement deity: God wants the Israelites, and the nations surrounding them, to know that his covenanted people are taking a stand against ingrained wickedness and are not conducting the usual military campaign for slaves (the women and children) or for spoil (the animals). In Hagar's history, could an evidently indifferent deity be defended?

After Jeanne brought up these questions, I looked again at the two Hagar chapters. I could see that ancient readers must have read the story differently from the way that I was reading it. The biblical author is consistent in characterization; an actor, introduced as good, does not suddenly turn bad. Individuals develop, but the reader is shown the reasons and the circumstances that lead to transformation. Sarah's first words in the Bible are those of a God-fearing woman with a sensible plan who addresses her husband with respect; the next time we hear her speak, she seems an irrational termagant, berating Abraham immoderately. Hagar apparently fails in subservience to Sarah, but would a servant's pertness engender so violent and misplaced a reaction? I stubbed my brain against the author's ostensibly contradictory representation of Sarah. Observant Jewish parents bless their daughters with the words: "May God make you like Sarah." Should they rather say, "May God give you Sarah's vision but not her vindictiveness"?

Nor did I understand the writer's portrayal of Hagar. The Bible's style is so concise that every word is consequential, but direct speech is more critical than exposition, for without it the author could be even more terse. When he is so expansive as to include dialogue, those words are important and revealing. Hagar's first words in the Bible are plain enough, but her next speech seems like gibberish; it was one of those "mistakes" that had been pointed out to me.

I accepted that God teaches lessons in a hard school, but what lesson is taught by Hagar and Ishmael's suffering? Though I am not observant, the Hebrew Bible was not only my people's book, it was my book. I felt tarnished by its depiction of God as complicit in Abraham and Sarah's callousness and by the story's failure to deprecate this couple's inhumanity toward their bondwoman and her son. When we were children, my little brother used to say, "My mind told me," when pressed to give an explanation for his beliefs or behavior. My mind told me there was more in these chapters than met my twentieth-century eye, but I could not figure it out.

The feminist breakfast, where I hoped I would learn the answers to these troubling questions, was held in the main ballroom of the hotel that hosted the conference. The huge room was packed with closely spaced tables of twelve. I am not good at estimating crowds, but as more than seven thousand academics attend the conference, I would guess that a thousand women were at that breakfast.

There were four speakers, all women, each presenting a paper on Sarah and Hagar. The first speaker made me only vaguely uncomfortable by her disparagement of Sarah and exaltation of Hagar. I did not feel personally maligned by her assessment of the two women, although since Sarah is respected as one of the matriarchs of my religion, it was not pleasing to hear her so soundly denigrated before this room packed with gentiles.

The second or third speaker, I do not now remember which, tagged herself by a label new to me: she said she was a womanist. I learned from a professor of history and woman's studies that a womanist is a feminist who is a woman of color. A womanist is, by definition, even more down-trodden and oppressed than the garden-variety feminist. If they are in the United States, they are not only not men in a man's world, they are not white in a white world, and not rich in a wealthy world. Because of their particular disadvantages, they distinguish themselves from more privi-leged feminists.

I sympathized with the speaker for the stumbling blocks chance and discrimination had set before her, but I was not in sympathy with her pres-entation. This speaker's vilification of Sarah went beyond the fringes of biblical exegesis into the outskirts of anti-Semitism. Her theme was the persistence of biblical models into the present day. She spoke of what she considered the racism of the ancient Hebrews, of their preoccupation with financial matters, of their insistence on their chosenness, and compared these traits with those of contemporary people. What contemporary people she had in mind was not explicitly stated. They were identified as people like Sarah: rich, white people who are well-educated, who profess to be religious, yet who cheat and rob vulnerable blacks, while all the while con-sidering themselves chosen for good fortune and superior to their victims. Again and again, as support for these conclusions, she quoted a book whose title she spoke too quickly for me to catch. Her talk received clam-orous approbation, and as she left the podium, she passed my table. I caught her eye and asked her the name of the book she had mentioned so often. "*Stony the Road We Trod*," she said. I would not forget it.

The last speaker, a nun or maybe an ex-nun, spoke about the "Sarahs" in her life and how she had overcome them, and then the floor was opened to anyone who wished to ask questions or to contribute. Women lined up at microphones placed at three locations in the room. Each woman got a turn to tell the story of the "Sarahs" in her life and how they had tortured or trampled or tyrannized her. I looked around to see if anyone other than myself was offended; all I could see were women nodding and clapping, eager for their turns to complain. I ate my breakfast; they ate my liver. My daughter, when I told her about it, asked why I did not get up and speak in Sarah's defense. I told her I could not because I knew nothing to say on her behalf, but Sarah's advocacy had now become my calling. I was going to concentrate on those Sarah/Hagar chapters until I understood them.

I realized that I was not coming to these chapters without preconcep-tions. Having twice taken classes that focused on them and having also read them in my Shabbos Group, I knew that I could not help but be influ-enced by accepted opinion. As much as I could, I tried to free my mind from assumptions about the story and about the characters. I wanted to read the chapters as though I were the first reader. All interpreters, for in-stance, believe that Sarah wants her husband to have a child by Hagar so that the childless Sarah can adopt that child as her own. Without depending on presuppositions, and using only the Bible as my authority, I saw that this is not so. Adoption is not Sarah's goal. Nor is it the goal of Rachel and Leah who also have their mutual husband father children by their maids.

I pored over the passages, looking up all the Hebrew words, using my Hebrew concordance to see if linguistic parallels provided clues. After a while I had the two chapters memorized, which was convenient, as it meant I could think about them wherever I was—in line at the supermarket, in the car, at the gym, and in bed at 3:00 A.M. My son says that I sound like one obsessed when I admit that my Bible habit murders sleep, but this is the truth. Whenever I am on a case, so to speak, I cannot sleep. I do not even want to sleep; I want to lie in the dark and try to think myself into the mind-set of past millennia.

Gradually, I succeeded. I saw that, contrary to prevailing analysis, Hagar does not become a true wife of Abraham. Sarah is not "temperamental," as previous commentators term her, nor does she "over-react" to Hagar's audacity. I saw, to my surprise, that a man *is* to blame—two men, in fact: Abraham gives Sarah ample reason for her wrath in chapter 16, and in chapter 21, Ishmael gives Sarah grounds for insisting upon ousting him from her son's milieu. Also, to one who had been provoked by the rapturous feminist exalting of maid over mistress, it was reparative to see Hagar deservedly demoted and chastised in both her encounters with the angel of the Lord.

I was excited by my reading of the chapters. Since I was unfettered by the perceptions of my predecessors and because I used more of the text than did earlier interpreters, I was able to solve narrative cruxes that had eluded them. For one, Hagar's speech in chapter 16 was no longer gibberish. For another, I understood Sarah's rancor toward the other actors in this family drama. Perhaps because I had begun as Sarah's advocate, I was primed to see the ameliorating argument for her bitterness and the inculpatory evidence against Abraham, Hagar, and Ishmael. What I could not see, however, was justice. I had not learned the answers to Jeanne's questions. What was the author's point in making Hagar return to hardship? The unchecked affliction Sarah visits on her and the injury Abraham and Sarah do to Hagar and Ishmael in expelling them with inadequate provisions is undeniable. Ishmael grows to be a thorn in the side of his adversaries and to found a nation. Is there no requital for Hagar, no punishment for her persecutors?

One night, I was thinking about Hagar's first conversation with the angel of God, about how unwilling she is to return to her mistress, and of how the angel has to convince her to go back to Sarah's affliction. It reminded me of Moses on his first meeting with God at the burning bush, of how reluctant Moses is to return to Egypt, where *his* people are under affliction, and of how God has to convince him.

Bingo!

The parallels between Hagar and Moses flooded my mind. There are so many similarities, I could not understand how I had been so thick for so long. Not only are their situations comparable, but the linguistic correspondences the biblical author seems to set as aural signals for the slow-witted sang in my ears. I saw why Hagar has to return to affliction for another seventeen or so years; I saw why she and her son have to be cast into the desert, and I saw the extensive punishment with which her pain is redressed. The Bible's intricate craft again astonished me, for I saw even further than I had looked. Hagar is requited with more than revenge; she is memorialized forever in Israelite law.

While I am reading an article, it interrupts my concentration to attend to the footnotes, but when I have finished it, I like to go back and read them so that I do not miss the rousing cut and thrust of scholastic belligerence. I hope you do this as well. If you do, you will see that I fence with woman-as-victim feminists who uncritically adulate Hagar. Of course I duel with my favorite opponents, the source critics, as well as with the author of one of the articles collected in *Stony the Road We Trod*. This book turned out to be an anthology of African-American biblical interpretation. Only one article, which I recognized as the one quoted by the womanist speaker, was about Sarah and Hagar. Notes 3, 57, and 67—skewering anti-Semitism, poor logic, and misstatement—refer to this article. As you will see, biblical scholarship is a blood sport.

"Shall the judge of all the earth not do justice?" (Genesis 18:25)

The story of Hagar is an embarrassment. The faithful find it difficult to reconcile their belief in a just and merciful creator with the account of God directing Hagar's return to certain oppression in Genesis 16 and of his encouraging Abraham's expulsion of wife and son in Genesis 21.[1] Those feminists who uncover male mastery and female victimhood deplore "the Bible's androcentric perspective" that fosters the customary interpretation of two women squabbling over status and appealing to a man's authority.[2] Jews, even the religiously detached, also find the story

---

[1] Karen Armstrong says, "God appears in a cruel and dubious light" (*In The Beginning* [New York: Knopf, 1996], 66). Phyllis Trible says, "All we who are heirs of Sarah and Abraham, by flesh and spirit, must answer for the terror in Hagar's story. To neglect the theological challenge she presents is to falsify faith" ("The Other Woman: A Literary and Theological Study of the Hagar Narratives," in *Understanding the Word: Essays in Honor of Bernhard W. Anderson* [ed. James T. Butler, Edgar W. Conrad, and Ben C. Ollenburger; JSOTSup 37; Sheffield: JSOT Press, 1985], 239).

[2] J. Cheryl Exum, " 'Mother in Israel': A Familiar Figure Reconsidered," in *Feminist Interpretation of the Bible* (ed. Letty M. Russell; Philadelphia: Westmin-

disconcerting. As some interpreters equate the mores of ancient Israelites with present-day Jewish ideology and practice, contemporary Jews, confronted with this equivalency, feel defensive about the behavior of the matriarch, Sarah, and the patriarch, Abraham.[3]

This chapter provides a unique and textually-justified reading that affords greater understanding of the biblical representation of Sarah, Hagar, Abraham, Ishmael, and God. It proves the privileged position of Hagar's suffering in God's precise economy of crime and punishment, details the conspicuous parallels between Hagar's ordeal and Moses' experience, and demonstrates that the biblical imperative to deal righteously with the stranger is the conscience-shaping ethical consequence of the sacrifice of Hagar. The Hagar stories are not about male or ethnic dominance, but about divine justice and human compassion.[4]

CHAPTER 16

> And Sarai, wife of Abram, did not bear to him; and she had a handmaid, Egyptian, and her name was Hagar. (Genesis 16:1)

The reader has already met Sarai and Abram and knows of their childlessness (11:30).[5] In this verse a new character in the Bible, Hagar, is introduced. The narrator identifies her by a position, a nationality, and a name—in that order. Each aspect of Hagar, in the sequence given, will be

---

ster John Knox, 1985), 85. Dolores Williams says, "a thoroughly patriarchical and androcentrically biased text: the Bible" (*Sisters in the Wilderness* [Maryknoll, N.Y.: Orbis, 1993], 242 n. 4).

[3] John Waters says, "In reading the Old Testament, it is possible to see an increasing tendency to portray the Hebrews/Israelites as superior to all their neighbors. This 'air' is incorporated in the concept of the 'chosen people'" ("Who Was Hagar," in *Stony the Road We Trod: African American Biblical Interpretation* [ed. Cain Hope Felder; Minneapolis: Fortress, 1991], 197). Katharina von Kellenbach says, "The Egyptian slave, Hagar, renounces racism and sexism by rejecting the God of Hebrew slave-holders. Anti-Judaism is adopted as a device to enhance Christian feminist and womanist theological argumentation by investing it with new values and visions" (*Anti-Judaism in Feminist Religious Writings* [Atlanta: Scholars Press, 1994], 89).

[4] Because chapters 16 and 21 use different names for God and tell, in broad outline, essentially the same story—a defenseless woman of low station flees or is driven from the security of Abraham and Sarah's home, meets the deity in the desert, and is given water and assurances—they are considered parade examples in support of the documentary hypothesis. Source critics attribute chapter 16 of the story of Hagar to J, chapter 21 to E, and both are said to contain certain verses by P. As a reader, however, I am not engaged if every difficult passage is handily explained as the expression of a different writer, clumsy redaction, or corrupt text. I prefer to read the Bible as though it left the hand of its author (authors, or perhaps, its final redactor) as a synchronous, integrated, aesthetic work of literary art, and that is the approach I bring to the Hagar chapters.

[5] Sarai and Abram's names are changed to Sarah and Abraham in Genesis 17:5, 15.

crucial to the drama. For now her position is of first importance; it enables Sarai to propose a fertility technique to Abram.

> And Sarai said to Abram: "Behold, please. The Lord has restrained me from bearing. Go in, please, to my handmaid in order that I may be built up through her." And Abram heard the voice of Sarai. (16:2)

Sarai's first speech in the Bible provides important clues to her character. Her mention of the Lord shows her to be God-fearing. The fact that she assumes infertility to be God's disposition on her, not on Abram, shows her faith. God has promised Abram a number of descendants equal to the number of stars in the sky (15:5); the infertility cannot lie with him.[6] Sarai has confidence in God's promise to Abram. He will have progeny; if not by her, then by another woman. Perhaps she will die and Abram will remarry.[7] In any case, Abram's posterity is assured, guaranteed by God. The fertility technique Sarai proposes is designed to give herself a chance to be "built up." Her husband's firstborn will not be Sarai's issue, but she is generous enough and desperate enough not to care.

Some medieval Jewish interpreters followed the opinion of the talmudic sages that Sarai intends to adopt Hagar's child in order to enhance her own fertility. Although contemporary commentators believe the phrase "that I may be built up through her" simply means that Sarai proposes to adopt the child of Hagar and thus be built up, Samson Kardimon offers that, for Sarai and Rachel, adoption itself was not the major goal.[8] He be-

---

[6] It is commonly thought that the Bible considers only women capable of infertility. See, however, Deuteronomy 7:14 in which God promises the Israelites that if they obey his laws there will be no infertile man or woman among them.

[7] Abraham does remarry in Genesis 25:1 and fathers six children by Keturah. Rashi says Keturah is actually Hagar, returned from exile (Abraham M. Silbermann, *Chumash with Rashi's Commentary: Bereshith* [Jerusalem: Routledge & Kegan Paul, 1934], 111). The verse, however, says both that Abraham יסף (added to, increased, did further) and that he took a wife; the unnecessarily stressed augmentation militates against the restoration of Hagar as does the reference to Abraham's concubines in Genesis 25:6 (see my note 19).

[8] Samson Kardimon says that most post-medieval commentators "have interpreted the said phrase in a *rational* way, in the sense that Sarah and Rachel each had merely attempted to adopt the children of her handmaid and thus 'be builded up through her'. . . . But since about the beginning of the twentieth century *all* Jewish commentators, from the ultra-liberal to the ultra-orthodox, have adopted the *rational* interpretation. . . . As to the non-Jewish commentators, as is well known to the informed, *all* of them, of *all* times, without any exception, interpret this phrase in the *rational* way, that the only aim of Sarah and Rachel was merely the adoption of the children of their maids" (123, emphasis his). Kardimon quotes a 1948 medical manual: "It is well known in adoption agencies that a high percentage of parents applying for babies have children of their own a year or two later" ("Adoption as a Remedy for Infertility in the Period of the Patriarchs," *JSS* 3 [1958]: 126). Since Kardimon's article, all Jewish commentators have not adopted the "rational interpretation." Nahum Sarna, for one, says: "In Sarai's

lieves that these women did intend to appropriate the children of their maids, but that this adoption was undertaken primarily as a stimulant to fertility. I agree that Sarah, Rachel, and, for that matter, Leah want their maids to bear children so that their own fertility will be increased, but I disagree with Kardimon, and all other commentators, that any of these matriarchs intended to adopt the child of her maid.[9]

Apparently there is benefit to be gained in sharing one's marital sexual prerogatives in order to effect the birth of a child.[10] It may be a superstitious folk belief, or an attempt to gain God's favor by furthering his command to propagate. When Leah bears Jacob a fifth son, she says, "God gave me my hire, because I gave my handmaid to my husband" (30:18). For her unselfish support of procreation, Leah is "paid" with a son of her own, not with the adopted offspring of her maid. Leah, Rachel, and Sarai, as owners of the handmaids, are the legal owners, not the putative mothers, of their maids' sons. Like their mothers, the children are property.[11]

Indeed, the Bible makes clear that these matriarchs have no maternal regard for their handmaids' sons. Sarah would not be likely to banish a boy she had raised as her own for about seventeen years.[12] When Jacob fears that Esau's approach threatens his family, he arranges his wives and children in order of their dearness to him (33:2). Bilhah and Zilpah and their sons are put in the least protected position and Rachel and her son in the most protected. If Rachel were raising Bilhah's sons as her own, she would have wanted them safeguarded with hers. When Joseph is old enough to help his brothers shepherd the herd, it is the sons of Bilhah and Zilpah that he joins (37:2). The enmity between him and the sons of Leah, his mother's true rival, must have been too great for him to work peacefully with them. Had the sons of Zilpah been brought up as Leah's own children, Joseph would not have been able to commune with these brothers either.[13]

---

case, it is unclear whether she had fully despaired of ever having children of her own or whether her action reflects the widespread popular belief that a woman who is unable to conceive may become fertile by adopting a child" (*Genesis: The Traditional Hebrew Text with New JPS Translation/Commentary* [Philadelphia: JPS, 1989], 119).

[9] All exegetes believe that Sarai intended to adopt Hagar's child. See, for example, Savina Teubal, *Hagar the Egyptian* (San Francisco: Harper & Row, 1990), 54–55; Hermann Gunkel, *Genesis* (trans. Mark E. Biddle; Macon, Ga.: Mercer University Press, 1997), 184.

[10] Rashi says that Sarah means to be built up (i.e., have children) "through the merit that I admit her as a rival into my house" (Silbermann, *Chumash*, 63).

[11] Compare Exodus 21:4.

[12] Depending upon Isaac's age when weaned, Ishmael is between sixteen and eighteen when he is exiled. See note 62.

[13] As all other commentators assume Sarai, Rachel, and Leah intend to adopt their maids' children, it is incumbent upon them to explain why these adoptions

The ancient Hebrews practiced both polygamy and concubinage.[14] Abram may legally bed another woman, but Sarai does not require a rival nor, from the ultra-polite entreaty she makes in v. 2, does it appear that Abram desires a second wife. Sarai needs a birthing mother and, because of her status, Hagar is a candidate for that office. Abram will comply with Sarai's fertility strategy and make Hagar his wife via sexual intercourse, but this union will have an inferior standing to his marriage to Sarai. As birthing mother, Hagar will have only a generative function; once pregnant, she will lose her copulation privileges. By sleeping with Abram until she conceives, Hagar does not attain wifely status equal to Sarai's, and as Sarai's servant the handmaid remains under her authority after conception.

Other interpreters assume that Sarai's plan provides Abram with a second sexual partner.[15] But why would Sarai, Rachel, and Leah establish competitors for themselves when all they need are birthing mothers? The mandrake scene of 30:14–16 manifests the handmaids' lack of entitlement: Bilhah and Zilpah, handmaids of Rachel and Leah, have borne children by Jacob, but these secondary wives seem to have no place in the rotation of his sexual favors. Since analysts posit that these handmaidens did enjoy regular sexual concourse with their mistresses' husbands, they must either admit three more childbearing miracles to the tally in Genesis or else provide a natural explanation for why three women of proven fecundity, with normal wifely access to husbands of confirmed fertility, bore no more children than the men's earlier wives wanted them to bear.

The primary wives must have controlled their husbands' consortium. Bilhah and Zilpah live out their lives within Jacob's domestic circle. Their sons grow up, get married, have children of their own, but Bilhah and Zilpah have no additional children. It is obvious that by limiting Jacob's sexual relations with these handmaids to those occasions required to produce two children each, Rachel and Leah maintain a parity of sons born to servants. In the seventeen or so years Hagar lives in Abram and Sarai's

---

never actually seem to take effect. Most choose not to address the problem. Matitiahu Tsevat, however, terms Sarai's attitude toward Ishmael as "this quite exceptional development" that confronts us with a rare "change in the social order." He is forced to admit: "Yet, against all expectation, the offspring is apparently not legally and socially the mistress's but the maid's" ("Hagar and the Birth of Ishmael," in *The Meaning of the Book of Job and Other Bible Studies* [Dallas: Ktav, 1980], 67).

[14] Ephraim Neufeld, *Ancient Hebrew Marriage Laws* (London: Longmans, Green, 1944), 121.

[15] Trible says, "In making Hagar Abram's wife, not concubine, Sarai has unwittingly diminished her own status in relationship to this servant" ("The Other Woman," 223). Bernadette Revicky says, "Sarai addresses Abram, her husband, who is also the husband of the one who brings her misery" (" 'Hagar, Maidservant of Sarai, from What Place Have You Come and Where Shall You Go?': A Rhetorical Critical Study of Genesis 16 and Genesis 21:8–21" [Master's thesis, Andover Newton Theological School, 1980], 28).

household after Ishmael's birth, she has no more children. Hagar, we must conclude, is not permitted to Abram once conception is achieved.[16]

The biblical author separates intention and act by his deft placement of the time span in 16:3. He could have written: "After ten years, Sarai, wife of Abram, took Hagar, the Egyptian, her handmaid, and gave her to Abram her husband to be his wife." Or he could have put the phrase at the end of the sentence. Instead, with incomparable literary finesse, he tells of the decade mid-verse so that it intervenes between plan and performance in syntax as well as in fact: "And Sarai, wife of Abram, took Hagar, the Egyptian, her handmaid, after Abram had lived in the land of Canaan ten years and gave her to Abram, her husband, to be his wife." Ten years is a long time to withstand the disappointment and frustration of childlessness, to endure every month for 120 months the fresh evidence of failed hope, while, with each passing year, the tick of the biological clock becomes more insistent. And Sarai and Abram have been married even longer than the ten years they lived in Canaan. They were married in 12:5 when Abram left his father's house in Haran. They were husband and wife in Egypt and in Gerar, where they must have lived as brother and sister in fact so as not to risk exposing Abram's lies by an obvious pregnancy (12:10–14; 20:1–2). They have lost opportunity to achieve conception, and opportunity is receding.

The delay in the transfer of Hagar stretches the already-prolonged interval and further underscores the couple's reluctance to resort to this fertility technique. Between the moment Sarai forms her resolve and takes Hagar and the actual giving of Hagar to Abram, there is the tension, insinuated or actual, of a decade's hesitation.[17] Since Abram assents to Sarai's request; one would expect *him* to take Hagar to be his wife, as marriage is usually delineated in the Bible.[18] That it is Sarai who is doing the protracted taking and giving at once emphasizes her authority in sexual matters, her hegemony over Hagar, and her and Abram's natural antipathy to the scheme. The couple's mutual disinclination is a meritorious tribute to their marital fidelity.

The verse begins with Sarai and ends with Abram. Artfully, its syntax does double duty; it interposes Hagar between wife and husband. The author also reiterates each character's status. Though we have long been

---

[16] The victimological school of feminist and womanist exegetes, vigilant detectors of biblical androcentrism, can now observe gynocentrism: matriarchal restriction on male sexual autonomy.

[17] Source critics do not credit the artistry I see here and attribute 16:3 to the interpolation of the P source. Claus Westermann says, "It is generally acknowledged that v. 3 belongs to P" (*Genesis 12–36: A Commentary* [trans. John J. Scullion, S. J.; Minneapolis: Augsburg, 1985], 239). See also Gerhard von Rad, *Genesis: A Commentary* (trans. John H. Marks; Philadelphia: Westminster John Knox, 1972), 191.

[18] In Genesis: 11:29; 24:67; 25:1, 20; 26:34; 28:9; 38:6.

aware of Sarai's relationship to Abram (since 11:29) and are reminded anew in the first verse of our chapter, 16:3 repeats again that Sarai is Abram's wife and also, superfluously, that Abram is Sarai's husband. Hagar, once again labeled the Egyptian handmaid, will also become a wife.[19] The terms "wife" and "husband" are hammered into our consciousness and given prominence by repetition.[20] Though we already know the characters' relationships, we are made to understand unequivocally that Sarai is the principal wife of Abram and that this partnership is paramount. Abram is identified as Sarai's husband—Sarai's alone; Abram is never denominated as Hagar's husband. The author stresses the entitlement that accrues to Sarai's position, and only to Sarai's position. We have previously noticed the value the couple places upon the exclusivity of their marital bond. Hagar, as has been pointed out above, is to be a wife in name only. Her duty is to have a child, not to enjoy the permanent prerogatives of the marital bed.

> And he went into Hagar, and she conceived; and she saw she conceived, and her mistress diminished in her eyes. (16:4)

After staying the reader ten years over the first three verses, the author now markedly accelerates the action. The use of four verbs within ten words (in Hebrew), rushes us past intercourse, through conception, realization of pregnancy, and to the effect of this awareness.[21] The universal interpretation of this effect is that, emboldened by the self-importance generated by her pregnancy, Hagar is insolent to Sarai. To understand, excuse, and accommodate Sarai's "vindictive" and "relentless" response to Hagar's behavior, exegetes intensify Hagar's transgression; translations say she "looked with contempt" (RSV), or that Sarai "was despised in her eyes" (KJV, ASV).[22] The Hebrew verb means to become scanty, small, or light; Sarai has become light in Hagar's estimation. The ensuing dialogue

---

[19] Though Hagar is not called a concubine in chapters 16 or 21, in 25:6 reference is made to the concubines of Abraham—presumably Hagar and Keturah. Bilhah, one of the secondary wives of Jacob is termed both "wife" (30:4) and "concubine" (35:22) as is Keturah ("wife," 25:1; "concubine," 1 Chronicles 1:32); apparently, either locution is appropriate for a subordinate wife.

[20] This effect is also used in the narrative describing the incestuous tryst of Amnon and Tamar; in 2 Samuel 13:1–22 the words "brother" or "sister" are repeated a total of eighteen times.

[21] Perhaps it is the sensation of speed in this verse that inspired the rabbinic opinion that Hagar became pregnant after one intimacy (*Genesis Rabbah* 45:4).

[22] Cynthia Gordon, "Hagar: A Throw-Away Character Among the Matriarchs?" *SBLSP* (Atlanta: Scholars Press, 1985), 274. John Skinner says Sarai was "passionate and most unjust" (*A Critical and Exegetical Commentary on Genesis* [repr. Edinburgh: T&T Clark, 1969], 286). Jo Ann Hackett says, "The diminished status angers Sarai, and it seems that it riles her more than it should" ("Rehabilitating Hagar: Fragments of an Epic Pattern," in *Gender and Difference in Ancient Israel* [ed. Peggy Day; Minneapolis: Fortress, 1989], 13).

reveals how Hagar expresses her disdain for Sarai's authority. Note that I have punctuated Sarai's words as though they were two separate statements; this individuation is necessary to my understanding of the passage and will be discussed below.

> And Sarai said to Abram, "The outrage done me is your responsibility. I put my handmaid in your bosom, and she saw she conceived and I diminished in her eyes." "The Lord judge between me and between you." (16:5)

First, a few words about translation. The word I have translated as "outrage," חמס, is usually rendered as "wrong" by interpreters who do not understand why Abram is the recipient of Sarai's vehemence (KJV, ASV, RSV). They suppose he has hurt her by a masculine disregard of Hagar's impudence. They believe he is castigated for refraining from involvement in the petty spats of women—a disengagement that seems more sensible than blameable to them.[23] The Hebrew word, חמס, is quite strong (stronger than "outrage" can express), and so seems excessive in the context they stipulate. Translators, therefore, soften the expression to make it suit what they regard as the meaning of the narrative.

חמס, however, is an offense so grave that God destroys a world because of it; it is the sin of Noah's generation that precipitates the flood. Speaking generally of חמס, Aviva Zornberg defines it as violent robbery with undertones of sexual rapacity.[24] Nahum Sarna says that "It means, in general, the flagrant subversion of the ordered processes of law."[25] The midrash says Sarai's expression, that I have translated as "the outrage done me," really means "what is stolen from me." The rabbis of the midrash support the robbery connotation by explaining that Abram robbed Sarai of the protection from insult he should have provided on her behalf (*Genesis Rabbah* 45:5).

In my translation of v. 5 above, I put Sarai's last sentence in separate quotation marks, rather than quote her whole speech as one utterance. I did this to show that Sarai has ended her rebuke to Abram and is now speaking to Hagar. That Sarai is addressing a woman is indicated in the Hebrew because, unlike English, Hebrew differentiates masculine and feminine forms of "you." In the words (one word in Hebrew) "and between you," the spelling is feminine. Rashi, the great medieval Hebraist, notes the feminine spelling of the expression and says the word should

---

[23] Gunkel says that "Abraham is good-natured and just." Sarai is "cruel and very subjective in her passion (thus she uses a more extreme expression than the circumstances of 'injured respect' allow). The Israelite husband, however, may well have sighed privately over his temperamental wife" (*Genesis,* 185). Sean McEvenue says, "The reader is not expected to blame Abram for Sarai's trouble" ("A Comparison of Narrative Styles in the Hagar Stories," *Semeia* 3 [1975]: 69).

[24] Aviva Zornberg, *The Beginning of Desire* (New York: Doubleday, 1995), 51–54.

[25] Sarna, *Genesis,* 51.

have been vocalized וּבֵינֵיִךְ.[26] He says that Sarai speaks first to Abram and then turns and addresses Hagar, but Rashi does not comment on the significance of Sarai speaking to both on the same occasion.[27] The anomaly of the feminine spelling is not even discussed by the majority of exegetes; the few who do mention it ascribe it to scribal error.[28]

There is no reason for Abram and Hagar to be together now that she has conceived. Her pregnancy is no secret—the narrator knows it, Hagar knows it, Sarai knows it. We can be sure that Abram also knows it, for Sarai would be eager to tell him in order to terminate sexual congress between him and Hagar. From Sarai's directly successive speeches to her husband and to her maid and from her accusation of חמס, we can deduce that she has surprised Abram and Hagar not only together but *flagrante delicto*.

Had the author written: "*And Sarai said to Hagar,* 'The Lord judge between me and between you,'" the feminine "you" would have been satisfied, but despite Sarai's use of the word חמס, we would no longer know that she caught Abram and Hagar together. We could think that Sarai spoke to Abram and then, on another occasion, she spoke to Hagar. The biblical author is skillful in what he includes and equally skillful in what he omits. The feminine "you" combined with the ingenious omission of "And Sarai said to Hagar" tells us what we need to know to discern this un-

---

[26] Every time the expression "between you" occurs in the Pentateuch (Genesis 3:15; 17:2, 7; 23:15; 26:28; 31:44, 48–51), other than in this verse, the speaker can only be talking to a man, and the word is spelled differently from the way it is spelled in our passage. The Hebrew Bible was originally written without vowels. Once Hebrew was no longer the vernacular it was necessary to add certain final and internal letters representing vowels to assist pronunciation. Still later, when the text was vocalized by the Masoretes, this fuller spelling was respected, and diacritical marks were added to it for greater precision. The spelling of the expression in our passage is consistent with the feminine "you"; by the time the Masoretes vocalized the word, however, they had their own interpretation of the meaning of the passage, and they vocalized the word to reflect the pronunciation of the masculine "you." Rashi corrects the diacritical marks of the Masoretes, indicating what he (and I) considers the proper understanding of the older, fuller spelling (Silbermann, *Chumash,* 64).

[27] Teubal is the only other commentator I have read who accepts Rashi's understanding that the word is "second person feminine singular and should not be vocalized as masculine." She suggests that Hagar's offense is "claiming equality regarding motherhood," and that, in this verse, Sarai invokes the Lord's decision, not Abram's, as to whom the social mother of the expected child should rightly be. As Rashi, Teubal also does not comment on the implication of Sarai's immediately consecutive speeches to the other two principals in this drama (*Hagar the Egyptian,* 79).

[28] See, for example, Skinner, *A Critical and Exegetical Commentary on Genesis,* 286; Gunkel, *Genesis,* 185; Westermann, *Genesis 12–36,* 234. Hugh White refers to "Sarah's appeal to Yahweh to be judge between her and Hagar in v. 5," but gives no rationalization for his opinion that Sarai's speech is directed to Hagar ("The Initiation Legend of Ishmael," *ZAW* 87 [1975]: 290).

seemly affair. The instant and unexpected redirection of invective from Abram to Hagar flags the sequential immediacy of Sarai's speeches and displays that she spoke first to one culprit and then to the other.[29] By sleeping with Hagar after her impregnation, Abram robs Sarai of an opportunity to conceive. She may experience this as her most severe loss, for not only is the time ripe for conception—since she has now (superstitiously or piously) provided for another pregnancy—but time is running out. Abram's forbidden love-making also robs Sarai of sexual pleasure, of the fidelity she once trusted, of her exclusive right to her husband's sexual services, and of her self-esteem. Abram once believed her so beautiful that every man would want her. And once men, wealthy and powerful men who had access to many women, did covet her because of her beauty (12:11–15; 20:2). Now Abram prefers to embrace a servant. Her own handmaid is more desirable than she. Robbery, injustice, and sexual rapacity are all connotations of the word חמס, and all of these meanings are relevant to this scenario. With this new understanding of the text, Sarai's outburst is no longer "unreasonable"; her fury no longer "seems overdone." This is no "mildly incriminating incident."[30] Sarai has justification for her rancor, a replete and rational reason to upbraid Abram.

The sequence of v. 4 suggests that Hagar initiates the rendezvous. After she has conceived and before Sarai discovers the illicit pair, her mistress is diminished in her eyes. Hagar evidences her newfound disrespect for Sarai's rights by sleeping with Sarai's husband.[31] Her motivation is understandable. In Sarai's domain, and in the servant's quarters, she is a handmaiden of little consequence. She is ordered about, given menial work, treated as an inferior, ignored. In bed with Abram, there is warmth, attention, affection, intimacy, tenderness. There she is not a servant but a desirable woman.[32]

---

[29] Elsa Tamez provides a fanciful feminist reading of Sarai's protest: "My offense falls on your shoulders; I let my slave sleep with you, but you look at me with distaste now that you see her pregnant" ("The Woman Who Complicated the History of Salvation," in New Eyes for Reading [ed. John S. Pobee and Barbel von Wartenberg-Potter; Geneva: World Council of Churches, 1986], 9). Exum also provides a feminist interpretation of Sarai's grievance for which I can find no textual justification: "When a critical feminist perspective is brought to bear upon the narrative, Sarah's anger at Abraham, 'May the Lord judge between you and me' (not 'between Hagar and me'; Genesis 16:5), becomes an indictment of the patriarchal system, which pits women against women and challenges their intrinsic worth with patriarchal presuppositions about women's role" ("Mother in Israel," 77).

[30] Hackett, "Rehabilitating Hagar," 13, 15, 17.

[31] Against Revicky who says, "The text remains silent about the manner in which Hagar expresses her belittlement of Sarai" ("Hagar, Maidservant of Sarai," 28).

[32] Williams, a womanist commentator, asserts that Hagar is "ravished" and that her predicament involved "rape" (Sisters in the Wilderness, 3–4).

By Sarai's repetition in v. 5 of the narrator's assessment in v. 4, we see Sarai too recognizes that Hagar finds her mistress's due less absolute after impregnation. Sarai acknowledges that Hagar is the instigator; nevertheless, the responsibility for the outrage is Abram's. He cannot claim exploitation; he is the master, the elder, the more powerful. Hagar may not be able to refuse him, but he can refuse Hagar. The handmaid, wrongly but understandably, looks to Abram for comfort and for the satisfaction of her sexual appetite, but the husband must look to his true wife, Sarai. Abram's capitulation to Hagar's initiative is all the more difficult for Sarai to bear when she considers that she herself promoted their liaison, that she is accountable for placing Hagar in Abram's bed. She berates Abram for his חמס, charges herself for inaugurating the sexual union, and scolds Hagar for her share of the blame.

Abram's fault is unquestionably the greatest, but Sarai bitterly shoulders guilt for disturbing the stability of the marriage. Hagar, however, is also culpable. She knew her place, and she left it. Perhaps she even aspires to a position beyond the bedroom and hopes to parlay her youth and fertility to achieve the status of favored wife. Sarai appeals to the Lord to assess the accountability of the two women, and, in so doing, injures herself. The Lord judges between Sarai and Hagar, and, as we shall see, Sarai's seed suffers.

> And Abram said to Sarai: "Behold, your handmaid is in your hand. Do to her what is good in your eyes." And Sarai oppressed her and she fled from her face. (16:6)

With the Bible's characteristic compactness, Abram tells Sarai exactly what she wants to hear.[33] I shall expand the message of Abram's terse words:

> "Look—this is how it is—she is your handmaid; she is not my wife. She is under your authority; I have neither the intention nor the desire to treat her as your co-wife. Whatever you do to her is fine with me, for I have no feelings for her whatsoever."

What is past is past. Abram does not deal with issues of wasted seed, infidelity, hurt feelings. He cannot justify himself, and he makes no apology. Abram addresses the present and the future. He reassures Sarai that she is still the sole wife, that she, alone, is loved, that her rightful authority over her servant has not been and will not be impaired. His subsequent deportment toward Hagar will evidence his truth and his remorse. As we are shown in chapter 21, he is completely indifferent to her; she is non-existent to him.[34]

---

[33] Gordon states, "Abraham remains utterly detached" ("Hagar: A Throw-Away Character," 274). McEvenue says, "Abram appears almost to have a modern husband's alacrity in ducking the attack" ("A Comparison of Narrative Styles," 69).

[34] Gordon says, "Years later, Hagar remains a nonperson in Abraham's ethical and emotional life" ("Hagar: A Throw-Away Character," 274).

Sarai's anger toward Hagar is justified, but her resulting behavior is not. The narrator rarely censures or approves explicitly; rather, the author guides the reader toward correct moral judgment by inference. The verb the author uses to describe Sarai's treatment of Hagar is an indictment.[35] To afflict or oppress, עָנָה, is wrong. First used in the Bible in the chapter immediately preceding ours (15:13), עָנָה describes the affliction Abram's seed will endure for four hundred years. It is frequently used in Exodus and Deuteronomy to refer to Israelite torment under the hand of Egypt. As God sees and punishes the perpetrators of Israelite suffering, so will he see and punish Sarai's oppression of Hagar.

Out of respect for the matriarch, or to make God's later collaboration (16:9) more tolerable, translators and commentators often ameliorate Sarai's treatment of Hagar. The KJV, NJPS, ASV, and RSV say that Sarai "dealt harshly" with Hagar, although they use "afflicted" or "oppressed" for the same verb in the preceding chapter, 15:13. "Dealt harshly" conveys severity without creating an identity between Sarai's cruelty and that of the oppressors of Abram's descendants. The midrash makes various suggestions to describe this harshness—that Sarai restrained Hagar from cohabitation with Abram, slapped her face, or required her to do work of a more menial nature than her status allowed (*Genesis Rabbah* 15:6). Rashi says Sarai compelled Hagar to work hard; Samson R. Hirsch says Sarai "humbled" her by constantly reminding her of her dependent condition.[36] Nachmanides, however, unequivocally states that Sarai sinned in her handling of Hagar and that Abram sinned in permitting it.

> And the angel of the Lord found her by a spring of water in the wilderness, by a spring in the way of Shur. And he said: "Hagar, handmaid of Sarai, from where did you come, and where are you going?" And she said: "I flee from the face of my mistress, Sarai." (16:7–8)

Exalted promises have been made about the seed of Abram. They shall have land (13:15); they shall be as numerous as the stars (15:5); they shall have great substance (15:14). Abram's reward will be "exceeding great" (15:1), and the issue of his loins will be his heir (15:4). In Genesis 16, the child Hagar carries in her womb is the only prospective progeny of Abram. There is no hint, as far as the first reader is concerned, that Abram will ever have another child. It is frequently noted that the angel's discourse with Hagar is Scripture's first record of such a theophany. It is

---

[35] Shimon Bar-Efrat quotes the Bible's use of this loaded word and says, "The narrator's attitude is sometimes expressed through the connotations of the words used to convey the characters' actions. . . . and thus, while giving what appears to be a factual account of events, the narrator's attitude is transmitted" (*Narrative Art in the Bible* [London: Almond, 1989], 33).

[36] Silbermann, *Chumash,* 64; Samson R. Hirsch, *The Pentateuch: Genesis* (vol. 1; trans. I. Levy, 1962; repr. Gateshead: Judaica, 1989), 286.

considered greatly to Hagar's credit that the Lord vouchsafes her this vision. Previous interpreters do not recognize that, during this encounter, Hagar does not gain glory but loses it. By her responses to the angel, she forfeits the opportunity to be the mother of the child of promise.

The Lord's messenger first identifies Hagar by name and station, thus disclosing deific knowledge. He asks two questions: where she has come from and where she is going. Hagar is able to answer one question but not the other[37]—she has no idea where she is going; she has no plan. Strike one. Had she, with prudent forethought, devised a viable course of action, one that would enable her and her baby to survive in the wilderness or to achieve safe reception in Egypt, perhaps the Lord would have set history on a different path. But with no survival strategy, Hagar will die in the desert. To stay alive, it is better for her to return to Sarai's malevolence—painful though the prospect may be.

> And the angel of the Lord said to her: "Return to your mistress and submit to affliction under her hands." And the angel of the Lord said to her: "I will greatly multiply your seed, and it will not be numbered for multitude." And the angel of the Lord said to her: "Behold, you have conceived and will bear a son, and you will call his name Ishmael, for the Lord has heard your affliction. And he will be a wild ass of a man; his hand will be against all, and the hand of all will be against him. And in the face of all his brothers he will dwell." (16:9–12)

Source critics leap upon the thrice repeated, "And the angel of the Lord said to her." John Skinner labels it a "fault of style which is in striking contrast to the exquisite artistic form of the original narrative" and considers v. 9 "a redactional excrescence obviously inserted in view of the expulsion of Hagar at a later date."[38] Hugh White argues with Skinner and others about v. 9 and states that it is vv. 10, 11, 12, rather, that are all later insertions by the E source which "would then account for the awkward repetition of the connecting phrases in vv. 10–11."[39] While disagreeing with other source critics, John Van Seters ("The real problem lies with v. 10") and Matitiahu Tsevat ("Vs. 10 has no place anywhere in this chapter and is particularly incongruous in its place before vs. 11") are in full agreement with each other.[40]

I believe that to serve his spare rhetorical style, the author utilizes even the smallest elements of narrative—the "he said" and the "she said."[41]

---

[37] Against Revicky who says, "One answer satisfies both of the messenger's questions" ("Hagar, Maidservant of Sarai," 3).

[38] Skinner, *A Critical and Exegetical Commentary on Genesis*, 285.

[39] White, "The Initiation Legend of Ishmael," 300.

[40] John Van Seters, *Abraham in History and Tradition* (New Haven: Yale University Press, 1975), 194; Tsevat, "Hagar and the Birth," 58.

[41] In a general discussion of the Bible's artistry, Bar-Efrat maintains that repetitions of "And he said" phrases are purposeful, and he provides a piquant example.

The astute omission of "And Sarai said to Hagar" in v. 5, when the object of Sarai's words is feminine, affords a synchroneity that situates Abram and Hagar together. In vv. 9–11, the author uses the literary device of profuse repetition of "And the angel of the Lord said" to disclose Hagar's character. The repetition indicates that Hagar obdurately makes no response to the angel's speeches in vv. 9 and 10. To return to certain abuse is not an attractive order, even if it does come from an angel; Hagar does not budge. The restatement of "And the angel of the Lord said to her," communicates this conversational void; the angel ceases his address, waits for an answer, and, receiving none, begins anew. In his second speech the angel offers an incentive; he will make her the mother of a multitude. This inducement was sufficient for Abram to leave his country and his kindred and his father's house (12:1–2), but it does not move Hagar. Before she agrees to return, the angel must start again—a commencement the author marks with the same preamble employed twice before. This time the angel offers the prospect of revenge. Only when Hagar hears that her son will be wild and free and a thorn in the side of her tormenters does she submit.[42] Strike two.

Source critics use the *Elohim* name of God and the tetragrammaton, יהוה (that I term "Lord"), as markers to differentiate the E source and the J source. Umberto Cassuto contests the tenets of the documentary hypothesis and offers an insightful analysis of the distinction between the two divine names:

> The designation *Elohim* was originally a common noun, an apellative, that was applied to both the One God of Israel and to the heathen gods (so, too, was the name *El*). On the other hand, the name YHVH [יהוה] is a proper noun, the

---

In 2 Samuel 11:6–8, David has recalled Uriah from combat, ostensibly to report on the war, in order to cover up the king's dalliance with Uriah's wife, Bathsheba. David's real aim is for Uriah to go to his home and make love to Bathsheba so that the child she has conceived by David will be attributed to Uriah. Scripture says, "And David asks," followed by many questions about the progress of the war, and then, with no recorded response from Uriah, we are told, "And David said to Uriah: 'Go down to your house and wash your feet.'" The reader assumes that Uriah must surely have answered his king, but the doubled report that David spoke discloses that he was not interested in whatever Uriah had to say and did not listen to his words. Anxious to effect his scheme, David could barely wait for Uriah to cease talking before sending him to Bathsheba's bed (*Narrative Art*, 45).

[42] Hirsch says v. 9 "is the condition, the second [v. 10] the promise, the third [v. 11] the task and its result." Hagar yields only when she hears: "Your descendent will become the freest man in the world" (*Genesis*, 287). Although T. D. Alexander endorses the documentary hypothesis (with his modifications), he concludes that the triple repetition is a purposeful stylistic feature employed to emphasize the eminence of the speaker, to accent the various elements of the angel's speech, or to give the reader a pause in which to comprehend the angel's preceding words ("The Hagar Traditions in Genesis 16 and 21," in *Studies in the Pentateuch* [VTSup 41; ed. John A. Emerton; Leiden: E. J. Brill, 1990], 139–40).

specific name of Israel's God, the God whom the Israelites acknowledge as the Sovereign of the universe and as the Divinity who chose them as his people.[43]

He specifies more particulars governing the usage of the divine names, but the above will suffice for me to explicate the next verses in our chapter.

> And she called the name of the Lord that spoke to her, "You are a god *[el]* of seeing." For she said, "Have I indeed [or 'also'] here seen after-me seeing?" Therefore the well was called the Well of Living-Seeing. (16:13–14)

Hagar's words have been called "nonsensical," "formidable," "corrupt," "difficult," and "awkward."[44] Revicky says that the text "defies precise interpretation."[45] Most scholars follow the rendering of Julius Wellhausen, the prominent nineteenth-century German documentary hypothesist. By adding a word here and subtracting a word there, he produces: "Have I seen God and remained alive after my seeing?"[46] The AB offers, "Did I not go on seeing here after he had seen me?" Skinner says that "the only sense that can be extracted from the MT" is, "Have I even here seen after him who sees me?" White renders, "Here have I also seen the effects of an appearance of God?" Hermann Gunkel goes rather farther afield with: "Here I have seen the end of my distress."[47]

Once the passage is correctly understood, Hagar's words are no longer enigmatic and need no additions or omissions. She is astonished by the long-sightedness of the being who appears to her; he is indeed a "god of seeing," for he can see beyond her to her descendants. The well is named the Well of Living-Seeing. "Living" is used in the sense given in 3:20 in which Eve is called the mother of all living. At this stage of the account, Eve is the mother of no one. Scripture looks ahead to the descendants that Eve will have and uses "living" as a collective noun for her posterity. The god Hagar names is capable of foreseeing immeasurable generations of Hagar's "living."

The phrase "after-me" (one word in Hebrew) is similarly used in the sense of descendants.[48] Had the author said "*seed* after-me," there would have been less confusion. It would have been plain that Hagar's words "seed after-me seeing" concern a prevision of progeny. The reader would

---

[43] Umberto Cassuto, *Documentary Hypothesis* (trans. Israel Abrahams from 1941 edition; Jerusalem: Magnus, 1983), 18.

[44] Respectively: Gunkel, *Genesis,* 188; Sarna, *Genesis,* 121; Skinner, *Critical and Exegetical,* 288; White, "The Initiation Legend of Ishmael," 285; Nick Wyatt, "The Meaning of *El Roi* and the Mythological Dimension in Genesis 16," *SJOT* 8 (1994): 143.

[45] Revicky, "Hagar, Maidservant of Sarai," 40.

[46] Thijs Booij says, "The most famous and most widely accepted conjecture is the one offered by Wellhausen" ("Hagar's Words in Genesis 16:13B," *VT* 30 [1980]: 1).

[47] Skinner, *A Critical and Exegetical Commentary on Genesis,* 288; White, "The Initiation Legend of Ishmael," 287; Gunkel, *Genesis,* 189.

[48] Compare Ecclesiastes 2:18.

readily grasp that Hagar exclaims over the supernatural precognition of the god she names.

Perhaps, however, including the word "seed" would have disturbed the sevenfold cycle of biblical information delivery. Abraham's seed, his progeny, is mentioned seven times before Hagar's interview with the angel; seven times after this passage God alludes to Abraham's seed.[49] The seventh reference in a category often bears special significance; in this second septet, the seventh, and final, reference is made to Abraham but is specific to the seed of Isaac. The number seven is a mystical number of wondrous potency that is invoked repeatedly in the Bible. From the first seven allusions to the seed of Abram, alert readers learn that this seed, these descendants, have a special relation to the diety. In Genesis 16:10 the angel of the Lord refers to the seed of Hagar just once. At this point, it could still be that the child of Abram and Hagar, the product of their combined seed, will be the child of promise. Hagar, however, abrogates that possibility by her words in v. 13. Her loss is evidenced by the fact that no additional reference to her seed occurs and by the corroborative reiteration of another septet of references to Abraham's seed, culminating with the pivotal allusion to the seed of Isaac.

Because she names God, Trible says, "Hagar is a theologian."[50] If so, she is a bad one. God has presented himself to Hagar as יהוה, the sole creator and sovereign of the universe and the solitary and unique diety who has chosen the Hebrews to be his people. Unlike Abram and Sarai, Hagar does not recognize the Lord as the one all-encompassing God. She names him, with a generic name for divinity, *el* (אל), as though he were the numen of a particular locality ("here") and phenomenon ("seeing").[51] Strike three. Until this moment Hagar had the opportunity to be the mother of the covenental child; now, though her son is the seed of Abraham, mother and child will have a different future. And the Lord will appear to Hagar and Ishmael, pagans, henceforth only as *Elohim* (אלהים).[52]

---

[49] Genesis 12:7; 13:15–16; 15:3, 5, 13, 18; and Genesis 17:7 (twice), 8–10, 12, 19.

[50] Trible, "The Other Woman," 229.

[51] Against Revicky who says, "Hagar acknowledges Yhwh as the God who perceives her circumstances" ("Hagar, Maidservant of Sarai," 87). Sarna says, "Hagar gives expression to her personal discovery by designating God after the particular aspect of His providence that she has experienced" (*Genesis*, 121 n. 13). Sharon Pace Jeansonne says, "Although the Hebrew of this phrase is difficult, it is clear that Hagar has named the Deity in response to her experience" (*The Women of Genesis* [Minneapolis: Fortress, 1990], 46). Both Sarna and Jeansonne agree that Hagar distinguishes a specific attribute in naming her god, but neither appreciates that she has failed to comprehend the singularity of יהוה.

[52] Wyatt says, "The whole point of the theophany narrative is Hagar's amazement at surviving a vision of a deity" ("The Meaning of *El Roi*," 143). Thomas Dozeman sees two separate, unharmonized histories in this chapter: a pre-Priestly history traced in Hagar's etiologies and a Priestly history focused on the angel's

And the child grew and was weaned. And Abraham made a great feast on the day Isaac was weaned. And Sarah saw the son of Hagar the Egyptian, that she bore to Abraham, מְצַחֵק. (Genesis 21:8–9)

The word, מְצַחֵק, is usually translated as "mocking" (KJV, ASV) or "playing" (NJPS, RSV; the RSV follows the LXX in adding "with her son Isaac"). The midrash offers several suggestions for Ishmael's conduct: immorality, idolatry, bloodshed, or claiming a firstborn's right to a double portion of Abraham's estate (*Genesis Rabbah* 53:11). Ephraim Speiser (AB) chooses "playing," for he says that "mocking" would require a preposition to designate an object of mockery.[53] Skinner says the Septuagint's addition of "with her son Isaac" is "essential to the sense and must be restored. . . . It is the spectacle of the two young children playing together, innocent of social distinctions, that excites Sarah's maternal jealousy and prompts her cruel demand."[54] Trible proposes that Ishmael was masturbating.[55] A number of scholars, conscious that מְצַחֵק has the same root (צחק, laughter) as Isaac's name, submit that Ishmael was "Isaac-ing"—that is, he was acting as a social equal to Isaac.[56]

Although they proffer no related pecuniary definition for מְצַחֵק, some interpreters see a financial motive for Sarah's reaction to her observation. A whiff of modern anti-Semitic stereotyping of Jews as racist and avaricious rises from African American Christian analyst John Waters's statement: "Sarah's command in Genesis 21:10 provides a basis for examination of ethnic 'purity,' as well as an examination of Sarah's vested economic interest."[57] Womanist commentator, Dolores Williams, agrees:

---

description of Ishmael's future. He says, "The interdependence of the two histories as literary supplements means that an interpretation in favor of one or the other will inevitably fail to account for the full range of details in the present form of the story" ("The Wilderness and Salvation History in the Hagar Story," *JBL* 117 [1998]: 43). Dozeman's analysis is correct that, independently, the "two histories" he stipulates "inevitably fail to account for the full range of details in the present form of the story"; however, the single literary interpretation of the present form of the story I provide here *does* account for the full range of details.

[53] Ephraim A. Speiser, *Genesis* (AB 1; Garden City, N.Y.: Doubleday, 1964), 155 n. 9. Westermann agrees that, in Hebrew, "to mock" would require a preposition. He says that a negative interpretation of Ishmael's act "is biased because it is looking for an explanation of Sarah's harshness (v. 10). But this is to misunderstand the text." Westermann's understanding is that Sarah looks into the future and sees that Ishmael will be a source of trouble for Isaac (*Genesis 12–36*, 339).

[54] Skinner, *A Critical and Exegetical Commentary on Genesis*, 322.

[55] Trible, "The Other Woman," 244 n. 46.

[56] For example, Hackett, "Rehabilitating Hagar," 21; Victor Hamilton, *The Book of Genesis: Chapters 18–50* (Grand Rapids, Mich.: Eerdmans, 1995), 79.

[57] Waters, "Who Was Hagar?" 205. Waters believes Egyptians were black. If so, the charge of Israelite racial (ethnic) bias, pervasive in his article, is rebutted by Joseph's marriage to an Egyptian woman and the full participation of their children, Ephraim and Manasseh, as progenitors of two of the twelve tribes of Israel.

"Economic realities, specifically inheritance, are the central issues here."[58] Jo Ann Hackett believes that a piece of the story is missing and says, "The original story must have said that he [Ishmael] did something to rile Sarah, to make her think or to remind her that he was also in a position to inherit, since that is her complaint to Abraham later in the episode."[59] If Sarah's motivation were economic, however, why did it take her years to repudiate Ishmael and Isaac's division of Abraham's legacy?

All previous definitions of מצחק share the same defect: none of them has anything to do with a weaning feast. The Bible is not concerned with the commonplace events of everyday life; the feast is not chronicled in order to record the customs and traditions of the ancient Israelites nor to keep us abreast of the social calendar of Abraham and Sarah. We would not have been told of the celebration unless it had a bearing on the plot. The distinguishing attribute of a feast, משתה, as opposed to any other meal, is that intoxicating beverages are served.[60] מצחק does not mean "playing"or "mocking"; it refers to drunkenness.[61] The Bible is not a temperance tract, but it could serve as one: when drink enters, trouble often follows.

Wine's first appearance in Scripture warns of its perils; Noah gets drunk and naked and something dissolute occurs (9:21–25). In 19:32–35, Lot, Abraham's nephew, impregnates his own daughters while in a drunken stupor. Before this scene, however, the Bible insinuates that Lot is no stranger to drink. When the two angels come to Lot to warn him of the destruction of Sodom, he entertains them with a feast, משתה (19:3). The menu consists of wine and bread. Why should the famously terse author pause to tell us Lot's bill of fare? What does it matter what he served? When Abraham fed the angels (18:6–8), he provided a sumptuous meal of veal, cheese, cakes, and milk: no alcoholic beverages. Abraham's reception serves as a paradigm for the reader. When, in the very next chapter, the recital of dining angels deviates from this standard, we are meant to take notice, and we notice the presence of liquor.

Lot's sons-in-law do not believe him when he warns them of Sodom's impending catastrophe (19:14). They think he is מצחק—the exact term

---

[58] Williams, *Sisters in the Wilderness,* 27.

[58] Hackett, "Rehabilitating Hagar," 20.

[60] In Ezra 3:7 the word for feast, משתה, is used as a synonym for wine. To indicate this particularity in Genesis, Everett Fox translates משתה, feast, as "meal-with-drink" (Genesis 19:3), and as a "drinking-feast" (21:8; 26:30; 29:22; and 40:20) (*The Five Books of Moses* [vol. 1; Schocken Bible; New York: Schocken, 1995]).

[61] This new definition of מצחק makes sense in Genesis 19:14 and 26:8, the only other uses of this specific word in the Pentateuch. The root is "laughter," צחק. Ishmael may exhibit a giggly, silly stage of drunkenness that is reflected in this root.

used to describe Ishmael two chapters later. In chapter 19 the word has always been translated, "as one who mocks" or "jests," but in view of Lot's menu preference prior to Sodom's destruction and the drunken debauch that follows, is it not more likely that his sons-in-law think he is as a drunk? The Bible gives no hint that Lot is a clown, always joking, but it does disclose that he is a tippler. I suggest that when he entreats his sons-in-law, and they assume he is מצחק, the word means drinking, not jesting.

> And she said to Abraham: "Cast out this [female] slave and her son, for the son of this [female] slave will not inherit with my son, with Isaac." (21:10)

Ishmael has become tipsy at the feast. He is of the right age to be curious, to experiment, and to make a spectacle of himself.[62] Foolishly, rather than hiding his drunkenness, he might have shown it off in a puerile attempt to look sophisticated. Sarah may even have pointed out to Abraham that Ishmael takes after his cousin, Lot. Abraham distanced himself from Lot (13:8–9), and Sarah demands the removal of this other bad influence.[63] Sarah's view of the danger to Isaac of Ishmael's companionship is artfully illustrated by the syntax of 21:10: the positioning of the word "with" immediately before and after "my son." Isaac, to his mother's eye, is hemmed in by the menacing fellowship of his half-brother.

> And the thing was very evil in the eyes of Abraham on account of his son. And God said to Abraham, "Let it not be evil in your eyes because of the lad and because of your slave. All that Sarah says to you, hear her voice, for in Isaac shall seed be called to you." (21:11–12)

Traditionally, source critics regarded the terms "handmaid" and "[female] slave" as markers for the J source and the E source respectively. This doctrine, however, has been challenged and all but abandoned.[64] Now scholars dispute the nuances of these words. Adele Berlin says that Hagar's status has been raised from handmaid (16:2, 3, 5, 6, 8) to slave (21:10, 12–13). Trible says slave is the more oppressive term; thus Hagar's status is lower in chapter 21.[65] If the change in terminology in-

---

[62] Abram was eighty-six years old when Ishmael was born (16:16). He was one hundred when Isaac was born (21:5); therefore, depending on the age of weaning, Ishmael is about sixteen to eighteen years old. In 2 Maccabees 7:27, a mother says that she nursed her child for three years.

[63] Unfortunately, Sarah's precaution is not altogether successful. Isaac is מצחק with his wife in Genesis 26:8—a carousing that relaxes caution and signals conjugality. Before deceiving Isaac concerning Esau's blessing, Jacob, perhaps to more easily fuddle his father, gives him wine that he has brought or found in his father's tent (27:25). The author makes a point of telling us that Isaac drinks the wine.

[64] Alfred Jepsen, "Ama[H] und Schiphcha[H]," VT (1958): 293; Van Seters, Abraham in History and Tradition, 202; Alexander, "The Hagar Traditions," 145.

[65] Adele Berlin, Poetics and Interpretation of the Biblical Narrative (Sheffield: Almond, 1983), 152 n. 5; Trible, "The Other Woman," 240 n. 11.

deed represents a change in status, then these commentators must explain Hagar's reversion to the status of handmaid in 25:12.

I concur with Frank C. Fensham that אמה is the female equivalent of עבד (male slave).[66] Both the handmaid and the אמה are slaves, but "handmaid" is the proper way to refer to such a woman.[67] Sarah is not interested in tact when she twice derisively labels Hagar, "*this* slave." In 21:12–13, God seems to show the same lack of consideration when he too twice identifies Hagar as a slave (though not as *this* slave, a contemptuous locution that expresses Sarah's enduring animosity toward Hagar). Sarah's lack of respectful address may be attributed to her tenacious resentment; God's terminology will be vital to Scripture's blueprint for history.

Abraham demonstrates his indifference to Hagar by deploring only the prospect of Ishmael's banishment. That Hagar too will be cast out seems to be of no concern to him. God, who reads his heart, chides him for his insensibility to the welfare of another human being by pointedly telling him not to be upset over the lad and over his *slave*. Abraham and the reader learn what Abraham's feelings should have been. God also tells Abraham to hear all that Sarah says to him. He could have said just, "Hear what Sarah says to you." We know what she says to Abraham, but, apparently, we do not know *all* that she says. She may have admonished him never to burden Isaac with co-heirs. Certainly in 25:5–6, Abraham gives his entire estate to Isaac and fobs off the sons of his concubines with gifts. Before his death, Abraham sends these sons away, literally "from upon Isaac," as though he were relieving him of the pressure of siblings.

> And Abraham arose in the morning and took bread and a bottle of water and gave it to Hagar, placing it on her shoulder, and the child, and sent her away. And they went and they wandered in the wilderness of Beer-sheba. (21:14)

---

[66] Frank C. Fensham, "The Son of a Handmaid in Northwest Semitic," *VT* 19 (1969): 321. Neufeld agrees that אמה is the female counterpart of the male slave, עבד, and discusses each use of the term in its biblical context. He says that אמה ranks socially lower than שפחה (handmaid) in each instance, though he believes that 1 Samuel 25:41 suggests otherwise. I think that אמה is the lower term in this example as well: Abigail, in a display of humility, calls herself an אמה, the more negative label, ready to serve the next lowest classification, the שפחה (*Ancient Hebrew Marriage Laws*, 122–23). Because Hagar is not called עֲבָדָה—a term he claims is the female correlative of עבד—Waters insists that she is not a slave. In support of his assertion, he cites five occurrences of עֲבָדָה in the Bible: Genesis 26:14; Job 1:3; Ezekiel 9:8, 9; Nehemiah 9:17 ("Who Was Hagar," 202–3). עֲבָדָה, however, is not the female correlative of עבד but is a collective noun referring to household servants, both male and female, and occurs twice in the Bible (Genesis 26:14; Job 1:3).

[67] This convention is similar to that of the cultivated antebellum American slave owner who spoke of "Negro property" and of "slaves" only in commercial, political, or theological contexts; in the domestic realm, whether in speaking to them or in speaking of them, the Africans were "servants" (Robert Manson Myers, *Children of Pride* [New Haven: Yale University Press, 1972]).

Many analysts note the correspondences between Abraham's loss of Ishmael and his near loss of Isaac in the following chapter.[68] One glaring difference is that when Abraham takes Isaac to be sacrificed, he also takes an ass. Here, rich man though he is, he does not even spare his firstborn son and the woman who has served his household for so many years an ass upon which to carry their personal belongings. Hagar seems to leave Abraham's house with nothing but her son and the bread and water she can carry on her shoulder. This meager disbursement is greatly to Abraham's discredit. Sarah is not alone in iniquity toward Hagar and her offspring.

Scholars have been much exercised over Ishmael's age in this passage. They see contradiction in the use of "lad" (נער, which designates a youth, an adolescent) in vv. 12, 17–20 and the use of "child" (ילד, which denotes a younger child or infant) in vv. 14–16. Also, there is an incongruity between Ishmael's indicated age of about seventeen with (what they understand as) Abraham's placing him on Hagar's shoulder. Documentary hypothesists see no psychologically penetrating reason for the author's choice of words and solve the problem expeditiously by dispensing with the chronological verses, 16:16; 17:24–25; and 21:5.[69] They assert that these verses had to have been later additions by the P source and have no place in either Hagar tradition. Ishmael is therefore a baby, and Abraham is free to balance him on Hagar's shoulder.[70] A woman, however, carries an infant or young child on her back or slung across her chest; she does not perch it on her shoulder like an organ-grinder's monkey.

Sharon Jeansonne tries to retain the chronological integrity of the passage and nevertheless resolve the lad/child dichotomy by stipulating that "child" is used when Ishmael's life is in danger in the desert, and "lad" is used when his life is not threatened.[71] Unfortunately, this solution breaks down in v. 14, for Ishmael is a "child" when Abraham gives him over to Hagar's care, but he is not yet in danger. Victor Hamilton suggests that Abraham and Hagar's use of "child" indicates a biological relationship, whereas God's use of "lad" shows that he aligns himself with Sarah in downplaying Abraham's paternity.[72]

My reading is that "lad" and "child" are aptly employed to illustrate different points of view. God calls Ishmael a lad because that is what he is. When the perspective is Abraham's or Hagar's, Ishmael is a child, the

---

[68] For example, Curt Leviant, "Ishmael and Hagar in the Wilderness: A Parallel *Akedah*," *Midstream*, 43, no. 8 (1997): 17–19.

[69] For example, Alexander, "The Hagar Traditions," 145–46.

[70] "Abraham places Ishmael, as well as food and water, on Hagar's shoulder" (Katheryn Pfisterer Darr, *Far More Precious Than Jewels* [Louisville: Westminster John Knox, 1991], 144–45); Gunkel, *Genesis*, 227; McEvenue, "A Comparison of Narrative Styles," 76; Alexander, "The Hagar Traditions," 146; Van Seters, *Abraham in History and Tradition*, 155; many others.

[71] Jeansonne, *The Women of Genesis*, 51.

[72] Hamilton, *The Book of Genesis*, 81.

more tender term, for, to them, he is their child whatever his age. Syntactically, v. 14 can be read that Abraham places bread and water on Hagar's shoulder and also gives their child into her charge. He may well, however, have set Ishmael's hand on his mother's shoulder. The boy may have felt somewhat frail and in need of support. If he had to close his eyes or squint against the morning light, he may have needed guidance. For Ishmael, after all, it is the morning after the night before.

Verse 14 reads, "Abraham sends *her* away." In fact, he sends both Hagar and Ishmael away, but I think the author narrows the "sends" to Hagar because the act of sending, שלח, constitutes divorce (Deuteronomy 22:19, 29; 24:1, 3–4; Isaiah 50:1; Jeremiah 3:1, 8; and Malachi 2:16). The stronger verb Sarah uses, "cast out," גרש, in v. 10 also often pertains to divorce; the passive participle of גרש, i.e., גרושה, means divorceé (Leviticus 21:7, 14; 22:13; Numbers 30:10; Ezekiel 44:22).

> And the water in the bottle was consumed, and she left the child under one of the shrubs. And she went and seated herself at a distance, about a bowshot, for she said, "Let me not see the death of the child." And she sat at a distance, and she lifted up her voice, and she wept. (21:15–16)

Ishmael dehydrates sooner than his mother (I contend that he was more dehydrated than she at their outset) and seems to her to be on the point of death. She abandons him beneath a bush and is able to continue walking a considerable distance.[73] We know the distance is extensive because it, or a measure of distance (bowshot), is repeated three times. She says that she does not want to see her son die, but her meaning is that she does not want to hear her son die, to hear when his moaning stops. The word "see" is used here in its sense of "to perceive"—just as she "saw" that she had conceived (16:4). Had she literally been speaking of vision, she could have settled herself next to Ishmael with her back to him. Scripture speaks of bowshot, but Hagar withdraws beyond earshot.

> And God heard the voice of the lad, and the angel of God called to Hagar from heaven and said, "What is with you, Hagar? Do not fear, for God has heard the voice of the lad, where he is. Arise, lift up the lad and grasp him strongly in your hand, for I will make him a great nation." (21:17–18)

Hagar is out of range of her son's voice, but God is not. Although we are told only of Hagar's weeping (and loud weeping at that: she "lifts up her voice"), it is the whimpering of Ishmael that God hears and stresses that he hears.[74] Not only are we twice told that God hears Ishmael, but

---

[73] The notion that Hagar "casts" Ishmael away feeds exegetic anxiety over his age. I accept Morton Cogan's convincing argument that the expression does not necessarily involve throwing an object but is the term for abandonment ("A Technical Term for Exposure," *JNES* 27 [1968]: 133–35).

[74] Skinner prefers to emend the text to: "And the boy lifted up his voice and wept" (*A Critical and Exegetical Commentary on Genesis*, 323).

Hagar is reproached by the words "where he is." No matter where she leaves Ishmael (and how far she distances herself from him and from her responsibility), she cannot leave the boy beyond God's ability to hear and to know.[75] In the imperative to "grasp him strongly," there is another note of admonishment; she is not to abandon him again. The Bible reassures the reader, concerned with the equity of God's plan, that Hagar does not have, in contemporary terms, "the right stuff" to be the mother of the covenantal child. Sarah and Isaac, on the other hand, are shown to be exceptionally close: Isaac is the only person in Scripture who needs to be comforted for the loss of his mother (24:67).

A frequently offered "proof" that chapters 16 and 21 are written by different authors is Hagar's character change from the first narrative to the second. Bernadette Revicky says, "In Genesis 21:8–21, Hagar loses her color and courage; she is no longer the tempestuous Bedouin woman. Here, she is depicted as passive and despondent."[76] Gunkel attributes this disparity in portrayal to the different "attitudes" of the J and E authors. The older J source, living in the wilderness, was imbued with the "robust local hues" of Bedouin matriarchy; whereas, the later E source, "a farmer or city-dweller" was unfamiliar with nomadic people, and only retained the concept of Hagar's misfortune.[77] I cannot guess the author's vocation or milieu, but I suggest that seventeen or so years of subjugation takes its toll on a personality. Sensitive to the corrosion of slavery, the author realistically delineates the formerly impertinent Hagar as submissive and quick to despair.

Slavery suppresses individuality and autonomy. With elegant literary economy, the author implies this loss of persona by denying Hagar and Ishmael their names. Only God names Hagar in this chapter, and Ishmael's name is never used. The author uses the same technique in Exodus, where, except for a Hebrew infant individuated by Pharaoh's daughter, the Israelite slaves are anonymous until after Moses' theophany. The Lord names Aaron, but the narrator does not restore the slaves' distinctive identities until Exodus 6:14.

Although Ishmael is depersonalized in this chapter, he is given a promise of future nationhood, a dwelling place, an occupation, and a wife (Genesis 21:18, 20–21). He is also accorded rapport with God. The "with," את, used in the phrase, "And God was with the lad" (v. 20) has a connotation different from the "with," עם, used twice in v. 10. The former expresses closer association, even companionship: "Enoch walked with God," 5:22, 24; "Noah walked with God," 6:9. In these examples it is as though Enoch and Noah took the initiative to follow in God's ways. With Ishmael, God takes the initiative.

---

[75] Westermann says that "where he is" does not suit v. 17b and moves it to v. 18a: "Lift up the boy from where he is." God's implied reproof of Hagar is effaced by this "improvement" (*Genesis 12–36*, 342).

[76] Revicky, "Hagar, Maidservant of Sarai," 87.

[77] Gunkel, *Genesis*, 230.

THE PARALLEL

In chapter 16, Hagar flees from the face of Sarai and encounters the Lord in the desert. The Lord tells her to return to the place from which she fled and makes concessions to induce her obedience. Hagar reluctantly returns as the Lord commands and, in chapter 21, is thrust out of the house of her bondage with her child. In the desert God rescues them by providing water. This time Hagar (and her child with her) remains free.

In Exodus 2:15 Moses flees from the face of Pharaoh. In 3:2 he encounters the Lord in the desert. The Lord tells him to return to the place from which he fled and makes concessions to induce his obedience (4:14–17). Moses reluctantly returns as the Lord commands and, in 12:39, is thrust out of the house of bondage with the people, Israel. In the desert the Lord rescues them by providing water (15:25). This time Moses (and his people with him) remains free.

Beside the striking thematic parallels, there are also lexical correspondences to guide the attentive reader to compare the narratives. In Genesis 16:8, Hagar says that she flees from the face (ברח מפני) of her mistress; in Exodus 2:15, we are told that Moses flees from the face (ברח מפני) of Pharaoh. In Genesis 16:11, the Lord tells Hagar that he has heard her affliction (ענה); in Exodus 3:7 the Lord tells Moses that he has seen the affliction (ענה) of his people and heard their cry. In Genesis 16:13, Hagar uses the word "here," "hither" (הלם), in naming her theophany; in Moses' theophany, the Lord also uses הלם (Exodus 3:5). The only instances of this word's use in the Pentateuch are in these two scenes. Contained in Hagar's theophany is the word גם, "indeed," "also." In analyzing the passage, I translate גם as though it were the intensifier, "indeed." Considering its context and its contiguity to the relatively rare word הלם, however, it could be that גם is meant to be read as "also"—a proleptic allusion to Moses' theophany. Other verbal links between Moses' deliverance and Hagar's are the words "send," שלח, "cast out," גרש, and "strong hand," יד שזק.[78]

In Genesis 15:13 the Lord makes a covenant with Abram. Abram is promised a certain land and numerous descendants. In the satisfaction of his part of the arrangement, Abram's seed will be strangers, גר (the root), will be slaves, עבד, and will be afflicted, ענה. When these three conditions are fulfilled, the Lord will redeem his people, Israel, and bring them up from subjugation, with great substance, into the promised land.[79] This

---

[78] For a lengthy discussion of many of these correlations, see Dozeman, "The Wilderness and Salvation History," 28–34.

[79] David Silber makes these observations in an audiotape explaining the Passover Seder. He does not enter into Hagar's story but does discuss these three key words as they relate to Jacob and Moses. The tape is distributed by The Drisha Institute, New York, N.Y.

consummation cannot take place for four hundred years because the Amorites, who are the inhabitants of the land, have not yet sinned sufficiently to deserve the punishment of exile (v. 16).[80] The Lord could, of course, displace the Amorites in favor of his chosen people whether or not they had earned punishment, but the author establishes that such arbitrary partisanship is not in the nature of God.[81]

In the first chapter of Exodus, two of the conditions required for redemption are fulfilled. We learn that the Israelites are afflicted, ענה, and enslaved, עבד. In fact, between them, these words are repeated seven times in four verses (vv. 11–14). The sevenfold repetition again bears an ethereal significance. The third condition, strangerhood, גר, is not met however, and so God does not respond to the affliction and enslavement. The Israelites have become so alienated from the Lord and so assimilated to Egyptian customs and values that they do not perceive themselves to be strangers in Egypt. Indeed, once free, this generation of Israelites continues to clamor for Egypt, and it is only the next generation that can advance to the promised land.

Moses runs from Pharaoh and settles in Midian where he marries and has a son. He names his son Gershom, "for he said, 'I was a stranger [גר, ger] in a foreign land'" (2:22). Embedded in his son's name is the all important profession of self-knowledge that will fulfill Israel's side of the covenant. Only Moses, who has left Egypt, has attained the geographic and cognitive distance to understand that he did not belong there, he was a stranger there. One man embodies the entire Hebrew people, and the third condition is finally achieved. In the next few verses, we are told that God heard, God remembered, God saw, and God knew (vv. 24–25); the series of events that will culminate in liberation are now initiated.

In the parallel story of Hagar, the key word גר is the first of the three we meet; in Hebrew, the expression "the stranger," הגר, and the name "Hagar," הגר, are the same word. We see the word "afflict" in Genesis 16:6, 9 referring to Sarai's mistreatment of Hagar. In Genesis 21, seventeen or so years later, Hagar is referred to as a slave, אמה, by Sarah and by God. As has been observed, אמה is the female counterpart for עבד, male slave. The third key concept is now fulfilled, and God hears and rescues Hagar and her child as he will later hear and rescue Moses and the children of Israel.

There is another possible pre-exodus correspondence between Hagar and the Israelites. Reuven Yaron proposes the following translation of

---

[80] Hallvard Hagelia says "Amorite" designates the original, pre-Israelite, population of Canaan (*Numbering the Stars: A Phraseological Analysis of Genesis 15* [Stockholm: Almqvist and Wiksell, 1994], 140–41).

[81] Nahum Sarna says, "There is no suggestion that Israel's right to the land results from any inherent superiority. On the contrary, the Book of Deuteronomy expressly warns against such a conceit" (*Understanding Genesis* [New York: Schocken, 1970], 125).

Exodus 11:1, "And the Lord said to Moses, 'Yet I will bring one plague more upon Pharaoh and upon Egypt, afterwards he will send you forth hence: as one sends away a bride, he will surely drive you out hence.' "[82] The word for "bride" and the word for "complete" are spelled the same in Hebrew. Most Bibles translate this word as "altogether" (KJV, ASV) or "completely" (RSV) in this verse, thus: " . . . afterwards he will send you forth hence; when he shall let you go, he will drive you out hence altogether." Yaron finds "when he shall let you go" unsatisfactory for there is no "you" in the Hebrew phrase and because, so translated, the whole verse bears no connection to the two verses that follow.

Yaron explains that the ancient Hebrew meaning of "bride" does not have the modern connotation, but refers instead to an inferior type of marriage such as Hagar's.[83] Although he compares the subordinate status of a bride to Hagar's situation, he does not suggest that the verse refers to Hagar specifically. It is tempting, however, to consider the possibility. Legally, a divorced slave-wife would be sent away with gifts; Abraham does not send Hagar away empty-handed, paltry though her gifts were. She is also the only slave-wife in Scripture who is summarily ejected, and the verse, as Yaron reads it, uses the same two expressions for divorce ("send," שלח; "cast out," גרש) that Sarah uses when she urges Abraham to get rid of Hagar and her son.[84] If "bride" is a reference to Hagar, then in this verse the author ventures past pointed parallels and links the two banishment narratives with the firm authority of God's words.

THE PLAN

Why does the Bible compare the story of Hagar's travail and deliverance to the story of God's redemption of his enslaved people, Israel? David Daube points out that the story of the exodus is a recurrent typology and recounts its similarity to Jacob's escape from Laban and the Philistines' release of the captured ark. He interprets the repeated exodus theme as the Bible's assurance that God's salvific intervention is not a singular occurrence. It has happened more than once in the past; it can happen again in the future.[85]

I do not disagree with his analysis, but I believe the Hagar/exodus affiliation is a unique correspondence, different from the typologies Daube discusses. Beyond ratifying that God has saved and will save; it also teaches

---

[82] Reuven Yaron, "On Divorce in Old Testament Times," *Revue International des Droits de L'antiquité* (1957), 122.

[83] Yaron, "On Divorce," 125.

[84] David Daube accepts "Yaron's brilliant solution" with enthusiasm and says, "One is reminded of Hagar, being rejected together with Ishmael and receiving not valuables, but at least some bread and water for the journey" (*The Exodus Pattern in the Bible* [All Souls Studies 2; London: Faber & Faber, 1963], 58).

[85] Daube, *The Exodus Pattern*, 13–14.

that, as the Lord deals with his faithful, so does he deal with deserving non-believers. Through the narrative of Israelite history, readers learn that afflicting the disadvantaged is an abomination to God, whoever the victims.

The duplicate stories of Hagar's deliverance and of the Israelite people's liberation impart still another essential message. They reveal the author's understanding of God's measure-for-measure standard of justice. God does not deliver Hagar in Genesis 16 but sends her back to her mistress because the iniquity of the patriarch and the matriarch is not yet complete. Just as God does not unjustly exile the Amorites but reserves sentence until they thoroughly deserve their punishment, so too does he permit Abraham and Sarah the full exercise of their free will before he wreaks judgment upon them. The Bible shows that God has foreknowledge of their ultimate guilt (15:13), but he does not control their behavior.

In its characteristic measure-for-measure mode, Scripture redresses Hagar's agony in witnessing her child's near death. In an ordeal similar to Hagar's, but more excruciating, Abraham suffers the fear not only of seeing but of causing the death of his son, Isaac, and according to medieval exegetes, Sarah dies of grief in the belief that Abraham will sacrifice her only child.[86] Their descendants too will pay for their forebears' maltreatment of Hagar. They will slave under Egyptian affliction as Hagar the Egyptian slaved under affliction. Hagar's nationality, the narrator's second ascription in 16:1 is no coincidence and gains relevance here. For so many people to suffer for so long in reparation for the injury of one individual may seem an excessive expiation, but Abraham and Sarah, as the progenitors of God's chosen people, are held to a high standard, and their sins are grave. Hagar will be requited thousands of times over, for four hundred years, and, ever after, all Israel will memorialize her in their laws and practices.

In Genesis 21, Hagar is referred to as a slave, אמה, by Sarah and by God. Ishmael, in this chapter, is called a בן־האמה, the son of the slave, also both by Sarah and by God (vv. 10, 13). As Bruce Rosenstock points out, this is an unusual denominative, for the only children of slaves discussed in the iteration of the laws pertaining to slavery (Exodus 21:1–11) are the children of male slaves. The form, בן־האמה, son of the female slave, occurs in the Pentateuch only in Genesis 21 and in the Sabbath law:[87] "Six days you will do your work, and the seventh day you will rest; that your ox and your ass may have rest, and the son of your [female] slave, and the stranger, may be refreshed" (Exodus 23:12). Rosenstock says that not only is "son of your [female] slave" anomalous, but

---

[86] Silbermann, *Chumash*, 98.

[87] The term occurs in Judges 9:18 as a derogatory designation for a specific individual: Abimelech, Gideon's son by his concubine. It is also used in Psalms 86:16 and 116:16 as self-referential expressions of humility.

the word *ha-ger* [the stranger] is also, in this context, anomalous. The previous three noun phrases ("your ox," "your ass," and "the son of your bondmaid") all end with the suffix *-kha* [your], but *v'ha-ger* [and the stranger] brings the series to an unexpected conclusion with the noun in the absolute state. Had *ha-ger* also ended with the second person suffix, the pun on Hagar would have been lost.[88]

According to Rosenstock, readers are expected to recollect Hagar when "the stranger" is denoted, and the repeated designation of Ishmael in Genesis 21:10, 13 as the "son of the slave" also primes us to recognize the reference to Ishmael in the Sabbath commandment. He concludes: "The observance of the Sabbath is Israel's manner of acknowledging the tragic misalignments of its history, and making restitution for the innocent victims whose collective identity is given its figuration in Hagar."[89]

Beyond the Sabbath law, the legislation aimed at the relief of the stranger, juridically, economically, and socially is recapitulated over and over. To list just a few of many examples: the Bible tells the Israelites that there should be the same law for the stranger and for the home-born (Exodus 12:49), that they should not glean all the produce of their fields but leave a corner for the stranger (Leviticus 19:10), and that they should not vex or wrong a stranger (Exodus 22:20). The Hebrews are adjured not only to treat the stranger justly but even empathically: "And a stranger you will not vex, for you know the heart of a stranger as you were strangers in the land of Egypt" (Exodus 23:9). Many of these laws explicitly bind equitable treatment of the stranger to the Israelite experience in Egypt: "And if a stranger sojourn with you in your land, do not do wrong to him. The stranger that sojourns with you shall be as the home-born to you. You shall love the stranger as yourself, for you were strangers in the land of Egypt: I am the Lord your God" (Leviticus 19:33–34). With few exceptions, the word, stranger, is expressed in the singular.[90] I believe this is because the plural "strangers," גרים, is not so immediately evocative of "the stranger," Hagar.

The author need not have used the word "stranger" at all; the Hebrew language has other words that express the separation and "otherness" of the foreign, heathen, and alien minority. Or he could have chosen expressions that precisely fit each verse's context. For example, in the injunction to spare a corner of one's field for the stranger, the author could have said "for the hungry." As Rosenstock observes, the anomalous use of "[female] slave" and "son of the [female] slave" in the Sabbath legislation is a cue to

---

[88] Bruce Rosenstock, "Inner-Biblical Exegesis in the Book of the Covenant," *Conservative Judaism* 44 (1993): 45 n. 13.

[89] Rosenstock, "Inner-Biblical Exegesis," 49.

[90] Rolf Rendtorff says, "The *ger* is mainly dealt with as an individual" ("The *Ger* in the Priestly Laws of the Pentateuch" in *Ethnicity and the Bible* [Leiden: E. J. Brill, 1996], 78).

readers that prompts us to think of Hagar. I submit that this coupling of Sabbath law with the description of Hagar encourages us to associate also the multiple commandments about "the stranger," הגר, with the name "Hagar," הגר.[91] The aspect of Hagar designated third by the narrator in Genesis 16:1 now rises to prominence as a profound commemorative.

Claus Westermann says, "A feels disadvantaged by B; A is liberated from the disadvantage; A disadvantages B. This happens in every area of human life, most notably in the political area; the oppressed when liberated becomes the oppressor."[92] We all know examples of Westermann's assertion: Northern Ireland, Bosnia, Rwanda, the Middle East. But the Bible does not share Westermann's pessimistic view of an inherently retributive human nature. The scriptural author believes in mankind's perfectibility and tries to refine and improve our characters so that, instead of cycling in an endless succession of reciprocal oppression and inequity, humanity progresses in righteousness and compassion.

The influence of the story of Hagar can be traced in the Bible's message for humankind. Hagar, the Egyptian, is oppressed, and her Ishmaelite heirs, along with the Midianites, representative descendants of Abraham's other disinherited children, sell Joseph into slavery in Egypt, thus beginning her countrymen's long oppression of the Israelites (Genesis 37:27–28, 36). When the Israelites are freed, however, they are forbidden to perpetuate the cycle of injury, and it is in the name of Hagar, the stranger, that they are forbidden it.

Israelite law, subsequent to the exodus, speaks to both the advance of ethical consciousness and to the perpetual commemoration of the suffering Hagar. In event and in precept, the two Hagar narratives mirror Moses' hegira from Egypt to freedom. As Moses embodies the Israelite people, initiating their release by his lone recognition that Egypt is not the spiritual home of the Hebrews, so Hagar is the embodiment of the downtrodden "other." She is not a demeaned and reduced woman as exegetes have maintained, but the prototypal stranger in name and in fate, an everlasting memorial to mold the conscience of the world.

---

[91] In Exodus 22:21–23, God says that if, despite his commandments, the stranger is at all afflicted and cries unto him, God will surely hear. This assurance merges remembrance of Ishmael with the law concerning the stranger; the name, Ishmael, means "God hears."

[92] Westermann, *Genesis 12–36*, 241.

CHAPTER FIVE

Dead Men Tell No Tales: On the Motivation of Joseph's Brothers

Sibling rivalry is both the theme of "Dead Men Tell No Tales," my first biblical essay, and the impetus for writing it. One Saturday, when I was at synagogue listening to Hebrew being spoken, the Torah reader chanted the story of Joseph, tattletale son of an over-fond father (Genesis 37). Joseph's father sent him to Shechem to find his hostile brothers and report back on them. In Shechem, Joseph encountered a nameless man who steered him to Dothan where his brothers went after leaving Shechem. When the brothers saw Joseph from afar, they discussed killing him. One of their number suggested that, rather than slaying him and having his blood on their hands, they profit by him. This plan was adopted, and Joseph was sold into slavery.

After the rabbi's talk on the Bible reading, he invited questions. I asked why the author employed a man simply to reroute Joseph to Dothan. Why were his brothers not in Shechem? The nameless man seemed to contribute nothing to the story, and Shechem would have been a fitting locale for the murder of Joseph. The brothers had made it a killing field in chapter 34 when they slaughtered all the men in Shechem to avenge their sister's rape.

The rabbi said the midrashists also wondered about the presence of the man and surmised that he was an angel. God sent a messenger to redirect Joseph so that he would not miss his brothers and thus thwart God's plan for history. This solution left unanswered the question of why the brothers left Shechem; had they stayed, God's plan for history would have been secure without an angel's intervention.

Angels, or messengers of God, had visited earlier in the Bible. They had told Abraham his nonagenarian, post-menopausal wife would bear a child and the cities of the plain would be destroyed by a rain of fire and brimstone from the heavens. This was news. An angel had told Hagar she would bear a son and be the mother of multitudes, and then he had saved her and Ishmael in the desert. This was important. An angel had prevented Abraham from sacrificing his son, Isaac. Also important. Now an angel was sent merely to give Joseph directions? I did not think so. Surely, God dispatched emissaries on more profound errands than that.

My bias in favor of the Bible's virtuosity led me to one deduction: the fact that his brothers were not where Joseph expected them to be was significant to the storyline, so significant in fact, that the author was willing to introduce a new character to advance it. Every night before I fell asleep, I tried to think of the author's reason for telling us the brothers had left Shechem for Dothan. One night, I thought of it. In the morning, I looked up the passage and reread it from the beginning of the chapter. Now, with the illumination of insight, I saw that each component of the story attested to my conclusion.

Once I arrived at a solution, I was satisfied and thought no more about Joseph and his brothers until, months later, I met with *my* brother. He told me he had written a short story and asked if I would read it for him before he submitted it for publication. I was honored to, but I drove away from our meeting thinking: "Well, if my little brother can write something, I can certainly write something!" But what to write? The only idea I had was the one about Joseph and his brothers, and even if I wrote about it, what then? I did not think a layman's article about the Bible could get published. Nevertheless, my brother's short story pricked so, I had to write down my only idea. Sibling rivalry is a sharp spur.

According to the laws of dramaturgy, if you show the audience a gun in the first act, it had better go off by the third. We are shown a gun in the first lines of the Joseph cycle when we are told that Joseph was a talebearer and brought his father evil reports of his brothers (Genesis 37:2). Joseph's tattling is not mentioned again, but the gun goes off in v. 18 when fear of his tale-bearing motivated his brothers to kill him. Although they resented Joseph because of their father's partiality and detested him because of his grandiose dreams, they did not plot against him for these reasons. The purpose of this chapter is to argue that Joseph discovered his brothers in wrong-doing, and they attempted murder to prevent him from divulging their misbehavior.

When their father, Jacob, sent Joseph to meet his brothers, he asked: "Do not thy brethren feed the flock in Shechem?" (v. 13). Why did he ask the question? We were just told in the preceding line, "And his brethren went to feed their father's flock in Shechem." The question plants a niggle of doubt in the reader's mind. Perhaps the brothers were not in Shechem. Perhaps Jacob suspected they were not and therefore sent Joseph to find them and to bring back word of them to him. We already knew that Joseph was a tattletale and need not be specifically enjoined to report on his brothers, but here, telling was part of his mission. He was charged by his father to do so.

Joseph did not, of course, find his brothers in Shechem but was directed to Dothan by a man who found him searching for them in the field.

Commentators speculate extensively about this encounter. They consider the identity of the man and examine the need for the dialogue between this man and Joseph. Surprise is expressed that the Bible describes their conversation in such detail, and some propose that the man was an angel.

For me, the man's identity is not critical, nor is the conversation puzzling. The anonymous man might have been a chance busybody, or he might have been an angel on an unusually trivial mission; either way, the conversation was necessary to get Joseph from where he expected his brothers to be to where they actually were. The conversation also tells us that the brothers did not lose their way or aimlessly follow the herd to Dothan; they went there purposefully, by a conscious decision: "And the man said: 'I heard them say: Let us go to Dothan'" (v. 17). Nothing I have read asks what is to me the more compelling question: why were Joseph's brothers in Dothan, not Shechem?

I submit that Joseph's brothers were not in Shechem feeding their father's flocks because they were in Dothan fooling around. The town name, Dothan, connotes no invidious overtones to modern ears, but it may have to the Bible's first readers. Imagine reading about a contemporary cattle rancher who sends his sons to herd cattle in Boulder City, Nevada, but finds they went instead a few miles away to Las Vegas. One would not assume they went there for better grazing. After reading the town name, Las Vegas, the modern reader would expect the boys' mischief and the father's anger. The ancient reader too must have made certain assumptions on hearing the name of the town to which the brothers had gone instead of Shechem.

In over 5,000 years a town's name can lose its implications; the reader is not left merely to guess, however, but is given a clue about the nature of Dothan. We are told that Ishmaelite and Midianite merchants passed through. Many explanations have been put forth as to why both groups are mentioned. My explanation is that it manifests for us that Dothan was a busy place.

Without the knowledge that Dothan was much-trafficked, one could suppose the brothers' murderous impulses were incited by the setting. Unlike Hebron, Dothan was not too near their father, and unlike Shechem it had no nameless man observing every move. Had Dothan been a bucolic, remote, secluded grazing area, the reader might think the brothers believed their deed would go unnoticed there. But that would not be an accurate description of Dothan. It must have been situated on an active trade route, a trade route that prostitutes were likely to frequent.

It is not unreasonable to suspect Joseph's brothers of seeking prostitutes. The story of their treatment of Joseph is bracketed by examples of their licentiousness. In 35:22 we are told of the sexual immorality of Reuben, even Reuben, the "good" brother who tried to spare Joseph. He was the oldest of Jacob's sons and therefore the one whom the others might be expected to emulate. We are told of Joseph's brother, Judah, and his sexual encounter with his daughter-in-law, Tamar, immediately after we are told of Joseph's sale into Egypt and before the story continues there. We can make assumptions about the brothers' probable conduct from these examples of their unchastity; however, we do not know, nor need to know, why the brothers went to Dothan. The Bible simply emphasizes that they were not where they were supposed to be.

Whatever the brother's misdeeds, they knew they could not keep their pursuits from their father's ears by persuading Joseph to join with them in their escapades. Joseph was informer not participant. They also knew they could not successfully plead for Joseph's silence. Not only would it have been demeaning to beg for favors from a younger brother with whom they had not previously had a peaceful word (37:4), but also Joseph was a habitual tattletale who, as the reader knows, had been pointedly instructed by his father to bring back word of his brothers' doings.

Most exegetes think the brothers' motivation to kill Joseph was their dread that his dreams would be realized. Their proof text is, "And they said to one another: 'Behold this master of dreams comes. Come now let us kill him'" (37:19–20). This epithet, however, sounds derisive, not apprehensive. The appellation "master of dreams" implied that Joseph manipulated his dreams at will, that he dreamed his self-aggrandizing prophecies to order, or that he improved upon them in the telling. Had the brothers continued, "Let us kill him lest his dreams come true," they would have voiced concern, but instead they said, "Let us kill him . . . and we shall see what will become of his dreams" (v. 20). Their tone was mocking and contemptuous. They seemed to have despised Joseph's arrogance rather than to have been anxious over his dreams' realization.

We are told Jacob rebuked Joseph for his dreams and words yet kept their message in mind. The brothers, in contrast, hated their sibling for his dreams and words yet disdained their message. Indeed, had the brothers credited the prophecy of Joseph's dreams, their shock at his ultimate elevation would have been lessened; it is their scornful attitude that makes the irony of the story so rich. Rather than establishing their motivation, this passage reveals their mocking assessment of Joseph's dreams.

In vv. 17–18 we are told, "And Joseph went after his brethren and found them in Dothan. And they saw him afar off, and before he came near unto them, they conspired against him to slay him." The Bible, with its usual economy of words, could have said just "And they saw him afar off, and they conspired against him to slay him." Why is it stressed that "before he came near unto them" they planned to kill him? Before he could brag about his dreams, before he could say, "Daddy loves me best," before he could strut about in his fancy coat, just the sight of him was enough to set off the conspiracy.

Joseph's brothers had reasons to hate him: his tale-bearing, his insulting dreams, their father's favoritism. Had they hated him enough to kill him for these reasons, they had their opportunity when he was shepherding with them in the fields of the vale of Hebron. They could have done it when he was telling them his dreams, when their rage presumably was the hottest. They hated his words and his deeds in Hebron, but they planned to kill him when they merely saw him approaching in Dothan. I suggest it is because *he* saw *them* in Dothan that they felt forced to kill him. They were afraid he would return to their father and disclose their whereabouts.

When Joseph approached Dothan and his brothers "saw him afar off," they must have said a collective "Uh-oh." Their father was not a wrathful man, but they knew that at the least they would sink in his eyes, and Joseph would be exalted above them even further. Their only recourse was to silence him. Joseph's brothers may have envied him for their father's attention to his pretentious dreams; they plotted to murder the tattler, however, for fear of their father's attention to the tale he was going to tell.

CHAPTER SIX

The Bridegroom of Blood: A New Reading

The Bridegroom of Blood verses, Exodus 4:24–26, unnerved me. Not only could I not make head or tail of them, but I found them repellent. There were many other passages in the Bible that I did not understand, but I did not need to hurry past them, refusing to think about them or even look at them, turning the page and missing what comes before and after the incomprehensible verses, lest they catch my eye. This was how I fled from the Bridegroom of Blood passage. I avoided these perplexing verses as some people avert their eyes from spiders.

Just before these verses we are told that God insists Moses go to Egypt to free the enslaved Israelites. Moses packs up wife and sons and starts on the journey to Egypt. At a lodging place on the way, the Lord meets him and seeks to kill him (v. 24). In the next two verses, Moses' wife, Zipporah, circumcises their son, God withdraws, and Zipporah calls Moses a "bridegroom of blood."

I am squeamish with blood, but my antipathy toward these verses had nothing to do with the few drops of blood spilled in them. It was neither the minor surgery nor what seemed like the threat of divine violence that repulsed me. I was anxious about the verses and tried to avoid them because I wanted to keep from admitting to myself that their only rational explanation was that there *was* a mistake in the Torah after all; my father had been wrong. Other difficult biblical passages generated either indifference or assurance. I could decide with equanimity that they did not interest me enough to reflect on them, or that I did not understand them *yet*. But these verses both screamed for attention and challenged my confidence.

What I glimpsed from the corner of my eye during my rapid transits past this passage looked alarmingly as though words or whole explanatory verses had been omitted. The absurdity of the passage advanced the, to me, heresy that it belonged in another location in the Bible where it would be appropriate and understandable. Maybe the verses were not even originally about Moses. Why would God want to kill Moses—especially at this juncture?

If there were a mistake in this chapter of Torah, then chances were the source critics were right, and there were mistakes all through the Bible. I would have to cede the perspective that had by now become part of my persona. Surrendering my point of view would be losing. I was a person with an attitude; I was attached to it; I did not want to give it up. It was preferable to dodge the passage and refuse to think about it.

If the documentary hypothesists were correct and this passage were poorly redacted, the editor who approved such glaring omissions or gross misplacement had not merely nodded, he must have been drugged. Why had he not noticed, on reading over his first draft, that these verses had gaps or were misplaced? Or maybe the redactor did an exemplary job, and it was the scribe who was at fault. But did not the first readers, or the first audience—before the Bible was canonized, when corrections of scribal errors were still possible—complain of bewilderment? Or did everyone then understand the passage perfectly well, and I was just too dense to grasp it? This was my best option, and though I am none too fond of admitting stupidity, I would have embraced it and grappled with the passage if it did not make me so uneasy.

During the synagogue service one Saturday, the rabbi read Numbers 12:1 in which we are told that Moses married a Cushite woman. After services, the rabbi said that some sages considered the Cushite woman to be Zipporah and others speculated that Moses had divorced Zipporah to marry this second wife. "Divorced Zipporah, the heroine of the life-saving circumcision scene!" I thought to myself, "Now this was an idea to conjure with." What if Moses and Zipporah did not get along? What if the emergency surgery Zipporah performed was done not to save Moses but to spite him in some way? What if Zipporah were not a heroine but an enraged wife on a tear?

These notions appealed strongly to my feminist bent. The men and women I had read who considered the women of the Bible at all, or who wrote about the Bible from a feminist perspective, seemed to me to assign female characters to one of two roles: they were either heroines or victims. The Bible depicted plenty of scheming or stupid or sinful men, and for all I then knew ("Bridegroom of Blood" was just the second article I wrote), biblical women were described as frankly, but all the women in conventional feminist commentaries were worthy of praise or pity. I had not yet analyzed a biblical passage that involved a woman, but I felt that true equality, analytic equality at any rate, would not be achieved until commentators admitted that women were just as warty as men.

The morsel of antique gossip repeated by my rabbi turned me to the Bridegroom of Blood passage with enthusiasm. I still could not imagine why God sought to kill Moses or why he let him alone, but I decided to address one issue at a time. For the present, I would see if I could find any reason for Zipporah to quarrel with her husband.

Clues make all the difference in solving a mystery. With an angle of approach, I saw the passage in a new light. Poor Zipporah, daughter of a prince, thought she had married an upper-class Egyptian; at the lodging place she discovered that her husband was a runaway fugitive of slave ethnicity. "Let me see," I thought, "would I be angry if my husband said to me:

'Honey, you know how all these years we've been married, you thought I was a Jew from Boston? Well, to tell the truth, I'm neither a Jew nor from Boston. I'm from Northern Ireland; I'm a wanted man there; my oppressed people are being afflicted, and tomorrow you, me, and the kids are going in harm's way to see if we can help them.' Would I be angry? Yes, I would."

Going back over Moses' career, I saw evidence of, if not outright deception, then certainly, selective truthfulness on his part. I saw a loveless match with the priest of Midian's daughter, a reluctance to identify himself as Hebrew, misgivings over meeting his own brother. Most shocking of all, I saw an ugly scene between Moses and Zipporah. Scripture tells us that Moses did send Zipporah away (Exodus 18:2), and it also tells us that he married a second time (Numbers 12:1). The rumor of divorce may or may not have been accurate, but I could see that Zipporah had reason to reproach her husband.

Not too long after this breakthrough, I was at a book sale. Among the books was a large workbook with ESL in the title. I did not know what ESL was, but I opened the book thinking that it might be some sort of school workbook a grandchild could someday use. I read one sentence from a list of idiomatic sentences: "The father turned the business over to his daughter," and set the book down. My grandchildren would have no use for it; it was a workbook for learning English as a second language. That was the ESL of the title.

The sentence I read stuck with me like a tune one cannot get out of one's head. In bed at night, I thought about it and mused over the fact that a foreigner could understand every word of it—"father," "turned," "business," "over," "daughter"—and still not know what the sentence meant. Night after night that sentence popped up. "What *is* it with this sentence?" I thought, "I'm boring myself!" I wished I had read a few more sentences on that list, just for variety, and then it occurred to me: what if the enigmatic verse, Exodus 4:24, were an idiom?

And it was on the way, in an inn, and the Lord met him and sought to kill him.

What did it mean that the Lord "sought" to kill him? If God wanted to kill Moses, why did he not just do it—a bolt of lightning, a heart attack? Maybe no first readers were flummoxed by this passage because all of them understood the phrase idiomatically to mean that the Lord caused Moses to contemplate suicide. (Suicide is not a modern phenomenon; there are biblical examples of suicide and assisted suicide: Abimelech in Judges 9:54, Samson in Judges 16:30, Saul in 1 Samuel 31:4, and Ahithophel in 2 Samuel 17:23. Jonah in Jonah 1:12 directs the frightened sailors to save their ship and themselves by throwing him into the sea, presumably to his death. In v. 14 the sailors acknowledge that God seeks this outcome. In 4:3 and 4:9, Jonah asks God to take his life and states that he is angry enough to die.) Moses' mood was undeniably dark; I could trace evidence of his psychological dissonance in the chapters prior to our verse. His emotional anguish could well have been sufficiently severe to make him seek death.

There are no other instances in the Bible in which "The Lord sought to kill" anyone, and so I could not confirm my conjecture with comparative references to God-provoked suicidal dispositions. But in the theology of the first readers, God can impose one's mental state. He hardened Pharaoh's heart, for a well-known example.

When the phrases "The Lord sought to kill" and "He withdrew from him" were perceived as idioms, Moses' God-induced depression before the enlightening clash with Zipporah and the divine lifting of his despair after the confrontation made consummate sense. Understood in this way, the episode at the lodging place was now both coherent and congruent to the circumstances of the narrative. It told us a little about Zipporah, a lot about Moses, and a discreet amount about their marital disharmony. My father was right after all; my aversion to this passage was the consequence of *my* deficiency, not the author's.

There are few passages in Scripture more initially mysterious than Exodus 4:24–26. In just three verses, verses that seem to move all the more rapidly because of the eight active verbs they contain, God encounters Moses and seeks to kill him; Zipporah circumcises either their son or Moses (the subject of the pronouns is unclear) and calls someone a bridegroom of blood; God withdraws, and Zipporah once again repeats the bridegroom of blood epithet. The incident is obviously problematic. God has just commanded Moses to go to Egypt and free the Israelites and has promised to be with him, and Moses is on his way. Why should God now want to kill him? How does God seek to kill Moses? Does Moses suddenly become deathly ill, or does he have only a presentiment of mortality? What makes Zipporah, a Midianite woman, think that by performing the Hebrew rite of circumcision she can save Moses' life? And what does "bridegroom of blood" mean?

Traditional and modern exegetes have tried to answer these questions. The traditional interpretation holds that Moses either neglects to circumcise his son or puts off circumcision because of concern that in a postoperative condition the newborn child will be unable to withstand the stress of the journey. God seeks to kill Moses because of his failure to perform the commandment. Some suggest that it is Moses himself who is circumcised by Zipporah and that her son is designated euphemistically to preserve Moses' modesty. In either case circumcision is life-saving, and the incident teaches the supreme importance of the commandment.

Unfortunately, this explanation raises as many questions as it answers. If Moses or his older son were uncircumcised, surely God knew this when he set Moses on his mission. Why, therefore, would he send him only to kill him? Were Moses' younger son born after God's call to Moses, and his circumcision postponed because of the impending journey, why would that delay displease God? We are told in Joshua 5:5 that the Israelites did not perform circumcisions during their forty-year wandering in the desert, presumably because of the hardships of travel.

Modern critical analysts offer that unless more information is unearthed this episode is forever largely inexplicable. They see these verses as only a fragment of what must once have been a longer narrative, and they speculate that perhaps this remnant is not even relevant here but instead belongs someplace else in the larger story. I believe that, far from being an enigmatic fragment, this passage is complete, revelatory, and relevant exactly as it is and where it is. I shall argue an interpretation of these verses, justified by a close reading of the text, that answers the questions raised above, advances the narrative, resonates with an earlier similar episode in Genesis, conforms with human nature, demonstrates Zipporah's autonomy, illuminates Moses' marital relationship, and points to the intended moral.

In Genesis 31:3 God tells Jacob, like Moses, to return to the land of his birth. Jacob, like Moses, leaves his father-in-law, packs up his family, and travels to his relatives in his native land. He sets out on that journey and, like Moses, suffers some sort of divine attack in the night (32:25). Bible scholars over the centuries have often interpreted this attack figuratively. They say Jacob experiences a prophetic dream or wrestles, not with God nor with a messenger of God, but with his own conscience. God initiates the combat, for it is God who prompts Jacob's conscience. Similarly, I interpret the incitement of Moses' dark night of the soul figuratively. The phrase, "The Lord met him and sought to kill him" (Exodus 4:24), can be understood to mean that Moses is overcome with a suicidal depression.

Just as Jacob earned his guilty conscience, Moses has reason to be depressed. Although he knows he was born an Israelite, he was raised as a patrician Egyptian with the attitudes and privileges of that class. During his years in Midian he becomes a thoroughly assimilated Midianite with the status of son-in-law of the priest. Now God reminds him that he is a Hebrew and makes him give up his comfortable life and throw in his lot with a despised, oppressed, subjugated underclass. God sets Moses a mighty task, but it is not fear of the mission that causes Moses' sickness unto death; it is the challenge to his persona. He can no longer be who he thinks he is or who he wishes he was; he has to recognize and become who he truly is. Moses has the archetypical identity crisis.

From the time he was weaned he lived in Pharaoh's court as a favorite of Pharaoh's daughter. Despite knowledge of his descent, it would have been natural for Moses to identify with the Egyptians with whom he lived rather than with his Israelite kindred. He is honored, educated, wealthy, and accustomed to all the luxuries the flesh-pots of Egypt can afford.

What has he to do with slaves? Some commentators maintain it is loyalty to kin that moves Moses to go out to his brethren. I think when he goes "out among his brethren" (2:11), he is impelled by curiosity not by fellowship. It is this same quality that God tests before he calls to Moses at the burning bush. Perhaps he wants to ascertain if the assimilated Moses has now become completely materialistic and self-absorbed or if he still retains the intellectual curiosity of his younger days: "And when the Lord saw that he turned aside to see, God called unto him" (3:4).

Moreover, Moses does not seem particularly biased in favor of his fellow Hebrews, but impartially pursues justice. We are given three examples in swift succession of Moses' moral intervention. In the first he kills an Egyptian who is smiting a Hebrew (2:12), in the second he chides one Hebrew for striving with another (2:13), and in the third he comes to the aid of Midianite young women (2:17). Whether the contenders are Egyptians, Hebrews, or women of neither stock, Moses flies to the side of the wronged.

The Midianite women whom Moses helps at the well turn out, serendipitously, to be the seven daughters of the priest of Midian. Or did Moses sit by that well designedly in order to approach the priest's daughters? We are first told that he settles in Midian and then that he sits by a well (2:15); once settled, he may have assessed the situation and decided that living in a ruler's household was not only his custom but his due.

Whether Moses meets the women by chance or by choice, we soon learn that he stays in Midian because of the father, not because of the daughters. After Moses meets Jethro, the priest of Midian, "Moses was content to dwell with the man" (2:21). The verb translated as "was content" may also be translated as "was pleased," "undertook," "resolved," "determined." Up to this point in the Bible many people go to dwell in lands not their own: Cain, Abram, Lot, Jacob, Joseph and his family. But in no case is this verb or any verb in addition to "dwell" used. Its use in this connection is unique and gives Moses' decision an air of calculation that is underscored by the designation "man" in the same verse. Why is this unspecific denominative used rather than the priest's name or title? I believe it is to emphasize that Moses stays because of the "man" not because of the "woman." The very sequence of the verse establishes this point: first Moses decides to dwell with the man, then he is given Zipporah to wed. There is certainly no suggestion here of a love-match such as Jacob's; Moses makes a socially advantageous marriage.

The priest's daughters told their father they were helped by an Egyptian. Moses' dress, regal bearing, and educated conversation enable the priest to judge for himself that this kind champion of women is not a commoner but is high-born. We do not know why Jethro accepts Moses, a stranger and a foreigner, as a son-in-law, but from his marriage to Zipporah we may deduce that Moses does not hasten to disabuse his new friends of their misapprehension about his origins. After all, fathers, particularly upper-class fathers, do not readily give their daughters to escaped felons of slave lineage.

Even when Moses takes leave of his father-in-law following God's call and is ready to return to Egypt, he cannot bring himself to disclose his secret. Orthodox exegesis says humility prevents Moses from mentioning God's charge; instead he tells his father-in-law he wants to return to his brethren in Egypt to see if they are still alive (4:18). My interpretation is that Moses constructs a very careful truth, one that permits him to retain the fiction that his brethren were Egyptian.

Moses avoids telling Jethro his background, but he can no longer dodge admitting the truth to his wife. She is shortly to meet his brother, Aaron. Moses is apprehensive of this meeting for reasons unrelated to Zipporah. We sense this uneasiness when God assures Moses Aaron will be glad to see him (4:14). Perhaps there was a custom of blood feud or guilt by kinship in Egypt, and Moses fears Aaron was made to suffer for the manslaughter and therefore resents him. Or perhaps Moses knows Aaron previously resented him because of his privileged position and life of safety and ease in Pharaoh's court. Zipporah, on the other hand, is probably looking forward to meeting her cultivated and refined in-laws, showing off her sons, seeing new sights. When Moses falls into his profound depression, one can almost hear Zipporah asking what ails him and bidding him cheer up. And then he tells her.

Zipporah is enraged. How could he build their marriage on a lie? How could he misrepresent himself to her father who was so hospitable and generous? How could he expect her, a priest's daughter, to live among slaves, and how could he intend exposing their children to such degradation? There is no compelling love here pressing Zipporah to cleave to her husband at any cost. She may not know much about the deprived and miserable Israelites, but she knows she does not want to be one with them.

Zipporah also knows the Israelites' *sine qua non* is infant circumcision. Even though many of them may not maintain the practice, it is probably known to be their custom, as today it is widely known that Jews do not eat pork even though many do. In her fury she snatches up a flint and circumcises their son as if to say to Moses: "You are a Hebrew? Then why not perform the disgusting and barbarous rite of the Hebrews!" Infant circumcision would not seem other than appalling to one whose custom dictated no circumcision or circumcision at puberty, just as most Americans would recoil from the Arabic ritual of pubertal circumcision even while looking benignly on infant observance.

It may seem unlikely to modern sensibilities that a mother would willingly cut her child, but circumcision then was a family affair. God commands Abraham to circumcise himself, his sons, and his servants (Genesis 17:12); he is not directed to engage a specialist. Furthermore, Zipporah is a pagan to whom ritual scarification may be commonplace. Other than circumcision, the Hebrews are expressly prohibited in Leviticus 19:28 and 21:5 from imitating this practice of their heathen neighbors.

Although the pronouns in the passage are equivocal, I believe Zipporah circumcises her son, not her husband, because I can imagine no man, however torpid, unable to fend off a hysterical woman who is reaching toward his genitals with a sharp rock and because it is infant, not adult, circumcision she intends to mock. I do not, however, think Moses was circumcised as an infant. Although this practice may be considered characteristic of the Hebrews, I infer it had fallen into disuse among perhaps the majority of the slaves. My proof texts are Joshua 5:2, 5, and 9. Just after the Israelites finally crossed the Jordan into Canaan, we are told God orders Joshua to circumcise the children of Israel "the second time." We are not told of a first mass circumcision; traditional exegetes, however, assume the Hebrews were circumcised en masse just before the exodus because they had not all had the operation in infancy. It has been suggested that blood from these procedures was added to the blood of the paschal lamb and put on their houses as a token.

If the commandment of circumcision were broken by many of the Hebrews, this dereliction would explain God's words in Joshua 5:9: "This day I have rolled the reproach [or shame] of Egypt from off you." It cannot mean, as some have thought, that God has removed from the Israelites the reproach of having once had the lowly status of slaves, as God himself, after this second circumcision, frequently adjures the Israelites to remember they were slaves in Egypt. Given the context, one may assume that it refers to the shame or reproach of their failure to fulfill the covenant of circumcision while under Pharaoh's yoke.

Scholars differ over whether or not the Egyptians practiced circumcision. If the Egyptians were uncircumcised and Moses were circumcised, this condition would have betrayed his nationality to Zipporah in Midian. If the Egyptians had practiced circumcision, then it is likely the Israelites would have maintained their covenant, as it would have conformed to the conventions of the dominant culture. Thus no mass circumcision before the exodus would have been necessary. It seems probable, therefore, that the Egyptians and most of the Hebrews, including Moses, were uncircumcised.

After Zipporah furiously circumcises their son, we are told she touches the foreskin to "his feet." This is where the euphemism is employed (see Isaiah 7:20). Others posit "feet" replaces "genitals" but proffer no explanation of Zipporah's action. I propose she touches the foreskin to Moses' genitals to make a sign in blood *on* the flesh where there should have been a sign *in* the flesh. Had there been such a sign, Moses' nationality would have been known to Jethro or betrayed in the marriage bed, and Zipporah, a chief's daughter, would not now be bound to a Hebrew fugitive of slave descent. Nor would she and her sons, the chief's grandsons, be on route to possible suppression and peonage.

Today, with bloody scenes ubiquitous on television and in the movies, it is hard to appreciate the potency of blood as a symbol in other times and among other peoples. The Bible tells us a man becomes ritually impure if he bleeds or if he touches another's blood or even the bedding of a bleeding person (Leviticus 15:5–15, 25–28). Jews are not permitted to eat blood or bloody meat because blood is considered to be the essence of life (Genesis 9:4, Leviticus 17:14, Deuteronomy 12:23, others). Even the word "blood" is powerful. When Zipporah calls Moses a "bridegroom of blood" she uses the strongest, most insulting language she can.

In Hebrew the word for bridegroom and the word for son-in-law are the same. The only appropriate occasion to call a man a bridegroom is his wedding day, but I suppose commentators find this passage troublesome enough without having to explain Zipporah's reference to her husband as a son-in-law. Yet, that is just how she refers to him. The sentence, "A bridegroom of blood you are to me" (Exodus 4:25), can be translated, "I have you, a son-in-law of blood!" as the prepositional phrase "to me" often indicates possession. Zipporah, remember, is one of seven daughters. Presumably her sisters made marriages befitting their high station. Suitably, they gave the priest of Midian sons-in-law of whom he could be proud. It is her lot, she flings at Moses bitterly, to have the son-in-law of blood. Because of respect, because of sexism, and because of his status, Zipporah uses her father as a referent. It is bad enough she is married to a man of blood, but it is even worse that her father, the priest of Midian, is disgraced by a son-in-law of blood. That the phrase "man of blood" is an execration is shown in 2 Samuel 16:7–8 in which Shimei curses King David with the expression. It is also used derogatorily in Psalms 5:7, 26:9, 55:24, 59:3, 139:19, and Proverbs 29:10. Lest one suppose Zipporah called Moses this because he had killed a man, the phrase is repeated and clarified: "A son-in-law of blood in regard to the circumcision" (Exodus 4:26). For Zipporah, this seemingly brutal and uncalled-for blood-letting symbolizes and epitomizes the odiousness of the Israelites.

The vehement repetition of the phrase "son-in-law" is echoed and exaggerated with wry irony in chapter 18 when the relative eminence of Jethro and Moses is reversed. At this time Moses has brought his people safely out of Egypt and across the Red Sea, vanquishing Pharaoh and his legions; he has become a hero. Jethro, with Zipporah and her children whom Moses had sent away (18:2), comes to Moses' encampment. Now luster is added to Jethro's name by his identification as Moses' father-in-law. The phrase "father-in-law" is repeated thirteen times in twenty-seven verses.

In the verse cited above we are told Moses sent Zipporah away. Conventional opinion asserts that he sends his family back to Midian at some later unrecorded time to keep them safe from the plagues and from Pharaoh's wrath. However, it would be impolitic for Moses to send his wife and children to safety when Aaron, the elders of Israel, and the other Hebrews could not protect their families. Also, if Zipporah saved Moses' life by her intuitive and immediate action as traditional interpretation affirms, what better helpmate could he have at times of danger? The fact that Moses sends Zipporah away supports my argument that the bridegroom of blood passage briefly lifts the veil from a violent scene of marital strife. Zipporah is dispatched in anger after the circumcision scene.

The Bible affords several examples of conjugal conflict. It is revealed to us briefly and without narrative assessment. Readers must judge for themselves the severity of the disaffection. In Genesis 16:5, Sarai blames Abram, "My outrage is on you"; that is, "The outrage done to me is your fault!" In chapter 27:6–17, Rebecca instructs and aids her favorite son, Jacob, to deceive her blind husband, Isaac. Jacob's wife, we are told, angers him in 30:2. And in 2 Samuel 6:16, we learn that David's wife, Michal, despises him in her heart. She mocks him in v. 20, and he retorts bitterly in v. 21. In none of these troubled marriages are we told that the wife is sent away. Zipporah's departure testifies to mutual enmity.

Zipporah's rampage is shock therapy to Moses. He is roused from his depression, "so he let him alone" (Exodus 4:26), and he rises a changed man. Moses' transformation parallels Jacob's. Jacob limps after his encounter with God. The trickster who once was quick—quick to usurp his brother, hoodwink his father, choose a wife, make a vow—from that time on drags his feet and reacts with deliberation as, for example, in his measured response to Reuben's offence, to Dinah's rape. Moses is also changed. He knows who he is and that his identity is bound up with the children of Israel; in 32:32 he offers his life for them. He marries a more congenial wife, a Cushite woman (Numbers 12:1), herself an object of prejudice, who cannot enhance his status; he is no longer interested in position.

Though some apologists assert "the Cushite woman" refers to Zipporah and not to a second wife, the redundancy of the reference is a distinct indicator of a second marriage: "the Cushite woman whom he had married; for he had married a Cushite woman" (12:1). If Zipporah were "the Cushite woman," the first phrase would suffice to denote her. Therefore the repetitive second phrase must signify a subsequent marriage. Perhaps Zipporah's abuse provokes Moses to seek out, and enables him to empathize with, a Cushite. As no other patriarch, on his own initiative, takes a second wife during the lifetime of his first wife, this emphatic allusion to a second marriage is further corroboration of the discord between Moses and Zipporah.

To sum up: my reading of the bridegroom of blood passage is that God seeks to kill Moses by permitting him to sink into a desperate depression engendered by his ambivalent self-image. In his distress he reveals his nativity to Zipporah. She is infuriated because of his prior duplicity and the abhorrent prospect of joining his people in slavery. Striking out, she circumcises their son in a travesty of the Israelite rite and contemptuously calls Moses a "son-in-law of blood." Though Zipporah acts as an adversary rather than a helpmate, her outburst is salutary, for her assault jolts Moses out of his despondency and forces him to recognize his essential allegiance.

The lesson inherent in the bridegroom of blood passage is not the supremacy of the covenant of circumcision; the moral, according to my analysis, is implied in the name God discloses to Moses at the burning bush: "I Am That I Am" (Exodus 3:14). The Hebrew admits of varying translations: "I Will Be That/What/Who I Will Be, I Am That/What/Who I Am." There are a great many philosophical and homiletical explanations of this name. Surely one more explanation for God's use of this particular name at this particular time is that it teaches Moses and all men that ultimately you are who you are. God, with sublime assurance, declares: "I Am Who I Am." Moses, made in God's image but just a man, has to struggle to embrace and integrate this fundamental credo.

CHAPTER SEVEN

Spoiled Child: A Fresh Look at Jephthah's Daughter

Ruth Fagen, whom I mentioned in Chapter Four, taught an eight-week class on the book of Judges. The class met for only one hour a week, and so we had to restrict our studies to "Topics in Judges." One week the topic was Judges 11, the story of Jephthah and his daughter.

Jephthah is a whore's son, frozen out of his father's estate and his home town of Gilead by his half-siblings. Since he is a "mighty man of valor," the town elders ask Jephthah to lead the army when Gilead is threatened by the Ammonites. Jephthah accepts the position none of Gilead's inhabitants want for themselves and bargains successfully for the civic as well as the military leadership. As commander in chief he accurately expounds to the king of the Ammonites, via messenger, Israel's historical right to the disputed land, but the Ammonites refuse to yield. Jephthah, with the spirit of the Lord descended upon him, makes a recruitment tour and, when he returns to his home in Mizpah, a pledge. He vows to the Lord that, if the Lord delivers the Ammonites to his hand, whatever comes out of the doors of his house to meet him when he returns to Mizpah in peace will be sacrificed. "I will offer it up for a burnt offering," Jephthah says.

He smites the Ammonites with a great slaughter, and when he arrives triumphantly in Mizpah, his daughter, his only child, meets him with music and dancing. Jephthah, grief-stricken, tells his daughter that he cannot go back on his word to the Lord. Seemingly aware of the vow, she responds that he should do as he promised but asks to go down on the mountains with her companions and mourn her virginity two months. He assents, and she bewails her virginity two months on the mountains. At the end of two months, Jephthah fulfills his vow, and we are told: "She had not known a man, and it was a custom in Israel" (v. 39). The last verse of the chapter says that the daughters of Israel lamented the daughter of Jephthah yearly, four days in the year.

Ruth asked the class to consider what Jephthah thought was likely to come out of his house. A faithful dog? Only certain animals, kosher animals, are eligible for sacrifice on God's altar, and a dog is not one of them. A cow or goat? Either may be sacrificed, but it is not such an impressive contract for a man to make: "Lord, if you grant me this tremendous victory over my enemies, I'll make you the sacrifice of a single cow." A human being? Israelites were taught by Abraham's intercepted sacrifice of Isaac that God does not desire such an offering, and human sacrifice is abhorred and denigrated throughout the Bible. Nor, according to Israelite law, does a man have the power of life and death over his slaves, children, or wives. Unless it is a case of self-defense, putting another human being to death is murder. Calling such a killing a "sacrifice" does not legalize homicide or render it less offensive to God.

What was Jephthah thinking? Why did he make a senseless vow, and how did he fulfill it? Was his daughter immolated or was she spared the flames but required to remain a virgin, and if the latter, in what way did permanent virginity satisfy the vow? What was "a custom in Israel"? And why do the English translations say "custom" when the Hebrew word usually means "statute"?

Together, class and teacher wrestled with the difficulties presented by this sorry tale. Some students thought the girl was made a burnt offering, and others believed she remained alive but virginal. I felt that, for the Hebrews, the issue of human sacrifice had been settled with Abraham and Isaac. Both human sacrifice and perpetual virginity seemed to be Christian, not Jewish, concepts to me. The salvific atonement of the singular human sacrifice of Jesus is a tenet of Christian faith, and lifelong celibacy has been a Christian ideal for centuries. It is anachronistic to apply the differences between Christian and Jewish belief to the period of history in Judges, but the roots of Judaism are here in these books. I could believe neither in propitiating God with human sacrifice nor in privileging sexual abstinence. Our class had to move on the next week to the rest of Judges, but every night my thoughts were faithful to Jephthah's daughter.

One of my classmates had seen Jephthah as a coarse, uneducated man capable of a stupid vow. She based her assessment on the fact that he was the son of a prostitute, was excluded from his father's house, and grew up, apparently, among a rag-tag band of similar outcasts. I thought the blot on his parentage could be a mark in his favor, as the biblical author always seems to prefer the underdog. Throughout Scripture, we see time and again that the second son, rather than the firstborn, is the recipient of the blessing—Isaac rather than Ishmael, Jacob rather than Esau, Ephraim rather than Manasseh. Or the younger of several siblings triumphs over his elders—Joseph, David, Solomon. The author emphasizes the point that status is bestowed as God wills, not as man wills.

The first words we hear about Jephthah are that he is a "mighty man of valor"; the phrase has a sterling ring to it. His astute and successful bargaining with the elders of Gilead also seems to me to exhibit the author's pro-Jephthah stance, as does Jephthah's ability to recite Israelite history to the Ammonite king. Jephthah not only appears educated, he also seems devout; he mentions the Lord in dealing with the elders, in his recitation to the Ammonite king, in his grief-stricken response to his daughter's unexpected appearance, and again in chapter 12 when he contends with the men of Ephraim. The Bible teaches that the leopard does not change its spots (Jeremiah 13:23). I could not accept the proposition that a man characterized as shrewd, knowledgeable, and pious suddenly becomes a fool—and becomes one while under the influence of the spirit of the Lord! Yet, the foolish vow is made.

Having reached an impasse in my contemplation of Jephthah, I began to ruminate over his daughter. In her first words to her father, she seems to know the terms of his vow. What if she *does* know the terms of the vow? But then, why is she the first one out of Jephthah's house? Could she be a spoiled child who does whatever she wants to do simply because she wants to do it? I could certainly understand that childish logic, having been the spoiled daughter of an indulgent father myself.

It was easier for me to recognize my father's lenience when it was applied to my brothers. I can remember once saying to him, "How can you let him do that?" when a brother was permitted a particularly egregious bit of folly. My father replied that in his youth, he had often believed his judgment superior to his father's, but he was never allowed to test his own opinion. While his father lived, he did not have a chance to learn if he were right or if his father were right, and he chafed under the restraint. Consequently, he always tried to let his five children do whatever they wanted and find out for themselves if they knew better than he.

I remember with shame a day I tried to drive the family car to high school after my father had told me the night before not to take it. When I woke up in the morning, the car was sitting in front of our house. I had thought he wanted to use it, or maybe he had said it needed service; I had not listened much after hearing I could not have it. Whatever he had said, he obviously was not using it or servicing it, and so I took it.

The car lurched along for a few blocks, while I, never having driven on a flat tire, tried to figure out the pitched progress. After getting out of the car, seeing the flat tire, and realizing what was wrong, I phoned my father at work from a stranger's house and asked him, rather accusingly, what I was supposed to do now. He told me to run along to school and leave the car for him to take care of. When I got home from school, the car was at our house with all four tires in good order, and the matter was never brought up to me—no scolding, no recriminations, no reference to how much trouble and annoyance my heedlessness had caused. For almost half a century, I have remembered my disobedience and my father's forbearance, and so maybe his permissive style was not the worst way to raise children. But the results of Jephthah's daughter's imprudence were more serious than a flat tire.

Once I was hot on the spore of the spoiled child notion, all of the textual problems melted before me. I saw the ingenious purpose of Jephthah's vow. I noticed the author's indication of how the daughter came to know of it. I realized who Jephthah supposed would emerge from his house, and I understood what that person's future would be. I recognized how rudely the spoiled girl addressed her agonized father, and how, with characteristic lenience, he continued to indulge her wishes though they went against his religious convictions. I even saw what virginity had to do with Jephthah's vow, and I knew why his daughter had to remain unmarried. The word in the second to last verse of the chapter, the one that is anomalously translated "custom" instead of "statute," could, in my interpretation, resume its usual meaning of "statute."

Commentators of both sexes disagree over whether Jephthah's daughter perishes or survives but remains a virgin in perpetuity. There is no gender division on this issue; some men say one thing, some say another; some women take one side, some take the other. On the character of the girl, however, there is a gender disparity. Male commentators admire what they see as typical feminine traits—intuition, resignation. Women analysts portray her as a saint, martyred by patriarchal oppression. Even if you do not care for footnotes, you will be forfeiting amusement if you do not read the notes in "Spoiled Child." I should like to add that the last sentence of the chapter was meant to be wry. I have been attacked as a female male-chauvinist by the feminists and, by those readers who do not find my final sarcasm droll, as too militantly feminist. I think I am just right, and I hold my father accountable for my egotism.

And his father had not vexed him all his life by saying: "Why have you done thus?" (1 Kings 1:6)

Fearful of the coming battle, the warrior chieftain makes a deal. In exchange for victory, he vows a significant sacrifice. The deity may select the particular sacrifice, for it is described in only general terms. Returning in triumph from his vanquished enemies, the warrior is horrified to find that, as punishment for his ill-considered vow, the victim chosen is a beloved family member.

The story outlined above, familiar to us from classical mythology and world folk literature, is also the story of Jephthah and his daughter (Judges 10:17–12:7). The reading I have given is universally accepted. All commentators agree that Jephthah makes a rash vow. Literalists, much in the majority, believe Jephthah's daughter is actually offered up as a burnt offering in fulfillment of the vow. Similarities they find in the binding of Isaac (Genesis 22:1–19) substantiate their position. Figurativists argue that she is only dedicated to the Lord in some way that requires perpetual virginity, though they adduce no scriptural model for this outcome.[1] Ad-

---

[1] David Marcus presents a historical study of the arguments on both sides of the question and of the problems arising from each. He also discusses the extra-biblical and intra-biblical parallels and the relation of the latter to the Jephthah story (*Jephthah and His Vow* [Lubbock, Tex.: Texas Tech Press, 1986], 7–55).

vocates of both persuasions, however, agree that Jephthah's vow is "hasty," "abusive," "foolish," "superfluous," "hideous," "brutal," "stupid," or "faithless" and tragically condemns his daughter.

The purpose of this chapter is to present a different interpretation of the story. A close reading of the text will show that Jephthah's vow is expressed astutely and is delivered in a manner well-calculated both to achieve his aim and to prevent the accident of targeting the wrong entity. Jephthah's daughter, in full knowledge of the vow, willfully chooses her own future. As my discussion will demonstrate, that prospect is not death but celibacy. I will explore her motivation, rescue her from her previous assignment as submissive victim, and reveal her to be a self-determining individual. My interpretation will also address and resolve persistent problems in the text: what internal situation necessitates such a vow? If war brings victory, what resolution of the vow do Jephthah and his auditors anticipate, and how does this expectation affect military commitment? Why does Jephthah's daughter seem cognizant of the terms of the vow when she greets her father? Why does the text stress her virginity? Why does she seek communion with her female companions? What is the meaning of the last clause of Judges 11:39, "It was a statute in Israel"?

The story begins with the children of Israel in imminent danger of attack from the Ammonites, who have been summoned to arms and have already encroached upon Gileadite territory (Judges 10:17–18). The Israelites are gathered in Mizpah of Gilead, verbally wringing their hands and crying for leadership. The princes of Gilead, from whose ranks a leader should naturally come, join the common people in asking, "each man to his neighbor," for someone, anyone, to take charge. In desperation they offer headship over all the inhabitants of Gilead to whomever comes forward, but no one does.

Jephthah, a Gileadite, is now introduced to us as a "mighty man of valor" and a whore's son. In a flashback we are told that he was exiled by the legitimate sons of Gilead (this proper noun may denominate a man known to be Jephthah's father, or it may refer to any of the men of Gilead who might have sired him by the prostitute) in a fight over money and property (11:1–2). Jephthah now lives in the land of Tob, where he heads a band of freebooters (v. 3).

In v. 4 the narrative returns to the present, and in v. 5 we are told that because (כאשר) the Ammonites are making war against them, the elders of Israel go to fetch Jephthah from Tob.[2] The elders seem to make an improbable choice in seeking out Jephthah. His low birth does not recommend him; he lives in Tob and thus has no home or family there, no threatened material stake in Gilead, and, because of their earlier rejection,

---

[2] The word כאשר is usually translated here as "when," but "because" is equally correct. I prefer the causal rather than the temporal force here, as the time has already been established in v. 4, and the Hebrew Bible is never prolix.

probably no emotional attachment to his Gileadite kin. There is one aspect of Jephthah, however, that is favorable to his selection and overcomes any distaste the elders may feel toward him—the elders know he will fight for money; he has been living on the spoils of his victories.[3]

The elders offer Jephthah military leadership and say that they will fight with him against the Ammonites (v. 6). Jephthah does not accede but reproves them for ousting him (v. 7). In v. 8 the elders increase their offer to headship over all the inhabitants of Gilead—the same prize they had dangled in vain before their own populace; in the bargain, however, they withdraw their offer of participation. They ask him to "go with them" (i.e., return to Gilead with them), but the "we may fight" of v. 6 (נלחמה) becomes "you may fight" in v. 8 (נלחמת).[4] Jephthah can be the chief of the army, and he can be the civilian head, but he can leave them out of the fighting and recruit an army on his own.

Jephthah accepts these qualifications, but instead of going immediately into battle, he initiates a dialogue with the king of the Ammonites. It is unlikely that Jephthah expects, or even desires, a negotiated peace with the Ammonites. No military leader in Israel's history has sought a mediated settlement with its attackers; the Bible does not approbate compromise with idolaters and endorse ceding God-granted land to pagans. Therefore, I believe Jephthah's lengthy, detailed, and accurate exposition of the historical events recorded in Numbers 20–21, justifying Israel's right to the land, is intended as a morale builder and a recruiting speech for his own people.[5]

From his previous contest with the elders, we learn that Jephthah is a clever man; he would not expend words ineffectually on intransigent Ammonites.[6] Under the guise of negotiation, he holds them off while he tactfully instructs the citizens of Gilead on the legality of Israel's claim and

---

[3] J. Cheryl Exum says his military prowess overcomes his unacceptability (*Tragedy and Biblical Narrative* [Cambridge: Cambridge University Press, 1992], 48).

[4] Exum also makes this observation (*Tragedy and Biblical Narrative*, 55).

[5] Jephthah's faithful grasp of Israelite history has received widespread approval by most commentators. Robert Boling says Jephthah's speech reflects "a high historicity" (*Judges* [AB 6A; Garden City, N.Y.: Doubleday, 1975], 205). Carl F. Keil and Franz Delitzsch find "marked agreement" to Numbers 20–21 (*Commentary on the Old Testament in Ten Volumes* [vol. 2; trans. James Martin; Edinburgh: T&T Clark, 1866–1891], 378 n. 1 [repr., Peabody, Mass.: Hendrickson, 1996], 273 n. 1). Lillian Klein, dissenting from the general assessment of Jephthah's knowledgeability, states that Jephthah displays his unfamiliarity with Hebrew law by offering a human sacrifice and attributes his ignorance to the lack of a father's instruction (*The Triumph of Irony in the Book of Judges* [Sheffield: Almond, 1988], 90–92). In my exegesis, Jephthah's conspicuous cognizance of his people's history and traditions is crucial to the understanding of his vow.

[6] As Benjamin Scolnic observes, the Ammonites certainly "could not be less interested" ("The Validity of Feminist Biblical Interpretation," *Conservative Judaism* 38 [1986]: 14).

the righteousness of their cause (Judges 11:15–27). Jephthah does not insult his constituency by lecturing them directly, as though they needed him, an outcast and an exile, to inform them of their history. Instead, diplomatically, he uses the pretext of briefing his messengers in order to motivate his people. Jephthah's disguised recruitment efforts are necessitated by the Gileadites' resistance to combat. The text discloses that, despite the lure of both martial and civil honor, the leaders of the Gileadites can find a champion neither from their own number nor from the rank and file. This reluctance is further accentuated by the elders' withdrawal of military support.

Apparently, the appeal to historical legitimacy is insufficient inducement for Jephthah's audience in Mizpah, for, after God's spirit comes upon him, he extends his recruitment to the rest of Gilead and to Manasseh before returning to Mizpah to try another tack (v. 29).[7] He does not pass over Mizpah as he does Gilead and Manasseh. The double mention of "Mizpah of Gilead" in v. 29 indicates an interruption in Jephthah's travels. Unlike the other destinations, we are first told he goes to Mizpah, and then that he leaves Mizpah. It is during this underscored interval in Mizpah that he makes his vow. Just as Jephthah earlier "spoke all his words before the Lord in Mizpah" (v. 11), he again speaks his words before the Lord in Mizpah.

The history given in Numbers 20–21 is followed by a prebattle vow (Numbers 21:2). Jephthah's reiteration of this history is also followed by a prebattle vow (Judges 11:30–31). The introductory clauses of the two vows are identical in all but the name of the enemy.[8] The final clauses of the two vows differ, however. In Numbers the Israelites promise to "utterly destroy" the captured cities; no captives, no spoil will be taken. Theirs will be a holy war, untainted by any trace of venality. The final clause of Jephthah's vow is devoted to the pecuniary interests of the citizens of Gilead. If they will not fight for honor (headship of the army and of the people, 10:18) or for the justice of their cause (11:15–27), perhaps they will fight for money.

---

[7] Barry Webb suggests that the purpose of Jephthah's parley with the enemy was to provide time for these later recruitment tours (*The Book of the Judges* [Sheffield: JSOT Press, 1987], 62). George Foot Moore states that, although recruitment tours here are conceivable, the reading cannot have been intended by the author, as the Israelites are already encamped in 10:17. Moore sees no need for enthusiastic reinforcements to bolster a timid militia. He also recognizes no narrative reason for Jephthah's public verbalization of Israel's right to the disputed land and believes vv. 12–28 are a later editorial interpolation: "In short, v. 29 is the result of a clumsy editorial pastiche, a somewhat unskillful attempt to fasten the new cloth, vv. 12–28, into the old garment" (*A Critical and Exegetical Commentary on Judges* [New York: Scribner, 1903], 298–99).

[8] Jephthah designates the Ammonites; in Numbers the enemy is called, "this people."

We know that the men of Gilead expelled Jephthah over a quarrel about inheritance, and they entreated him to be their chief despite his origins, his lack of ties to Gilead, and the dislike they may have borne toward one whom they had injured. They must have believed he would take the field for booty. To these men, money is the only motivator. In order to spur the Gileadites to fervent commitment, Jephthah highlights the economic rewards of war by specifying a sacrifice chosen to suggest that participation in this conflict will result in enrichment.[9]

In vowing to sacrifice the one who comes out of the doors of his house to greet him, Jephthah is not thinking of an animal. A single animal would be too ludicrously trivial a sacrifice in exchange for a bounteous victory.[10] Nor does he plan to put a human being to death. Jephthah has already exhibited a detailed knowledge of Israelite history; there is no warrant to suppose his ignorance of Israelite laws prohibiting murder, for that is what the literal sacrifice of a human being would be.[11] Hebrews may not take human life except in cases of self-defense, God-sanctioned warfare, and capital punishment. Hebrew men have no sovereignty over the lives of their wives, children, and slaves.[12]

Jephthah intends to dedicate and redeem a slave. Leviticus 27:1–8 lists the redemptive value by sex and age of any person vowed to the Lord. For example, if one vows to the Lord a male between the ages of twenty and sixty, that person is not slaughtered, but rather, a gift of fifty shekels of silver, a not inconsiderable sum, is given to the priests, and the human being is redeemed.[13] Verse 2 uses the word נדר, "vow," to denote a dedication of

---

[9] Tony Cartledge says it is for the sake of his own band of freebooters that Jephthah does not forswear the taking of spoil (*Vows in the Hebrew Bible and the Ancient Near East* [JSOTSup 147; Sheffield: JSOT Press, 1992], 179).

[10] Marcus, *Jephthah and His Vow*, 15.

[11] Though documentary theorists debate compositional order of the biblical canon, sequence of authorship is immaterial to my holistic, literary view of the Bible. For a discussion of this integrated exegetical approach, see Johannes de Moor, ed., *Synchronic or Diachronic? A Debate on Method in Old Testament Exegesis* (Leiden: E. J. Brill, 1995).

[12] According to W. Gunther Plaut, "Unlike Roman law, the Torah never granted power of life and death to a father over his children or to a master over his slaves" (*The Torah: A Modern Commentary* [New York: Union of American Hebrew Congregations, 1981], 966). Exum says, "The ritual act of sacrifice transforms murder in this story into a socially acceptable act of execution" (*Tragedy and Biblical Narrative*, 65). This is an audacious statement in the face of repeated scriptural injunctions against murder and against immolation of children. As proof that human sacrifice was a "socially acceptable act," Exum begs the question by observing that "no outright condemnation of Jephthah's sacrifice appears in the text" (166 n. 29). She does not discuss the possibility that there was no disapprobation because there was no sacrifice.

[13] In order to support their belief in literal sacrifice, commentators have had to assert that Jephthah was unaware of the laws of Leviticus. Klein says, "Had Jephthah 'known' his faith, he would have known that the observance of the

persons to the Lord, ליהוה. Jephthah also uses a vow, נדר, to effect the dedication of his intended sacrifice to the Lord, ליהוה (Judges 11:30–31). There
is, of course, no hint or mention of burnt offering in the legal language of
Leviticus in regard to this dedication of persons, as Israelites are forbidden human sacrifice. In the parallel situation of vowing a suitable animal
to the Lord, however, Leviticus 27:9 alludes to קרבן, a general term for offering that can refer to monetary gifts but also includes burnt offering.[14]

I suggest that this dedicated person, once redeemed, can no longer do
work. Although it is not stated in the Bible, I believe the status of a dedicated and redeemed person is analogous to that of an animal that has been
dedicated for sacrifice but is instead redeemed with money or with a substitute animal. The once-dedicated animal, even though redeemed, remains holy and may never be shorn or worked.[15] The discrimination
between workaday secularity and the unworked and unworkable nature
of the sanctified is made frequently in the Bible. The Sabbath day and holi-
days are considered "holy convocations" when no work can be done (for
example, Leviticus 23:3, 24–25). The altar must be built of unhewn stone

---

burnt offerings had been increasingly commuted: that Yahweh gave the best
of his offerings to his priests and that, in any case, man must not be sacrificed"
(*The Triumph of Irony in the Book of Judges*, 92). Scolnic says Jephthah may not
have known the Levitical system ("The Validity of Feminist Biblical Interpretation," 14). Jephthah, is limned by the author (authors, redactor) as cognizant of Israelite history and even with the sequence of verses in Numbers that
locates, as he does, a prebattle vow—essentially identical in protasis with his
prebattle vow—directly after the recitation of that history. In order to deduce
that Jephthah, because of ignorance of the redemption procedure in Leviticus, literally sacrifices his daughter, the reader must disregard this confirmation of conversance with the details of Israelite tradition.

[14] In the legalities describing the procedure for vowing a person to the Lord,
what Jon Levenson terms the "telltale verb," נתן (give, dedicate), is not used. This
verb, according to Levenson, a key element in dedication, is used in Exodus
22:28; Numbers 8:16; 1 Samuel 1:11, as well as in the passage pertaining to vowing animals in Leviticus 27:9. Contrariwise, in Leviticus 27:1–8, as the individual
who makes the pledge intends redemption of the human from the vow's very inception, this verb is not employed. Similarly, it is used neither in the apodosis of
Jephthah's vow, pledging a burnt offering, nor in his fulfillment of the vow. For a
discussion of the significance of נתן, see Jon Levenson, *The Death and Resurrection of the Beloved Son: The Transformation of Child Sacrifice in Judaism and
Christianity* (New Haven: Yale University Press, 1993), 48.

[15] "And if it be a beast, whereof men bring an offering unto the Lord, all that
any man giveth of such shall be holy. He shall not alter it or change it, a good for a
bad or a bad for a good; and if he shall at all change beast for beast, then both it
and that for which it is exchanged shall be holy" (Leviticus 27:9–10). See also
v. 33. The talmudic understanding of these verses, refining the proscription
against working or shearing the exchanged animal, is the subject of the tractate
Temurah. For a modern gloss on the enduring sanctity of what is redeemed, see
Samson R. Hirsch, *The Pentateuch: Leviticus* (vol. 3; trans. I. Levy; 1962; repr.,
Gateshead: Judaica, 1989), 820.

upon which no chisel has come (Deuteronomy 27:5; Joshua 8:31). In the purification ceremony utilizing a red heifer, that heifer must never have been yoked (Numbers 19:2), and in the ceremony of expiation for the unknown slayer, a heifer that has not been worked or yoked (Deuteronomy 21:3) is slain in a "rough valley that may neither be plowed nor sown" (v. 4). Sanctified time, stone, animals, and land are separated from the profanation of secular work. My conviction that a dedicated and redeemed person, like a dedicated and redeemed animal, may no longer work is based on these ordinances.

Jephthah speaks in the language of men, not of law, as in Leviticus 27. His words represent the dedicated and redeemed individual as symbolically reduced to nothing. Like a sacrificed or redeemed animal, the redeemed slave does not exist as a working, productive creature. He is like the dead in that one can no longer receive benefit from him. The reader's job would have been easier had Jephthah uttered a simile rather than a metaphor. Had he said, "Whatever is first to greet me will become *like* a burnt offering," it is unlikely that anyone would have supposed him willing to countenance the disproportion of offering a single animal in exchange for a resounding victory, to chance being met by a ritually impure animal, or to defy the interdiction against human sacrifice.[16] The story would also be less emotional and less suspenseful.

Jephthah is portrayed as devout, knowledgeable, and measured of speech. He is shown to mention God in his every conversation. His comprehension of Israel's history is presented as accurately informed. His prudent self-command is demonstrated in his verbal exchange with the elders, with his constituency, with the enemy and, later we shall see, with his daughter. The reader is, therefore, not free to suppose that Jephthah steps completely out of character to make an impious, murderous, or ill-considered vow. Mindful only of the demands of literary consistency, his words, "I will offer it up for a burnt offering" (Judges 11:31), must be interpreted metaphorically.[17]

Jephthah's vow sends a double message to the money-minded men of Gilead. In the expensive undertaking both to pay fifty shekels to redeem a slave and to provide lifelong support for that individual, he demonstrates

---

[16] To accept Jephthah's words literally, one must concede the legality of human sacrifice. Levenson says, "Jephthah's actions are intelligible only on the assumption that his daughter—he had no son—could legitimately be sacrificed as a burnt offering to YHWH" (*Death and Resurrection of the Beloved Son*, 14).

[17] This verse does not appear in the linguistic "zero-context" of a philosopher's imagination, but against a rich contextual background of history, custom, commandment, and characterization. If one rejects the presumption of Jephthah's obliviousness to the pervasive laws against murder and child sacrifice, then the verse must be construed as a metaphor. According to Stephen Garfinkel, "The *peshat* [apparent meaning] may, and often must, comprise a metaphorical understanding of the text" ("Applied *Peshat*: Historical-Critical Method and Religious Meaning," *JANES* 22 [1993]: 21).

to his men that their chief is not greedy. He will not exact more than his appropriate share of the spoils. His willingness to relinquish a slave also suggests that the coming battle will be profitable; there will be plenty more slaves to be had.

Jephthah must have intended a slave rather than a son, say, if he had one, for supporting a nonworking slave is a more onerous and impressive obligation than supporting one's own son. I say son, rather than daughter, because I do not think Jephthah had a woman in mind. Women's work includes childbearing. When God punishes Eve and Adam in Genesis 3:16–17, he curses them with the toil (עֶצֶב) of childbirth (v. 16) and the toil (עִצָּבוֹן) of earning a living (v. 17). The work of each sex is allocated and designated with the same word. If a woman were to come out of Jephthah's house to greet him, she would be required to remain celibate after her redemption in order to ensure that she would never labor with child. In her inability to generate, she would be as the dead. This hypothesis explains why Jephthah's daughter weeps over her virginity; she laments the compelled perpetual abstinence.[18] Had she been facing death, she would have had graver cause for tears.

Equivalency between redeemed humans and redeemed animals in regard to work restriction is not explicitly stated in Leviticus. Nevertheless, I find justification for this inference in the thrust of the redemption laws of Leviticus 27, which seem designed to discourage voluntary gifts in excess of those imposed by the law.[19] The legally required redemption of the firstborn son, for example, does not demand the prohibition on work, for obstacles are not put in the way of proper statutory observance. The conditions for self-generated vows and the penalties for their non-fulfillment are, however, purposely exacting to inhibit their use.[20] My inference both

---

[18] It has been argued that בְּתוּלִי does not necessarily imply virginity. According to Gordon Wenham, it may also refer to a nubile young woman, married or unmarried, who has not yet born a child ("BETÛLAH 'A Girl of Marriageable Age,' " VT 22 [1972]: 326–48). Peggy Day says, "There is a growing recognition amongst biblical scholars that betûlîm typically does not mean virginity, but rather designates an age group. Likewise, the related word, betûlâ, does not mean virgin, but rather denotes a female who has reached a certain stage in her life" ("From the Child Is Born the Woman: The Story of Jephthah's Daughter," in Gender and Difference in Ancient Israel [ed. Peggy Day; Minneapolis: Fortress, 1989], 59). Though either meaning accords with my analysis that, after redemption, Jephthah's daughter must remain celibate and never experience childbirth, neither meaning supports the contention of the literalists that at the end of two months she will die. See Marcus for a good summary of the argument on this issue (Jephthah and His Vow, 31).

[19] On the "strikingly separated" laws of this chapter from the rest of the Levitical laws, Hirsch says, "The Jewish codex of the laws of the priests declares temple endowments and vows of gifts as being not such specially pious God-pleasing acts" (Leviticus, 811).

[20] In speaking of the impediments to self-made vows put forward in Leviticus 27, Gordon Wenham says, "It may well be part of the purpose of this chapter to discourage rash swearing by fixing a relatively high price for the discharge of these vows" (The Book of Leviticus [NICOT 3; Grand Rapids, Mich.: Eerdmans, 1979], 337).

conforms to the spirit of Leviticus 27 and increases Jephthah's liability from a maximum of fifty shekels to an obligation of more serious magnitude.

Jephthah's vow is not designed to bribe God.[21] Nor is it proof of his insecurity or lack of faith.[22] He makes the vow, in the security of his investiture with the spirit of the Lord (Judges 11:29), in order to bribe men. Jephthah supposed an appeal to justice would suffice to raise a zealous force; the spirit of the Lord renders him more sensitive to his particular listeners.

In his groundbreaking *The Art of Biblical Narrative*, Robert Alter discusses recurrent intra-biblical type-scenes—that is, repetitive motifs that develop according to conventions familiar to the reader. An example he gives is the meeting of the to-be-betrothed at a well. He compares these literary conventions to American movie Westerns in which the hero is always faster on the draw than the villain. The audience does not think, "Uh-oh, I've already seen this one," but settles back with pleasure to see how yet another version of the tale will be resolved. In the architecture of the Bible, God is in the details; the variations in these type-scenes from set pattern to set pattern are purposeful and significant.[23]

The story of Jephthah's vow is just such a type-scene, but it is extra-biblical. Many accounts of familial tragedies precipitated by open-ended vows have come down to us.[24] Perhaps the most familiar is the Iliad's account of Agamemnon and his daughter, Iphigeneia. Many more such tales may have been extant in ancient times but failed to survive the erosion of millennia. I believe that the Bible's first audience, on hearing Jephthah's vow, knows just what is in store: a beloved family member—specifically, a wife or daughter (for if the son of a wealthy father could no longer work, it would be no great tragedy)—will come out to greet Jephthah, satisfying the indeterminate terms of the vow. After the war, Jephthah will have money enough to pay the redemption fee, but, if the greeter is Jephthah's wife, he will be unable to have conjugal relations with her lest she labor with child, and if it is an unmarried daughter, she will not be able to marry for the same reason. The contemporary reader may not immediately grasp all the implications, but from the open-ended vow type-scenes with which we are familiar, we, too, expect a loved one to come forth.

---

[21] Although he admits the act seems at variance with Jephthah's evident confidence in God's judgment (11:9, 27), Webb says the vow is an attempt to bribe Yahweh (*Book of the Judges,* 64).

[22] Trible says, "The meaning of his vow is doubt, not faith; it is control, not courage. To such a vow the deity makes no reply" (*Texts of Terror* [Philadelphia: Fortress, 1984], 97). On the contrary, the deity makes the same reply that he makes to the Israelites in Numbers 21:3—victory in battle.

[23] Robert Alter, *The Art of Biblical Narrative* (New York: Basic, 1981), 47–62.

[24] Marcus (*Jephthah and His Vow,* 40–43) compares and contrasts these type-scenes to the story of Jephthah and his daughter.

The war, a great victory, is dealt with in two quick verses (Judges 11:32–33), and in v. 34 the reader is told that Jephthah's house is in Mizpah. This intelligence completely confounds our anticipation. Jephthah made his vow publicly in Mizpah; his home is also in Mizpah. Surely, his entire household knows the terms of the vow—his womenfolk will stay safely inside, and his male slaves will vie with one another to be first out the door. We understand now how a man shown to be skillful in speech, controlled, and pious has the ostensible temerity to entrust his destiny to an open-ended vow. Even if his family were not in the gathering that witnessed it, word of such a dramatic vow would doubtless have reached them while Jephthah was smiting the Ammonites from Aroer to Abel-cheramim. Indeed, while taking leave of his household before the war, so prudent a man probably cautioned them himself.

Now that the reader is reassured, apprehension gone, behold: Jephthah's daughter, his only child, dances out of the house to greet him! We are almost as surprised and appalled as Jephthah. With the Bible's brilliant economy, and while still telling a typical story in the conventional way, it manages with just one word, Mizpah, to give us an emotional roller-coaster ride. That one word relieves our foreboding and relaxes our guard so that the rest of the verse plunges us all the more joltingly into astonishment.[25] What is the girl thinking?[26] Why does she come out? Doesn't she know about the vow?

Jephthah is stunned. He tears his garment in a mourning gesture and utters a wordless outcry (usually translated as "alas," v. 35). The ensuing dialogue between father and daughter rewards careful examination:

> And it was when he saw her, that he rent his clothes, and said: "Alas, my daughter! You have brought me very low, and you have become my troubler; for I have opened my mouth to the Lord, and I am not able to return." (v. 35)

Even at this nadir of his life, Jephthah's speech is careful and considerate. It is as though he had taken a course called "How to Communicate Effectively with Your Teenager." He describes what he sees: "My daughter." He describes the emotional effect her action has wrought in him: she has brought him low, has troubled him. And lastly, he tells her he is unable to ameliorate the situation.[27] Translators say, "I cannot," but "I am not able"

---

[25] The Bible is not concerned with mundane detail; were there no plot point associated with the information, there would be no need for the narrator to tell us where Jephthah lives.

[26] I call Jephthah's daughter a "girl" because her words, acts, and marital status lead me to think she is between thirteen and fifteen years of age.

[27] Child psychologist Haim Ginott instructs parents on handling sudden anger: "Describe what you see. Describe what you feel. Describe what needs to be done" (*Between Parent and Teenager* [New York: Macmillan, 1969], 100). Jephthah's behavior may seem exemplary to psychologists, but biblical commentators invariably describe him as "displacing the blame onto the victim" (J. Cheryl Exum,

is a better rendering of the phrase לא אוכל. Jephthah thus implies that he wishes he were permitted to revoke the vow, but he is constrained by God's law.[28] "Return" (שוב) is the word for both apostasy and return from apostasy (BDB, 997). Jephthah may also be saying that, because of his faith in the Lord, he is unable to turn to other gods for release from his vow. At no time does he vex his daughter by asking her why she did such a foolish thing. He has probably never pressed her to account for her behavior. In my epigraph, 1 Kings 1:6, the Bible gives us a prescription for spoiling a child, and Jephthah gives us an object lesson.

Jephthah's four dialogues are the only expressions of his character. Each time he speaks, he reveals his piety by referring to God. In three of these dialogues he does not hesitate to take his adversaries to task, to insist on an explanation for their actions. In Judges 11:7 he asks the elders of Gilead, "Why are you come to me now when you are in distress?" Speaking to the king about three-hundred-year-old Ammonite claims to Israelite towns, he demands, "Why did you not attempt to recover them in that time?" (v. 26). And in 12:3 he questions the Ephraimites, "Why have you come up against me this day to fight me?" It can be no coincidence that in each dialogue, except the one with his daughter, there is a calling to account, a vigorous "why" question. The reader is meant to notice the obvious lack of a "why" question in this single dialogue and to recognize, thereby, that Jephthah's daughter has been, and is continuing to be, spoiled.

In her reply, Jephthah's daughter makes no excuse, gives no reason. One learns from her rejoinder, however, that she did know of the vow:[29]

"Feminist Criticism: Whose Interests Are Being Served?" in *Judges and Method* [ed. Gale Yee; Minneapolis: Fortress, 1995], 75). Mieke Bal accuses him of "blaming the victim" for becoming pubertal and thus of an age to marry and leave him ("Between Altar and Wondering Rock: Toward a Feminist Philology" in *Anti-Covenant: Counter-Reading Women's Lives in the Hebrew Bible* [ed. Mieke Bal; Sheffield: Almond, 1989], 224). Danna Fewell and David Gunn say, "He blames her for the predicament he has brought upon them" (*Gender, Power, and Promise* [Nashville: Abingdon, 1993], 127).

[28] "When a man vows a vow unto the Lord, or swears an oath to bind his soul with a bond, he shall not break his word; he shall do according to all that came out of his mouth" (Numbers 30:3).

[29] Among many others, Exum says, "The narrative does not tell us how she knows or surmises the terms of the vow" (*Tragedy and Biblical Narrative*, 58). Moore says she intuits the implication of her father's speech "with a woman's quick presentiment" (*A Critical and Exegetical Commentary on Judges*, 302). Fewell and Gunn agree that the vow was made publicly in Mizpah and Jephthah's daughter knew of it. They propose that she "steps forward aware of her fate" in order to teach her father a "lesson about recklessness, thoughtlessness, and human worth." They add, "Others knew of the vow—why else would they have stayed indoors as their troops returned victorious" (*Gender, Power, and Promise*, 127). On the contrary, the townspeople may have thronged to salute Jephthah. The Bible does not mention the welcome afforded by others, for only the greeting of the designee of the vow is germane.

And she said to him: "My father, *you* have opened *your* mouth to the Lord; [*you*] do to me that which came out of *your* mouth; as the Lord has taken vengeance for *you* from *your* enemies, from the children of Ammon." (11:36)

Not only does she know that he "has opened his mouth to the Lord," but her response is fresh. I have put the words "you" and "your" in italics (the "you" in brackets is expressed as an integral part of the verb in Hebrew). Though she begins with the familiar, "My father," the six repetitions on the "you" theme are an attempt to cast the onus for her fate onto him; that is: "You did it. It was your vow, your mouth, your revenge, your enemies." Instead of explaining her incomprehensible act, she tries to displace blame.[30]

To Jephthah, too, his daughter's answer must sound insolent, for a silence now falls on the text. Verse 36 began with the words, "And she said," and v. 37, when she again speaks, begins with the same words. Unless there were a hiatus, a gap in which Jephthah's daughter waited for her father to speak, there would have been no need to repeat the introductory phrase; she could simply have continued the speech of v. 36 in v. 37. She may have waited minutes, hours, or days for her father to break his silence, but he does not. He knows that she, not he, is the blameworthy party, but he is too indulgent and too deeply distressed to chastise her. Bafflement, grief, love, pity, and rage furnish Jephthah's silence.[31]

Jephthah's daughter takes advantage of her father's numb misery over the termination of his line and of his pity for his now ever-virginal daughter to ask a favor—a favor, it appears, he would not ordinarily grant:

And she said to her father: "Let this thing be done for me: let me alone two months, and I will go, and I will [go] down on the mountains and bewail my virginity, I and my girlfriends." (v. 37)

She begins by asking him to let an unspecified thing be done for her. The verb is expressed in the passive to make it easier for him to accede: he does not have to do anything actively, just to permit something, as yet unknown, to happen. Without disclosing her objective, she then tells him to

---

[30] Most exegetes write that she responds with wisdom and noble resignation. Moore, to cite just one example, says she "answers with tragic heroism" (*A Critical and Exegetical Commentary on Judges,* 302). Some commentators, however, agree with me, if only tentatively. Cartledge says of her speech, "The daughter quickly turns the tables" (*Vows in the Hebrew Bible,* 180). Exum says, "Her speech bears traces of her attempt to assert herself" ("Feminist Criticism," 77). Webb says Jephthah's daughter is "wholly good" but nevertheless, feels the need for a disclaimer on her behalf and assures us that her speech is not "counterrecrimination" (*Book of the Judges,* 230, 67).

[31] Fruitful marriage is the scriptural standard for the good life. Jephthah's daughter has both cut herself off from this ideal and terminated her father's hope of grandchildren, considered, even in a patrilineal society, to be life's crowning blessing (see Psalm 128:6 and Proverbs 17:6).

let her alone two months. Literalists interpret this as a request for a brief remission from slaughter. I understand it to mean, "let me have my way; do not forbid me." In either case, the verb is in the imperative. Jephthah's daughter is thus further delineated as a spoiled brat by her failure to address her father with proper expressions of respect. The particle of entreaty, נָא, "please," "I pray thee," is customarily used in speaking to one's elders or superiors and is certainly used in asking a favor.[32] Her use of the imperative, absent any courteous moderation, augments the impression of effrontery given by her earlier impertinent speech.

Two more phrases intervene before Jephthah's daughter divulges her destination: "two months" and "and I will go." I shall deal with the "two months" when the phrase is repeated. "I will go" denotes leaving Jephthah's house and connotes another departure. When she finally divulges where she wants to go, "down" on the mountains, we learn that she intends to depart both from Jephthah's house and from his religion.

One cannot physically go "down" on mountains; one goes "up" to mountains.[33] The anomalous use of the word here alerts the reader that the word is being employed in a spiritual, not physical, sense. The direction, down, is used ubiquitously in Scripture to signal a spiritual descent.[34] For example, when anyone leaves the Holy Land, he is said to be going down; entering the Holy Land is always a spiritual gain, a trip upward. Whatever it is Jephthah's daughter wants to do on the mountains, it will be done on a lower spiritual level than obtains in her father's house.[35]

---

[32] As a matter of common courtesy, David uses it in making a request of his daughter even though he is both her father and her king (2 Samuel 13:7).

[33] It is for this reason, perhaps, that the RSV, the AB, and many exegetes translate this word as "wander." Though she offers no explanation for the peculiar use of "down," Day criticizes the substitution of "wander": "This emendation is unnecessary; MT is intelligible both syntactically and semantically" ("From the Child Is Born the Woman," 69).

[34] See also Genesis 38:1–2 and Judges 14:1, where men, to their spiritual loss, go "down" to either wanton or exogamous women. Spirituality is specifically tied to direction in Ecclesiastes 3:21.

[35] Bal notices that "to go down onto the mountains" produces the strange effect of going in opposing directions and asserts that "down" is used in an emotional sense: "to go 'down' (emotionally) 'toward the mountains' in order to be confronted with the solitude in the wilderness (the site of negative 'down' feelings because threatening)" (*Death and Dissymmetry: The Politics of Coherence in the Book of Judges* [Chicago: University of Chicago Press, 1988], 48). This is a poetic interpretation, but one for which I can find no justification in the Bible. Beth Gerstein also notes the odd spatial relationship between going down and mountains and says: " 'To go down' might indicate that she sees herself as being high up or above something, which could be symbolic of her power and sexual independence as a virgin and her command of the fateful situation her father presents her with" ("A Ritual Processed: A Look at Judges 11:40," in *Anti-Covenant: Counter-Reading Women's Lives in the Hebrew Bible* [ed. Mieke Bal; Sheffield: Almond, 1989], 188). If Gerstein's conjecture is correct and Jephthah's daughter sees her-

At the end of v. 37 she fully exposes that she wants to "bewail" (בכה) her virginity, her childlessness (בתולי), with her girlfriends.[36] That her concern is virginity, not immolation, is further justification for a metaphorical reading. In 20:23 the children of Israel go "up" to weep (בכה) before the Lord. I believe Jephthah's daughter wants to go "down" to weep (בכה) before other gods. Her father refuses to go back on his vow, but perhaps other gods can intervene. Now that she has seen Jephthah's anguish at the death of his hopes for her and for his grandchildren and heard him express his inability to renege on his promise to the Lord, she seeks assuagement from another quarter. The Israelites' attraction to idolatry is a pervasive theme of Judges.

Jephthah's daughter shrewdly gauges the extent of her father's leniency—devout though he is, he will let her do even this. With manifest aversion, he bites off a single word, "And he said: 'Go'" (11:38).[37] Excessive permissiveness and lack of parental discipline lead him to make what will prove to be a fateful mistake. We are also told that "he sends her." The author need not have mentioned that. In Exodus 2:8 when another young woman is given the same monosyllabic command, the Bible says, "And Pharaoh's daughter said to her: 'Go.' And the maiden went." The seemingly unnecessary information that Jephthah sends his daughter is provided to illustrate his involvement and to accent his transgression in permitting her this heterodox excursion. The added detail helps to justify the punishment that awaits him for putting his devotion to his pampered only child before his reverence to the one God.

The Bible says Jephthah sends his daughter "two months." Many translations provide the preposition "for" (KJV, RSV, NJPS, and AB, among others); I think this word is supplied because it agrees better with the unanimous opinion that the girl remains away about sixty days. Without the added "for," however, the verse implies that he sends her away twice on a monthly cycle, and that is precisely what I think she requests and what Jephthah does.

My reasons for this conclusion are several. One is that the logistics of provisioning, maintaining, and protecting a group of young women on the mountains for sixty days would be burdensome and expensive. We know what happened to Dinah when she went out (Genesis 34:1–2), and in Judges 21:21–23 we see what happens to a gathering of young women

---

self as being high up, symbolic of her power and command, why would she ask permission to go down and thereby give up her enviable position?

[36] See note 18.

[37] Interpreters have so firmly cast Jephthah's daughter as the heroine of this drama and Jephthah as the miscreant, that Exum (*Tragedy and Biblical Narrative*, 63), while ignoring the girl's lack of courtesy when asking a favor of her father, remarks disparagingly on Jephthah's saying "'go,' without any accompanying mollifying particle (such as the customary particle of politeness, '*na*,' usually translated as 'please' or 'I pray you')."

who go out. Even discounting the religious aspects, venturing out is not safe. Jephthah's daughter can play on her father's sympathy, but how would the other young women get *their* fathers to permit them to go? I can imagine the parental indignation: "You will do no such thing, Missy. You will stay home where you belong. Whatever happens between Jephthah and his daughter is their business, but no daughter of mine is traipsing *down* on the mountains!"

When it is generally known that a certain event occurs periodically, people make such statements as, "I have watched the Super Bowl five years," without fear that anyone will misunderstand and suppose they have been thus engaged for 1,826 days. Similarly, the Bible says "two months" to mean "two times, a month apart," not sixty consecutive days. If a period of sixty days had been intended, the Bible could have clarified this time span by using a phrase similar to that in 19:2, "the days of four months." I offer that in Jephthah's time it was general practice for women, from homes less orthodox than his, to assemble monthly for idolatrous worship, probably connected to the moon. The observance may have lasted only a few hours, for all we know. That is the reason Jephthah's daughter's participation in such a gathering constitutes a spiritual descent, a going down. And it is the reason the other young women are allowed to attend. It is an ordinary ritual, but a ritual in which Jephthah's daughter has not hitherto been permitted to take part.

A number of commentators have suggested that the reference to four days in v. 40 provides an etiology for a Jewish festival. There is no such festival in the Jewish calendar, however, nor is there any historical indication that such a festival ever existed. On the other hand, there is ample attestation in both the contemporary Jewish calendar and the historical record of a connection between a specifically women's holiday and the phases of the moon. Rosh Hodesh, the celebration of the new moon, is honored by observant Jews and is considered, in a vague sort of way, to be particularly a women's holiday.[38] I propose that Jephthah's daughter's monthly meetings were early pagan precursors of Rosh Hodesh and that the Jews co-opted that heathen worship and sanctified it.

Examination of the narrator's role in the exchange between Jephthah and his daughter yields further information. Both father and daughter speak twice. Jephthah's words are preceded only by the expression, "He said" (11:35, 38). Her two speeches, however, are preceded by, "She said *to him*" and "She said *to her father*" (vv. 36–37). By the narrator's intervening words, the biblical author effects a subtle distinction between Jephthah and his daughter. Delicately, the father is shown to speak more

---

[38] T. C. G. Thornton, "Jewish New Moon Festivals, Galatians 4:3–11 and Colossians 2:16," *JTS* 40 (1989): 97–100. Arlene Agus, "This Month is for You: Observing Rosh Hodesh as a Woman's Holiday," in *The Jewish Woman: New Perspectives* (ed. Elizabeth Koltun; New York: Schocken, 1976), 84–93.

intimately to his daughter than she speaks to him. With his two speeches, it is as though the words fly directly from his mouth to his daughter. The narrator, by contrast, not only creates a distance by interposing between the daughter and her words to her father, but also, tellingly, characterizes each of her speeches by the epithet employed. Jephthah's daughter addresses her first speech, the one I label impudent, to "him," to a pronoun. This detachment supports my assertion of rudeness in her answer and even hints that her first words, "My father," are but a mocking echo of his astonished, "My daughter." Her second speech is addressed to "her father." The separation between speech and speaker is sustained by the intrusion of the narrator, but now she appeals to the familial bond, to her father's parental tenderness and vulnerability, for she needs his permission.

The story of Jephthah and his daughter is invariably compared to the story of Abraham and Isaac in Genesis 22. Abraham's averted sacrifice of Isaac is recalled both to prove and to disprove the literal slaughter of Jephthah's daughter.[39] I shall not examine the story in Genesis for this purpose but only to note a contrast between the two father-child dialogues that has not, to my knowledge, been previously observed. In Genesis 22:7–8, Abraham and Isaac each speak twice. They speak alternately; there is no silence, no hiatus in their exchange. In all four of their speeches, their own words immediately follow the word "said." No distancing or difference in their attitudes toward one another is implied by any narrative interjection. Heart speaks directly to heart, and the narrator ends v. 8: "And they went two of them together." The redundant "two of them" and "together" doubly stresses the intimacy and mutuality we see present in this dialogue and missing in the colloquy between Jephthah and his daughter. He speaks to her with the all-embracing parental love of even an errant child, but she does not return his affection in equal measure.

We are told that after her second moon-meeting, Jephthah's daughter "returned to her father" (Judges 11:39a). If the Bible had said: "At the end of two months, Jephthah did according to his vow," we would readily have assumed her return. The phrase, "returned to her father," therefore, gains significance. It indicates that the pagan deity appealed to has failed to rescue her from her virginal fate. Realizing the ineffectuality of idol worship, the girl abandons her heterodoxy and returns, שׁוּב (repents, turns back), both to her father and to his faith. Scripture does not track the obvious. Other than to record the girl's repentance (and to manifest the futility of appealing to idols), there is no reason to stipulate her return. The inclusion of this phrase further supports my argument that Jephthah reluctantly, but culpably, complies in his daughter's pursuit of heretical relief.

"And he did with her according to the vow that he had vowed" (v. 39b). To me, this means that Jephthah, heartsick that as a "burnt offering" she

---

[39] Marcus, *Jephthah and His Vow*, 38–40.

cannot know the fulfillment of marriage and children, redeems his daughter with the appropriate fee and fulfills the conditions of his vow. To figurativists, this clause means that Jephthah cloisters her in a separate establishment where she remains an isolated virgin for life.[40] The text dictates enduring virginity; solitary confinement is a requisite imposed by the exegetes.[41] Literalists claim that this laconic phrase masks an event too sadistic to recount. The details dwelled upon in the near-sacrifice of Isaac—the wood, the fire, the knife—are omitted here, they assert, because the reader would find them unbearable in view of "the despicable outcome."[42] Unlike classical Greek theater, however, the murders in the Bible are not committed offstage. In the book of Judges alone, the excrement spews from a king stabbed in the belly (3:22); a woman drives a tent peg through the head of a sleeping man (4:21); a concubine, gang-raped to death, is hacked into pieces (19:25–29). Scripture does not spare the squeamish. If there had been a literal sacrifice, I believe we would have been told of it.

The phrase "And she did not know a man" (11:39c) may be considered circumstantial or consequential.[43] The literalists deem it circumstantial; "she had not known a man" at the time of her death. The figurativists say it is consequential; she maintained permanent virginity in the fulfillment of the vow and "did not know a man." Partisans of both persuasions venerate Jephthah's daughter's virginity to a degree unsubstantiated by the Hebrew Bible and the Jewish faith. Scripture and Jewish mores value virginity as an attractive and proper commodity in a never-married woman, but as a lifestyle, celibacy is deplored; fruitful marriage is the appropriate paradigm for both men and women.

Figurativists Keil and Delitzsch say that dedicating a virgin as a spiritual offering to the Lord means that, for the rest of her life, she can belong to no man, but only to God.[44] This conclusion, however, has the Christianized character of a spiritual marriage unknown to Judaism. The Hebrews, men and women, could be dedicated to God, or could dedicate themselves, for a specific period or for life (Numbers 6:2–21), but this consecration did not preclude marriage (Judges 14:2) or fornication (16:1).

In a supposition typical of literalist thought, Exum says Jephthah's daughter had to be a virgin for "reasons of sacrificial purity."[45] The notion of virginity as a source of "sacrificial purity" is, however, unattested

---

[40] Trible says that Jephthah's daughter's "seclusion is living death" and "Whether secluded or sacrificed, the female is the innocent victim of violence" (*Texts of Terror*, 116 n. 59).

[41] For example, Moore, *A Critical and Exegetical Commentary on Judges*, 304.

[42] Trible, *Texts of Terror*, 105; Exum, *Tragedy and Biblical Narrative*, 52.

[43] Marcus, *Jephthah and His Vow*, 33–34.

[44] Keil and Delitzsch, *Commentary on the Old Testament*, 395.

[45] Exum, *Tragedy and Biblical Narrative*, 65. Anne Tapp says virgin daughters are suitable for sacrifice because they exist in a dangerous liminal state between

in the Bible. Isaac is unmarried when his father is told to sacrifice him, but if he were a virgin, this status is not considered sufficiently important for Scripture to impart. Priests with a physical blemish cannot approach the altar to offer sacrifice, but marriage does not preclude their service (Leviticus 21:17–23). Animals, to be suitable for sacrifice, also cannot bear a blemish, but there is no restriction on their mating (22:20). According to my exegesis, it is not because of any hypothesized and unsubstantiated sacral quality attached to virginity that Jephthah's daughter must never know a man; it is so that, as a redeemed entity, she never performs the labor of childbearing, "for it was a statute in Israel" (Judges 11:39d).

This final clause of v. 39 above has been handled roughly by interpreters. It has been wrenched from its place at the end of v. 39 and affixed to the beginning of v. 40. They explain that the MT reflects a "false division" of verses by placing this clause in v. 39, and by relocating it, they are rectifying the mistake.[46] They know the MT's placement is a mistake because, left where it is, it does not accord with their analyses. English translations either actually renumber the verses (AB, 207), or translate the concluding clause of v. 39 as though it were the introductory clause of v. 40: "And it was a custom in Israel that the daughters of Israel," and so on (KJV, RSV, NJPS).

The word חק (specific decree, law, statute) has been translated as "custom" or "tradition," in order that it make sense in its new location. Some commentators even render the phrase, "*She* was/became a tradition/custom in Israel."[47] Their argument is that, as "it was" is expressed by a feminine verb, its subject cannot be חק, which is masculine. That is, the verse cannot be saying, "It (the law) became a statute in Israel." Though their grammar is correct, their argument that חק alludes to Jephthah's daughter is rather strained, for nowhere in the MT is a חק an individual.[48]

My analysis assumes no false division and leaves the last clause of v. 39 in its place. "It" refers to the obligatory virginity mentioned in the preceding clause (בתוליה is a feminine noun), and the whole verse confirms my reading that Jephthah's daughter is now prohibited the labor of childbirth: "[He] did with her according to his vow which he had vowed, and she did not know a man, for it [virginity, childlessness] was a statute in Israel."[49] In v. 39 we are thus told that there *is* a statute imposing work restriction on redeemed women, and we no longer have to extrapolate from time, stones, fields, and animals to humans.

---

the opposing forces of father and husband ("An Ideology of Expendability: Virgin Daughter Sacrifice," in Bal, *Anti-Covenant,* 172).

[46] Moore, *A Critical and Exegetical Commentary on Judges,* 303; Webb, *Book of the Judges,* 229. I cite two; however, every commentator I have read emends the text.

[47] Trible, *Texts of Terror,* 106. Exum translates, "She became an example in Israel" (*Tragedy and Biblical Narrative,* 66).

[48] Webb, *Book of the Judges,* 229.

[49] See note 18.

Why does she do it? Why does Jephthah's daughter come out to greet her father in full knowledge of his vow and of its consequences? I see two reasons. One, it is traditional for women to welcome the victorious warrior with music and dance, and, childlike, she wants to do as others do.[50] She knows the repercussions of the vow, but she thinks her father can resolve the difficulty. Jephthah is an important man, the head of the people. Can he not do whatever he wants, vow or no vow, and can she not, therefore, do whatever she wants? This answer reflects both what a spoiled child might think and Jephthah's apparent estimation of her reasoning, for such a deduction must have prompted his statement: "I am not able to return" (v. 35). He lets her know that, contrary to what she may think, he is constrained by God's laws from doing whatever he wants.

The other reason is more profound. She may not consciously have articulated it to herself, but I think she chooses, on at least a subconscious level, to remain unmarried. She would rather defy convention and continue to be the one and only love of an extremely indulgent father than become some man's first wife. Without the restraint of the vow, she would surely be married off, will she or nil she, because of cultural pressures and because Jephthah's only prospect of grandchildren is through her.[51]

In her immaturity, Jephthah's daughter may not consider the impact of her appearance at all. Or, as above, she may think that her father can repair any predicament her impulsivity precipitates. Perhaps she hopes that, despite any warning he may have given, Jephthah will welcome the sight of her upon his return from war, and that he will rejoice in the marriage prohibition attendant on the vow, knowing that his little girl, with full societal sanction, can now never leave him. If so, her father's reception of her and his silent grief teaches her otherwise. Anxious to expunge her miscalculation (or lack of any calculation) and to get back into her father's good graces, she asks permission to appeal to the local gods for intervention.

Jephthah's mother was a זונה. A recent study suggests that the word does not necessarily mean "prostitute" but could refer to a self-supporting woman who prefers to live independent of any man's protection or authority.[52] Jephthah's father, a Gileadite, was presumably as acquisitive as his fellow Gileadites. In preferring emancipation and affluence over marriage and dependence, Jephthah's daughter may embody a third-generation reversion to familial traits.

---

[50] For examples of this practice among Israelites, see Exodus 15:20 and 1 Samuel 18:6. Deborah may be envisioning the same custom among Canaanites in Judges 5:28 when she describes Sisera's mother and her princesses waiting by the window for their hero's return from battle.

[51] See note 31.

[52] Hannelis Schulte, "Beobachtungen zum Begriff der Zônâ im Alten Testament," ZAW 104 (1992): 255–62. I am grateful to Ruth Fagen for bringing this issue to my attention.

Jephthah is a man of means and, now, high-standing. Life with father would be quite comfortable; his daughter would be cosseted while he lived and independently wealthy after his death—other Gileadite women, the daughters of Zelophehad had established that, in the absence of sons, daughters inherit (Numbers 27:1–8). The biblical author inspires the inference above by giving the girl no name other than "Jephthah's daughter." Other feminist exegetes take umbrage at the namelessness they consider an androcentric ideological position that violates the girl.[53] In writing of her, they give her the name "Bat" (transliteration of the Hebrew "daughter"), thus, I believe, blunting the author's pointed clue to the reader that she is first, last, always, and only Jephthah's daughter—both in his eyes and in hers. She is the archetypal "daddy's girl."

Jephthah's daughter's choice of independence and self-determination may be what the daughters of Israel are celebrating, or commemorating, four days in the year (Judges 11:40).[54] Because of what translators have considered the context of the "rash vow" story, they have translated לתנות as "to mourn" or "to lament"; the verb's only other use in Scripture, however, is in Deborah's victory song, where its object is "the righteous acts of the Lord," and its connotation is hardly negative (5:11). The daughters of Israel, in the triumphant mode of Deborah's song, may be recounting one young woman's achievement of autonomy and celebrating her success in shaping her own life. It has often been noted that the women of Judges are remarkably assertive. Just as this trait is valued today, their four-day commemoration of Jephthah's daughter may be proof that it was also prized and praised by an ancient sisterhood.[55]

Commentators repeatedly deplore what they see as the silence of God in this episode.[56] Why did he not intervene to save Jephthah's daughter as he did to save Abraham's son (Genesis 22:12)? Why does Jephthah receive neither punishment nor condemnation in the text? If, as I maintain, there was no bloody sacrifice, there was no need for the intercession of God or of the people.[57] Nor has God reason to rebuke Jephthah for making a

---

[53] Bal, *Death and Dissymmetry*, 43; Gerstein, "A Ritual Processed," 176.

[54] Against Tapp, who defines her as one of the virgin daughter "paradigm victims," the "passive, resigned and helpless" ("An Ideology of Expendability," 171).

[55] These four days could be consecutive or discrete. I conceive them as occurring at four separate women's monthly rituals, perhaps when the moon is in alignment with certain heavenly bodies or geographical features.

[56] Klein, *The Triumph of Irony in the Book of Judges*, 95; Bal, "Between Altar and Wondering Rock," 221; Fewell and Gunn, *Gender, Power, and Promise*, 128; Webb, *Book of the Judges*, 69; Cheryl Brown, *No Longer Be Silent: First Century Jewish Portraits of Biblical Women: Studies in Pseudo-Philo's Biblical Antiquities and Josephus's Jewish Antiquities* (Louisville: Westminster John Knox, 1992), 93; and Trible, who says, "My God, my God, why hast thou forsaken her?" (*Texts of Terror*, 106).

[57] The populace rescues Jonathan from death at the hands of his father (1 Samuel 14:45).

foolish vow. He has, however, another reason to penalize Jephthah: paternal overindulgence extending to heresy. And both punishment and condemnation are indeed recorded in the text.

Three punishments are recorded: the end of Jephthah's line, his brief judgeship, and the manner of his burial. In Judges 12:7, we are told that Jephthah judges Israel six years, dies, and is buried in the cities of Gilead.[58] His reign is shorter than that of any other judge except for Abimelech, of whom we are told, "Thus God requited the wickedness of Abimelech" (9:56).[59] Jephthah's short term of office is a sign of divine displeasure. Another sign is the intimation of multiple gravesites. The midrash (*Genesis Rabbah* 60:3) copes with the plural "cities" by propounding that Jephthah dies of a protracted disease, causing his limbs to wither and drop away one by one; his parts are buried where they fall in the various cities of Gilead that he tours in his judicial circuit. Though this resolution seems unlikely (if not medically impossible) to the modern reader, one might readily suppose that Jephthah is mutilated in battle or by accident. Whatever the circumstances, the Bible's description of his interment is antithetic to the Israelite ideal in which the integrity of the corpse is respected, and all the remains are buried in one grave.

We are meant to learn a lesson from Jephthah's tragedy. Scripture does not recall the extra-biblical type-scene of the open-ended vow merely to give the reader the pleasure of seeing how the familiar story will unfold. It is used to convey a didactic and theological message. In the variations between our rendition and any other, the reader learns the wages of parental overindulgence, the futility of appealing to false gods, and the inevitability of divine judgment.

The unanimous opinion of centuries weighs in favor of the "rash vow" interpretation. To oppose it may seem bold, even radical, but I believe that my analysis adheres more closely to the plain, surface meaning of the text than does the accepted reading. Why should the author take such pains to record Jephthah's shrewdness with words if he wants the reader to believe Jephthah capable of an ill-spoken vow? Why is Jephthah shown to be minutely conversant with the Israelite history detailed in Numbers, and even with its sequence of verses locating a prebattle vow just after the recitation of this history, if the reader is to believe him totally ignorant of Israelite laws against murder and of the redemption laws of Leviticus?[60]

---

[58] Translators often "correct" this to "one of the cities of Gilead" (NJPS), "in his own city in Gilead" (AB), "in his city in Gilead" (RSV).

[59] We are not told the length of Shamgar's reign (3:31).

[60] Meir Sternberg says, "Even an outlaw like Jephthah, once he opens negotiations with the king of Ammon, exhibits a remarkable but entirely creditable command of the minutiae of the ancestral migration from the Nile to Jordan (11:12–28)" (*The Poetics of Biblical Narrative* [Bloomington: University of Indiana Press, 1987], 116).

As noted, many commentators have written that Jephthah appears to blame his daughter for coming to greet him. I do not think he blames her, but even if he does, is it not reasonable to suppose that he blames her because she is to blame? It is also obvious to interpreters that she seems to know the terms of the vow. Some say she intuits the vow or that the verses in which a grieving Jephthah tells her of the vow are omitted.[61] Others mistranslate the MT to their purpose, adding "if"—"*If* you have opened your mouth to the Lord" (Judges 11:36)—to make it seem as though Jephthah's daughter has no prior awareness, but is only guessing.[62] My analysis does not depend on intuition, missing verses, or mistranslation. That the vow is broadcast in Mizpah, that the daughter lives in Mizpah, and that she seems to know the terms of the vow lead me to assume that she does indeed have this information. Her impertinent words confirm my assumption of her knowledge and my perception of her willfulness.

Jephthah's character and personality, his excellences and his flaws, are not stated by the narrator but are revealed in four dialogues. In three of these dialogues, he firmly and peremptorily demands an explanation for his opponent's behavior. "Why?" he asks, in every conversation but one—the one in which both he and the reader are most anxious to know the answer. This conspicuously repeated use of "why" in his other dialogues makes his reserve in the case of his daughter all the more revelatory of his spoiling indulgence. The girl's rude manner of appealing to her father without a moderating "please" corroborates this conclusion.

Neither literalists, who consider virginity a prerequisite for sacrifice, nor figurativists, who believe virginity in perpetuity *is* the sacrifice, offer any scriptural support for their theories. My analysis, that a vowed and redeemed person is regarded as though he/she had been a burnt offering and may no longer do productive work (which, for women, includes childbearing), is supported by several biblical passages—both those defining childbearing as work and those expressly ordaining the detachment of work from the holy. My reading of v. 39d, "for it [virginity] was a statute in Israel," has advantages over the typical, "it became a custom in Israel," as the usual meaning of the word חק (statute) can be retained, the last clause of v. 39 need not be relocated to the beginning of v. 40, and the full stop indicated by the MT to mark the end of the verse can be preserved.

The Bible looks at women steadily and sees them whole, but after hundreds and thousands of years, male exegetes view the female characters through a man-made lens of idealized femininity. If the witch of Endor seems to act against her self-interest by nurturing her mortal enemy, it is a woman's tenderness that moves her. If Jephthah's daughter seems to know the conditions of her father's vow, it is a woman's intuition that informs her.

---

[61] Moore, *A Critical and Exegetical Commentary on Judges*, 302.
[62] Boling, *Judges*, 206.

Conventional feminist exegetes, schooled in this perspective, proffer essentially the same analysis filtered through two additional lenses: one, a reductive understanding of gender relations that reflexively regards biblical women as casualties of male subjugation and, the second, a stereotypical perception of masculinity. They propound that in this "gyno-sadistic text"[63] Jephthah is a reprehensible patriarchal oppressor who blames his victim because of a man's predilection for displacement, projection, and castration anxiety.[64] His daughter, too powerless to protest her fate, can only seek solace in solidarity with her equally-oppressed sisters. In previous readings, Jephthah, despite his evident heartbreak at his daughter's actions and his malleability in her hands, continues to be depicted as the all-powerful figure, and his daughter, with full honors for docility, is placed still higher on the pedestal of innocent victimhood.

My analysis brings Jephthah's daughter down to earth. On the solid ground of the (undoctored) textual evidence and via an equitable feminist interpretation that frees her from passivity's bonds, I show that, far from powerless, she manipulates her father, gets him to permit her even what is most offensive, and ultimately ruinous to him, and secures for herself a life of comfortable independence. The daughters of Israel have something to celebrate.

---

[63] Tapp, "An Ideology of Expendability," 172.
[64] Bal, *Death and Dissymmetry*, 64.

CHAPTER EIGHT

Collusion At Nob: A New Reading of 1 Samuel 21–22

An internationally-known Bible scholar attended my Saturday afternoon Shabbos Group during his term as visiting professor at Yale. He was reserved during the study sessions and barely participated in the conversation. Though he would answer specific questions when asked, he took care not to dominate the discussion, lest he intimidate us with his superior insight and erudition. He had been attending the gathering for some months when we reached 1 Samuel 21, and he asked to lead the study of that chapter.

As the leader, he was imperious in his analysis. He went through the chapter, verse by verse, explicating it to us decisively and firmly. He was a forbidding man with whom to differ, and I was too timid to contend with so distinguished an academic. Though I disagreed with him, I did not express my opinion—especially since my demurral seemed to be over an insignificant point.

First Samuel 21 tells of David's flight from King Saul. David is Saul's music therapist, son-in-law, and armor bearer. Saul had once loved him greatly. David is so charismatic a figure that he has won the hearts of the entire population of Israel and Judah (18:16). Even Saul's putative heir, Jonathan, loves David, and Saul begins to fear a palace coup. David, realizing that Saul is suspicious of him and wants him dead, disappears from the palace and runs to Nob, to the priest, Ahimelech, who meets him trembling (21:2). David tells Ahimelech that the king sent him on a secret errand, and that he needs five loaves of bread, or whatever food is at hand, for his men. The narrator now mentions that Doeg, one of Saul's head servants, happens to be in the sanctuary. David asks Ahimelech for a weapon, for, he says, he left so hurriedly on his mission that he had not had time to arm himself. Ahimelech gives him bread and Goliath's sword, and David flees to the land of the Philistines.

I read the chapter before I went to the discussion, so that I could familiarize myself with it and make sure I understood it. It seemed clear enough, except that I could not understand why Ahimelech meets David trembling. We are told that all the people love David, and so why should Ahimelech tremble before him? I asked the leader this question, and he said that it was unusual and therefore alarming for David, a high court functionary, to appear without escort. "If a highly placed member of your government came to your door alone, you would be fearful, would you not?" he asked. George Bush was the (41st, not 43rd) president then, and though I might be surprised that he turned up at my doorstep without his usual entourage of Secret Service men, or that he turned up at my doorstep at all, I would not be frightened by his solitude. Nor, imagining George Schultz ringing my front doorbell, would I fear the solitary arrival of a high government functionary. America is the land of the free and the home of the brave, and the professor was from Israel, but I did not think I, or he, would be afraid of the unaccompanied approach of *his* country's president either. It did not seem worthwhile, however, to press the point.

That night I thought over the passage and tried to decide for myself why Ahimelech trembles at the sight of David. Well, of course, Saul's man, Doeg, is in the sanctuary and Ahimelech, as priest, must have been aware of his presence well before the narrator informs the reader, but so what? Ahimelech does not take David's side in a coup d'etat. As far as Ahimelech knows, David, like Doeg, is also Saul's man. At least, the words between David and Ahimelech sound like a dialogue between a servant of Saul's and a loyal subject of Saul's, both working to advance the king's mission. Doeg must have thought their conversation innocent and appropriate, because the reader learns that he does not run to tell Saul about the overheard encounter. In fact, even when he is back at the palace in the next chapter, standing around Saul with the other servants, he does not mention it until Saul complains that all conspire against him and no one helps him in his conflict with David (22:8). Saul is a mercurial man; he can enjoy David's music one moment and throw a javelin at him the next (18:10–11). Saul's minions therefore might not always be sure who is in favor and who is out of favor. When Doeg learns by Saul's complaint that David is not in his good graces, he tells what he knows.

The trembling was one problem; another question was raised by Ahimelech's defense when, in 22:13, Saul accuses him of conspiring with David against the crown. Why does not Ahimelech tell the simple truth? From their dialogue, it appears that David lies to and tricks Ahimelech; there is no collusion. Why does Ahimelech fail to say so? Ahimelech maintains that he knows nothing about anything, but he does not say that he is innocent of treachery.

Again I went to the library and read what others had written about this pericope (I had learned that story segments of a book were called pericopes). Every article and book I read agreed with the visiting professor's interpretation that David hoodwinks Ahimelech. No one wrote about why Ahimelech trembles to see David, and the few who addressed the issue of Ahimelech's feeble defense said that he does not try the truth because he thinks he would not be believed.

I was not satisfied. The trembling troubled me. The anemic defense troubled me. And, the following week, after the Shabbos Group read the next chapter, what troubled me most of all were the words of David to Ahimelech's son. This son was the only escapee from the merciless slaughter, ordered by Saul, of every priest, man, woman, child, and animal in Nob. David said to him, "I knew it that day, when Doeg the Edomite was there, that he would surely tell Saul" (22:22). David knew Doeg was there? How did he know, and when did he know it? He knew Doeg would surely tell Saul what? What could Doeg tell Saul that would incriminate Ahimelech? David had experience of Saul's paranoia; how could he run to Philistia to save his own skin if he thought he had compromised Ahimelech? If David knew Doeg would tell Saul something detrimental to Ahimelech, why did he not act on the knowledge in Nob and kill Doeg with Goliath's sword? Speaking of which, why did David make a fuss over the sword—"There is none like it" (21:10)—leading the reader to think it would become an important element of the plot when it does not? Doeg is impressed with Goliath's sword, and tells Saul about it, but Saul does not care about the weapon's origin, and it is never mentioned again. Would a laconic author introduce a plot device for no reason?

To understand the pericope, I tried to imagine myself in David's shoes, in Doeg's shoes, in Saul's shoes, and most of all, in Ahimelech's shoes. What would make me tremble at David's approach? It may or may not be unusual for a court dignitary to travel alone, but it is certainly unusual for this author to give the reader a hint about a character's feelings. Ahimelech must be terrified indeed. But of what, of David whom everyone loves? When I pretended to be Ahimelech, in the unselfconscious privacy of my thoughts, I was afraid of the madman Saul via his servant, Doeg. I trembled at the sight of David because I knew he was fleeing the court. If David were a traitor to Saul, would Doeg consider me a partner in treason because David had sought me out?

Once it occurred to me that Ahimelech was afraid of being denounced as a traitor, my questions found ready answers in the text. The dialogue that had seemed drab and innocuous on a casual reading, now glittered with guile. Solutions to all of the problems outlined above are elaborated and clarified in this chapter. Only one question remained: my interpretation defied the unanimous consensus of scholarly opinion; if my exegesis were valid, why had no one else arrived at it? Friends have suggested that, because I am a woman, I can empathize with the female characters' probable emotions and bring that sensibility to the service of the text. Biblical commentators over the centuries have been predominately male, but my gender cannot be cited as the muse of intuition, as the biblical chapters concerning Nob, unlike those about Hagar, the wife/sister stories, Zipporah, and Jephthah's daughter, have nothing to do with women or with feminine sensitivities. It is possible that I differ from everyone else because I am wrong. I could be far from the mark, my reasoning flawed, and my argument far-fetched, but since my analysis is supported by the text and resolves all of the difficulties attending previous commentaries, it does not seem so to me.

I believe that I am able to see what others do not see because I have two advantages. The first is my point of view. Unlike the concerns of medieval commentators, my investigation is not centered on legal, moral, religious, or historical values. It focuses on literary considerations. Modern scholars also are interested in literary qualities, but rather than weighing what makes a good story, rather than crediting the author for knowing what he is about, the majority of these exegetes concentrate on distinguishing the pericope's sources by analyzing (what they see as) diverse literary language or styles. I see what others do not see because I am looking where others have not looked.

My second advantage is my state of ignorance. Contemporary exegetes who are nevertheless traditional in their analytic approach, like the renowned professor who led the Shabbos Group through this passage, bear a great chain of learning forged by scholars and passed from teacher to teacher to teacher down the generations. I have reached mature years, years crammed with experience of human nature and of the vicissitudes of life, yet because of my educational background I do not also bear the weight of received opinion.

It is obvious that no one today has the mind-set of the Bible's first readers or first listeners, and that interpreters over the years have laid the tracing paper of their own theological, political, and critical agendas on the writer's words. My own preconception of the aesthetic unity and understandability of the Bible tints my personal tracing-paper a rosy shade. But my imagination is free from other agendas precisely because of my ignorance of past commentaries. My desire to solve riddles prods me to try to assume the persona of the actors in the biblical story, basing my characterizations exclusively on the scant but sufficient information provided by the writer. A lamentable lacuna in professional training has perversely worked in my favor. Perhaps because I am lightened by this lack, I can spring from my platform of respect for the artistry and integrity of the text and enter the wavelength of the biblical author.

From earlier biblical commentaries to the most recent, David's encounter at Nob with the priest, Ahimelech, and the resulting massacre of every living thing in that city has been interpreted similarly. It does not seem to matter whether the point of view is twelfth century or twenty-first century, whether religious or purely literary; neither changing cultural assumptions nor fluctuating fashions in critical analysis disturb the surprising unanimity. There is variation in detail and emphasis, but the overall consensus (cited copiously below) is that David deceived

Ahimelech at Nob and that the priest therefore replied in innocence to Saul's interrogation and went guiltlessly to his death.

Despite the imprimatur conferred by this accord, the exegesis is awkward. The problems it raises for one generation of scholars remain to plague the next. I propose a close reading of 1 Samuel 21–22 radically different from that above. Far from falling prey to David's ruse, Ahimelech connives with David to deceive Doeg, one of Saul's head servants. Though Saul's exaggerated hatred of David perverts his judgment, there is, nevertheless, a twisted justice in his condemnation of the priest, for Ahimelech and David are, in fact, partners in intrigue. As we shall see, this understanding of the narrative answers the questions attendant upon the usual exegesis, amplifies the characterization of David, Ahimelech, Doeg, and Saul, and adheres to both the letter and the spirit of the text.

The incident begins, "Then came David to Nob to Ahimelech" (21:2).[1] The order of city and person could have been reversed as it is in 19:18 when David flees "to Samuel to Ramah." There David's object is the person, Samuel; here his objective is the city of Nob. The sequence reported in the narrative reveals his design; David deals with Ahimelech because he is the head priest, but it is the entire populace he is after.

Besides Samuel, who could not or would not help David (19:18–24), the ecclesiastical establishment is a potential counter authority to the state. Whether David is contemplating rebellion or seeking intercession with Saul, it is wise to secure the backing of this influential body. By the time Doeg informs on David and Ahimelech, he has become sensitive to David's aim and his dialogue repeats the order of precedence given in the narration (22:9).

Commentators struggle with David's reason for coming to Nob. Jan Fokkelman points out that Nob is not on the route from Gibeah to Gath—David's next destination.[2] In my reading, Nob is not out of David's way. Prior to his visit to Ahimelech, David had no plan to go to Gath. I shall show that he is compelled to go to Gath by his experience in Nob.

Nob is a city of priests, an unlikely place to seek food and a weapon if that is David's aim. One would not expect priests to have arms, and the food brought to them as offerings (תרומה) may be eaten only by priests and their families.[3] Peter Ackroyd says there must have been unsanctified bread in Nob.[4] A town of eighty-six priests would need lay people to furnish goods and services; they could have provided David with common food.

---

[1] *The Holy Scriptures* (Philadelphia: JPS, 1917). I use this JPS translation throughout this chapter.

[2] Jan P. Fokkelman, *The Crossing Fates* (vol. 2; *Narrative Art and Poetry in the Books of Samuel;* Assen: van Gorcum, 1986), 353.

[3] Exodus 29:28.

[4] Peter Ackroyd, *The First Book of Samuel* (CamB, 9; Cambridge: Cambridge University Press, 1971), 170. He therefore agrees with Fokkelman (see note 6 below) that David came to Nob in order to get consecrated bread.

David Kimchi, however, says that David takes the specially-prepared holy bread from Ahimelech, for in the whole city of Nob there is only תרומה, which is even more hallowed.[5] Because of the dearth of permissible food in the town and because Goliath's sword is kept in Nob, Fokkelman reasons that David comes to Nob expressly to attain sanctified bread and this particular sword. He argues that David's consumption of holy bread and possession of Goliath's sword damages Saul's prestige.[6]

If so, there is no reflection of this injury in Doeg's account to Saul of the transaction in Nob and in Saul's reaction to this account. Doeg does not even mention holy bread but merely says that David was given "victuals" (22:10). Saul is told David was given Goliath's sword, but, in questioning Ahimelech, Saul accuses him simply of giving David "a sword" (22:13). Surely if Goliath's sword were a significant symbol of state, Saul would not fail to identify it in order to aggravate Ahimelech's culpability.

Before David approaches Nob, I posit that Ahimelech knows that Doeg is somewhere about the sanctuary. How could he not know? Doeg is "detained before the Lord" (21:8). He has obviously come to the sanctuary for a religious reason, and he has been there for some time. This is indicated by the use of the same verb, עצר, in the phrases "women have been kept from us about these three days" (21:6) and "detained before the Lord." After the specificity of those three days in the first use of the word, it is difficult to conceive that in the second instance, describing Doeg's detention, only a fleeting visit to the sanctuary is connoted. The temporal quality of the first usage extends to the second. Doeg may have a skin blemish that requires a quarantine of at least seven days under a priest's diagnostic eye (Leviticus 13:2–5, 24–28, 29–32, 38, 39). Or perhaps he has an issue from his body for which the priest must offer sacrifice and make vicarious atonement (15:15). There are a number of reasons why a man visits the sanctuary, but for each he needs the services of a priest.[7]

Knowing that Saul's officer is near, Ahimelech meets David "trembling" (21:2). Why does he tremble? I propose that as head priest of the

---

[5] Cited in Adolph J. Rosenberg, *Samuel 1: A New English Translation of the Text, Rashi and Commentary Digest* (New York: Judaica Press, 1988), 182.

[6] Fokkelman, *The Crossing Fates*, 352. See also Diana Edelman, *King Saul in the Historiography of Judah* (JSOTSup 121; Sheffield: JSOT Press, 1991), 166–67.

[7] Edelman, however, imputes no religious connotation to the phrase "detained before the Lord." She translates עצר as "constrained" and reminds us that God uses the same verb in introducing Saul to Samuel as the man who "shall have authority over [constrain] my people" (9:17). Doeg is one of the people "constrained" by Saul. He is under his control, Saul's minion. His presence, therefore, is an ominous reference to Saul's power. She labels Doeg a non-Israelite, a status which, she reasons, makes him willing to perpetrate the crime (22:17–18) Saul's Israelite servants refuse (*King Saul*, 179). See also Fokkelman, *The Crossing Fates*, 387. Even if Doeg were an Israelite, his readiness to slaughter the priests could be attributed to the pernicious influence of his Edomite birth. The Bible considers any country other than the Holy Land a bad neighborhood.

kingdom, Ahimelech comprehends or suspects that David is in flight from Saul. He meets David trembling, in an agony of terror, lest, by his first words, David incriminate them both. Should David say, for example, "I am running from Saul; help me," they would both be executed as conspiring traitors. The priesthood sympathizes with David, I believe, and Ahimelech wants to help him, but, with Doeg listening, he cannot receive such a supplication with impunity.[8] Nor can he safely rebuff it. David's assumption of Ahimelech's assistance would be sufficiently incriminating to such a hot-headed tyrant as Saul.[9] Even were Ahimelech ostentatiously to refuse David aid, his repudiation might be seen as occasioned by his knowledge that Doeg could overhear. His subsequent protestations of non-complicity would not establish his fidelity to the king; they would be seen as self-serving and without credibility.

Many readers compare Ahimelech's fear with the trembling of the elders in 16:4 when Samuel arrives in Bethlehem.[10] Of the latter, Walter Brueggemann says:

> Whenever the high officials of the court come to the village, there can only be trouble and risk. Such officials never come to give but always take. Either Samuel is Saul's man . . . or he is not Saul's man. The elders assume themselves to be in a no-win situation.[11]

The same apprehension is attributed to Ahimelech. Is David Saul's man, or is he not Saul's man? If he is Saul's man, for what troublesome reason has he come? If he is not Saul's man, as his lack of retinue suggests, is it dangerous to consort with him?[12] But Ahimelech's inquiry does not suggest that he trembles because he fears David. If he thought, as the elders in 16:4 thought, that Saul's man had come to the village for some oppressive

---

[8] P. Kyle McCarter Jr. says that though Ahimelech does not knowingly help David, his son, Abiathar, later does, and so "the theme of the conscious contribution of the priesthood to David's rise is not really clouded by what we see here" (*I Samuel: A New Translation with Introduction and Commentary* [AB 8; Garden City, N.Y.: Doubleday, 1980], 350 n. 1). According to my exegesis, that Ahimelech deliberately intrigues with David, this theme is clarified by the example of both priests.

[9] We know that Saul is quick to murderous rage from his sudden spear attacks on David and Jonathan (18:11; 19:10; 20:33). We learn that his reign has become despotic in 14:52 when we are told, "and when Saul saw any mighty man, or any valiant man he took him unto him." Compare this impressment to the earlier God-sanctioned volition in 10:26: "And there went with him [Saul] the men of valour, whose hearts God had touched." Saul fulfills Samuel's pessimistic prediction of royal tyranny, "he will take your sons" (8:11), and his flagrant misdeeds are known to the head priest.

[10] See, for example, Peter Miscall, *1 Samuel: A Literary Reading* (Bloomington: Indiana University Press, 1986), 131.

[11] Walter Brueggemann, *Interpretation, First and Second Samuel* (Louisville: Westminster John Knox, 1990), 121.

[12] Fokkelman, *The Crossing Fates,* 353.

official purpose, he would have met David trembling and, like them, asked anxiously, "Comest thou peaceably?" Only the same question as that in the earlier passage, or one similar, would indicate such a trepidation.[13]

Nor would the sight of David with no retinue, however unusual, cause Ahimelech to tremble. He might be curious, but Doeg, after all, is also one of Saul's officers and has come to the sanctuary alone to be before the Lord. Perhaps David, too, requires the exercise of Ahimelech's priestly function. He might have a blemish or an unusual genital discharge that he prefers to conceal from his escort. Privacy, not insurgency, could be his motivation.

Diana Edelman notes that Ahimelech's trembling precludes the possibility that David comes to Nob seeking sanctuary; there is no reason to fear a supplicant for asylum.[14] Against this conclusion, however, one might contend that Ahimelech fears Saul's wrath if he grants asylum and David's wrath if he refuses. A better argument against the likelihood that David seeks sanctuary is his understanding of Saul. In 16:2 we learn that Samuel fears for his life at Saul's hands. If Saul were capable of killing a God-appointed prophet, David knows that he would not hesitate to kill an ordinary (as far as Saul knew) man in defiance of the priest's protection. Indeed, as we later learn in chapter 22, Saul does not scruple to order the slaying of eighty-six priests, their families, and their livestock.[15]

Some commentators and translators avoid the problem of the priest's trembling by translating חרד as "rushed," "hastened," or "hurried."[16] With this translation, Ahimelech's bearing in meeting David is only an expression of appropriate respect for authority and conveys no hint of peril. My explanation maintains the usual meaning of חרד; the priest knows that he is in jeopardy. His interrogative first words to David, communicated before David can open his mouth, are ingenious. They inform David that Ahimelech is not alone and yet appear completely innocuous and perfectly consistent with the priest's feigned assumption that David is still Saul's officer: "Why art thou alone, and no man with thee?"(21:2). Biblical narrative does not needlessly multiply words. Ahimelech's first phrase suffices to question David's solitude; the reiteration of the same theme in the second phrase, emphasizing David's unattended state, imparts to

---

[13] Contra Brueggemann as quoted above, Samuel's standing with respect to Saul was not ambiguous to the elders, for in 15:30–31 Saul persuades Samuel to make a public display of their unity. In 15:25 Saul asks Samuel to pardon and return with him so that they might worship the Lord together. Samuel does not pardon him but does return and worship with him before the elders and before Israel. Whatever Samuel may have thought, the elders believed the prophet to be in league with Saul.

[14] Edelman, King Saul, 162.

[15] In the event, one priest escapes and eighty-five are killed.

[16] Robert Alter, The Art of Biblical Narrative (New York: Basic Books, 1981), 64; David Kimchi, David Altshul, Joseph Kara cited in Rosenberg, Samuel 1, 170; Ackroyd, The First Book of Samuel, 168.

David, himself so prudent in speech and sensitive to nuance, that he is uniquely solitary—unlike the priest. Ahimelech's repetitiveness alerts the attentive reader to the import of his words, though we can only fully understand them in retrospect after reading 21:8.

Robert Alter proposes that the repetition suggests "a certain slowness or obtuseness on the part of Ahimelech."[17] My exegesis, on the contrary, not only shows the repetition to be purposeful, but also provides a solution to a difficulty imposed by the usual explication. In 22:22 David admits that he knew of Doeg's propinquity on that day. How did David know on that day that Doeg was there, and when did he know it? None of my sources concern themselves with this mystery, though Alter asks why, if David knew Doeg was there, he did not eliminate him. Why did he let Doeg live to inform?[18] McCarter comments only on the second sentence in v. 22, "I have brought about the death of all the persons of thy father's house." He writes that, with these words to Abiathar, Ahimelech's son, David acknowledges responsibility for the aftermath of his selfish and deceitful appeal to Ahimelech.[19]

In my reading, Ahimelech's redundancy is David's initial indication of a menacing presence. Following this, David himself may plainly see Doeg once he enters the sanctuary. The knowledge of Doeg is hidden from the reader until 21:8, but we are never told that Doeg is actually hiding; indeed, he has no reason to hide.

Although David learns that Doeg is there and perceives the danger, he does not try to eliminate him. Perhaps the reason he does not, and the answer to Alter's question, is that, unlike Saul who is liable to throw a spear even at his own son, David has not yet begun to kill Israelites. Nevertheless, he does use the information for his own safety, as we shall see below.

Responding appropriately to Ahimelech's resourcefulness, David pretends, for the benefit of their unwanted auditor, to be on the king's confidential errand. As befits a rushed, impatient emissary of the king, he brusquely and peremptorily demands five loaves of bread for himself and his men, who, he says, are at "such and such a place." David has not come to Nob in search of provision; his demand for bread is but a credible pretext before Doeg to account for his approach to Achimelech.

Alter suggests that the author employs the phrase "such and such a place" to enhance the reader's impression that David is inventing a false story to dupe Ahimelech. David could have named a plausible but fictitious place, or he could have said, "I have told my men where to meet me." Either alternative would lend David's story a concrete reality and ring of truth that the abstraction "such and such a place" avoids.[20]

---

[17] Alter, *The Art of Biblical Narrative*, 71.
[18] Alter, *The Art of Biblical Narrative*, 70.
[19] McCarter, *I Samuel*, 350, 365.
[20] Alter, *The Art of Biblical Narrative*, 71.

I agree that David's use of the evasive phrase "such and such a place" lends an air of fabrication to his story. The author does give us a hint that David is lying, but the lie is fashioned to mislead Doeg, not Ahimelech. The subtlety of the author is such that I also believe David specifies five loaves deliberately. David chose five smooth stones before going into battle with Goliath (17:40); with this numerical reminder of a previous successful encounter with danger, David calms and encourages Ahimelech and perhaps himself as well. And if, by this intimation, Doeg too is reminded of David's prowess, all the better.

In the popular interpretation David may name five loaves of bread by chance simply because, as he speaks, he observes five loaves of bread displayed, or the number may be mentioned for a reason. Fokkelman suggests that if David brought five loaves of bread with him when he joined Saul's court (16:20), removing five loaves from the state sanctuary might be a way of symbolizing his withdrawal from court.[21] There is, however, no reason to suppose that he entered Saul's employ with precisely five loaves. Rashi says that David may want five loaves so that his stores will last several days. Naming a larger amount than is sufficient to satisfy one man also helps convince Ahimelech that David has an escort.[22]

According to this understanding of the text, David mendaciously tells Ahimelech that he is on a secret mission for the king. Fokkelman, among others, notices that David does not designate King Saul as the author of his mission. "The king" is a generic term that could refer to the Lord, and David's mission could be the divinely ordained kingship of Israel. He writes that David may be tempering his dishonesty to Ahimelech with a sly double entendre.[23]

Achimelech, in this usual reading, is completely taken in by David's duplicitous assertion of authority and need for bread. He has only holy bread—the shewbread that has been removed from before the Lord so that it can be replaced by hot bread, but he offers it to David provided David's men have kept themselves from women. Apparently, it would be indelicate of the priest to inquire if David, too, had kept from women. David includes himself in his reply that "women have been kept from us about these three days" (21:5–7).

Word that Ahimelech gave David sanctified bread never comes to Saul's ears. This desecration, if desecration it is, is not troubling for Saul, but it is a problem for biblical scholars. Kimchi quotes his father's opinion that the bread David received had been a thanksgiving offering; such bread, though holy, is permitted to the ritually clean. Therefore, v. 7 means that other than the holy bread of the thanksgiving offering, the only bread present was the shewbread, which of course could not be of-

[21] Fokkelman, *The Crossing Fates,* 356.
[22] Rosenberg, *Samuel 1,* 180.
[23] Fokkelman, *The Crossing Fates,* 355.

fered to David.[24] The Talmud says that David's need for sustenance was life-threatening, and therefore Ahimelech could properly abrogate the prohibition against non-priests eating the shewbread.[25] According to Alter, v. 7 is narrated to tell us that David is given only bread no longer needed for worship and thus allowed.[26]

In my analysis, David's request for bread places Ahimelech in a quandary. He wants to cooperate in David's cover story, and he needs to convince Doeg that he is loyally abetting the king's interest; however, he cannot commit sacrilege nor even give the appearance of impiety. Much as he would like to expedite David's speedy departure, he takes the time to ascertain that David and his non-existent men are fit to receive the only bread he has to give. The narrator too, in 21:7, suspends the dialogue to tell us that the bread Ahimelech gives has already been removed from before the Lord. Therefore I concur with Alter, above, that this verse is interjected to inform us that the bread may now be given to David. Ahimelech will stand guilty of collusion, not profanation, before Saul.[27]

Interpreters agree that the narrator introduces Doeg here in anticipation of future events, but most maintain that this introduction is inserted into the dialogue digressively and could have entered at any point in the exchange.[28] Alter, on the other hand, contends that the narrator cleverly relates this verse just before David asks for a spear or sword, as the threat implied by the presence of Saul's man is intensified by the immediate talk of weapons. He also asserts that giving Goliath's sword to David will be the strongest charge against Ahimelech, and he points out that the city of Nob will fall to the sword. The mention of Doeg, therefore, adjoining the mention of a sword, adroitly foreshadows these events.[29]

As Alter does, I consider Doeg's presence purposefully revealed at this point in the narrative, but I differ on the reason the discovery is relevant here. David wants to make his getaway. He hopes the scene he and Ahimelech have played is sufficient to fool Doeg, but, if it is not, he dares not leave the sanctuary unarmed; Doeg might follow and kill him. The

---

[24] Rosenberg, *Samuel 1*, 182.

[25] *b. Menaḥot* 95b. See *The Hebrew-English Edition of the BabylonianTalmud*, ed. Isidore Epstein (30 vols.; London: Soncino, 1960), 585. The rabbis state there is "no doubt at all" that David may have bread that has already been removed from before the Lord: "Since it is no more subject to the law of sacrilege it is in a manner common. But even that which has been sanctified this day in the vessel you may give him to eat for he is in danger of his life."

[26] Alter, *The Art of Biblical Narrative*, 65.

[27] Doeg's mention of "victuals" (22:10) rather than "holy bread" illuminates the contemporary understanding of the legality of this gift. If Doeg had thought Ahimelech impious, he would have been eager to tell Saul and increase the gravity of the charge.

[28] See, for example, McCarter, *I Samuel*, 349.

[29] Alter, *The Art of Biblical Narrative*, 66.

menace of Doeg is exposed here to explain to the reader why David asks for a weapon, any weapon, and why he accepts Goliath's sword, a sword that must be too long and heavy for him.[30] It is fortuitous that the sanctuary contains a weapon, and it is only such a souvenir, a sort of national trophy, that would be there.

David takes the sword with an expression of admiration; he appreciatively proclaims its uniqueness, "There is none like that." If he is to discourage Doeg's zeal, it is well to build up the mystique of this particular sword. Surely, Doeg will not presume to engage the bearer of such a sword, a man moreover who, as Ahimelech intentionally observes, has slain Goliath. All David and Ahimelech's dialogue appears as shrewd improvisation in the reader's hindsight. After we learn of David's (and thus, necessarily, Ahimelech's) awareness of Doeg's presence in 22:22, their every word seems to have been directed at Doeg.

Once David is safely away from the sanctuary, the sword is of no further use to him. Except for Doeg's report to Saul, we never hear of it again. Certainly David must dispose of it before he enters Gath, as it would be grossly impolitic and even provocative in Philistia to brandish spoil taken from the vanquished Philistine champion. This argues further against Fokkelman's supposition that David sought possession of that particular weapon. Nor do I agree with Alter that permitting David to take Goliath's sword will be the strongest charge against Ahimelech. The puffery David confers upon the sword impresses Doeg, and Doeg passes the sword's pedigree on to Saul in 22:10. Saul, however, could not care less; he does not mention the sword's provenance in his indictment of Ahimelech. He is furious that Ahimelech gave David any weapon; it does not matter which one (22:13).

Exegetes differ on why David goes next to Gath. Fokkelman thinks it probable that David plans detente with Achish, king of Gath.[31] Brueggemann says David has no particular destination in mind as long as it is one far from Saul.[32] I submit that David boldly enters Gath to shake off any possible tail that might be in pursuit. A Hollywood cowboy on the run can cross the Mexican border to elude the following U. S. Marshal. David can step in and out of enemy territory, a venture neither Doeg nor Saul nor Saul's soldiers would risk.

There are no followers. Doeg is completely hoodwinked by the collusion of David and Ahimelech. We learn this when Doeg does not immediately race back to Saul with his knowledge of David's whereabouts and Ahimelech's treason.[33] The whole court knows that Saul has tried to kill

---

[30] We do not know the size of Goliath's sword, but the shaft of the giant's spear is "like a weaver's beam" (17:7). His sword is probably equally unwieldy.

[31] Fokkelman, *The Crossing Fates*, 363.

[32] Brueggemann, *First and Second Samuel*, 155.

[33] See also Miscall, *1 Samuel*, 135.

David on several occasions, but, with so mercurial and erratic king, these murder attempts seem not to spoil their relationship. Saul twice tries to impale David in 18:11 but promotes him to captain in 18:13 and takes him as a son-in-law in 18:27. Saul may have ulterior motives, but the court sees only a love-hate pattern. Even after Saul pronounces David a "son of death" in 20:31, Doeg could well believe that Saul sends him on a covert royal mission and that Ahimelech's assistance is the appropriate behavior of a loyal subject confronting the king's representative.

In chapter 22 the scene shifts to Saul who has learned the whereabouts of David. Surrounded by his standing and, one assumes, uneasy courtiers, Saul sits upbraiding them, spear in hand. He seesaws between paranoid rage and maudlin self-pity as he complains that no one informed him of Jonathan's covenant with David, nor of Jonathan's supposed incitement of disloyalty in David (22:6–8).[34] Only now, when Doeg hears Saul's rancorous diatribe, does he realize that, for this moment at least, it is expedient to declare against David. He discloses in two swift sentences that he saw David come to Nob to Ahimelech, the son of Ahitub, and that Ahimelech gave him food and the sword of Goliath the Philistine (22:9–10).[35] Recognizing that he was played a fool, he comes forward with a more lethal case than the facts allow and also tells Saul that Ahimelech inquired of the Lord for David.

This report of Doeg's brings the customary exegesis again into difficulty. The narrator has not told us that Ahimelech inquired of the Lord for David. Is Doeg lying? Interpreters disagree. Ralbag, in support of Doeg's account, says that general terms rather than specific questions were used to consult the oracle in order to maintain the fiction that David was acting on Saul's behalf.[36] Brueggemann flatly rejects Doeg's assertion, calling it false.[37] Peter Miscall accepts it readily, for he considers it confirmed by Ahimelech's response to Saul's accusation.[38] Fokkelman provides an extensive evaluation of both options and finally decides to leave the dilemma unresolved.[39]

On this question of whether or not Ahimelech actually did act as oracle-giver for David, I come down firmly in the negative. In my reading he could not have done so. To question the Lord in the context of the charade he and David were enacting would have been sacrilege. If they had asked a question consistent with the supposed secret mission in which

---

[34] To call either of these putative traitors by name would be too intimate. Saul names neither David nor Jonathan throughout this speech, calling the former "the son of Jesse" and the latter, "my son."

[35] When we read Ahimelech's father's name, we learn that he is of the doomed house of Eli. See 1 Samuel 2:31 and 14:3.

[36] Rosenberg, *Samuel 1,* 179.

[37] Brueggemann, *First and Second Samuel,* 159.

[38] Miscall, *1 Samuel,* 134.

[39] Fokkelman, *The Crossing Fates,* 389–91, 415.

David claimed to be engaged, they would have been inquiring of the Lord in vain. And that, they would not do. Doeg, however, may have suspected that they had done so. Presumably, he was attending to his own devotions and not listening to their every word; he may have heard Ahimelech say "ephod" in reference to the sword ("Behold, it is wrapped in a cloth behind the ephod," 21:10) and elaborated on this cue.[40]

Reacting to Doeg's report, Saul summons Ahimelech and all his father's house. Despite the priest's respectful demeanor, Saul belittles him by addressing him disparagingly as "son of Ahitub." He accuses him of conspiring with David and providing the renegade with food, a sword, and the word of God (22:11–13).

Ahimelech begins his defense with warmly enthusiastic praise of David. He then responds only to Saul's last charge and asks, "Have I today begun to inquire of God for him?" As is often noted, his rhetoric may be understood two ways. Ahimelech may be confirming incredulously that Saul thinks him capable of such a transgression, or he may be affirming dismissively that he has often inquired of God for David in the past. Considering the emphatic denial he then makes, the former sense seems more likely. Ahimelech concludes rather vaguely by telling the king not to impute any of the דבר, "matter," "affair," "business," "thing," to him or to his father's house, for he knows neither much nor little about all this דבר (22:14–15).[41]

Ahimelech's defense is problematic in the context of the accepted interpretation. One wonders why he does not simply tell the exculpatory truth. Why does he not frankly tell Saul that David deceived him into believing that donating food and a sword would further the king's business? Such straightforward veracity would both affirm his fealty to the crown and please Saul by denigrating David.

According to Fokkelman, Ahimelech perceives that no argument or apologia will prevail over the vehemence of his accuser. Therefore the priest determines to go to his death in an affirmative way, without disparaging David, merely stating innocence and upholding truth.[42] Yet Fokkelman's own rendering, consonant with the common consensus, is that David did mislead Ahimelech. Consequently, his conclusion that Ahimelech's defense relies on the truth is inconsistent, for had the priest been David's victim, as Fokkelman asserts, rebutting Saul's indictment with this fact would be the outright, unequivocal, and perhaps life-saving truth.

Ahimelech's line of defense, so incomprehensible if one subscribes to the standard exegesis, is entirely justified by my new interpretation. We

---

[40] See also Fokkelman, *The Crossing Fates*, 390.

[41] Ahimelech maintains a respectful attitude throughout, referring to himself only as Saul's servant.

[42] Fokkelman, *The Crossing Fates*, 401. For his analysis of the incident at Nob, see 379–416.

know that Ahimelech cannot claim that he was deceived because, in truth, he was a party in deceit. Because of this conscious complicity, he cannot even claim to be a faithful subject of the king.

Heroically maintaining a posture of precise honesty, the priest makes the only defense he can. There are two strategies available to him. The first is to convince Saul that there is no foundation for his paranoid suspicion of David. If Saul accepts this proposition, the trial ceases. Even if Saul refuses to accept Ahimelech's attempt to exonerate David, he may imply from it, without any prevarication on Ahimelech's part, that the priest believed in David's allegiance to the crown and thus was blameless in his conduct. The second, weaker strategy is to deny the one accusation of which he is innocent. This he does with all the emphasis he can muster, first reframing the charge into an ironic question. With this sarcasm he hopes to make evident not only that he is guiltless of such lese majesty, but also that he can scarcely conceive of the possibility. He ends by saying that he and his house know nothing of this thing, דבר. By דבר, I am sure, he refers to Saul's irrational hatred. Ahimelech sincerely sees no cause for Saul to hate David.

Saul, of course, is not to be reasoned out of his insane jealousy and distrust of David, and he responds aggressively to Ahimelech's omissions. The priest does not repudiate the conspiracy; he does not deny giving food and a weapon to David; he makes no excuses or explanations: he is a traitor. All the priests, Saul judges, must support David, else why would he have come to Nob? Saul feels surrounded by treason and is more isolated in his madness than ever. He orders the death of Ahimelech and all the priests of the Lord "because their hand also is with David."[43]

By the late introduction of Doeg, the author artfully arouses our suspense. He sustains the tension until after the grisly denouement at Nob by reserving till then the information that David and Ahimelech knew of Doeg's threatening proximity. After the climactic slaughter, anxiety fulfilled, the reader is apprized of their foreknowledge and can review and appreciate the intelligence and humanity of their collusive performance.

An advantage of this reading is that it makes more use of the text than do earlier commentaries. David's concluding statement, that he knew of Doeg on that day, is not glossed over but informs both chapters. Many questions are answered in the reader's retrospective review: why did David go to Nob? Why did the priest tremble? Was it licit for Ahimelech to give David holy bread? Why is the allusion to Doeg so placed in the story? Why did David want Goliath's sword? Why did David go to Gath? Why did Doeg delay reporting to Saul? Did Ahimelech inquire of the Lord for David? Why did Ahimelech make

---

[43] Saul's thoroughness in killing Israelites is regularly contrasted with his failure to completely exterminate the Amalekites (15:9).

such a feeble defense? Why did Saul order the death of every priest in Nob? And how did David know that Doeg was there on that day? Besides elucidating these problems, there is another advantage of this interpretation over the traditional exegesis: conforming strictly to the evidence of the text, it reveals the quick-wittedness and integrity of David and Ahimelech and makes more understandable, though no less heinous, the massacre at Nob.

CHAPTER NINE

Eating the Blood: Saul and the Witch of Endor

I typed the name of an eminent professor of Bible in the field labeled "Author" so that the library's computer database of articles about religion would list all the articles he had written. "Vindicating God" was just finished, and I was seeking a venue other than those journals that had already accepted my work. As an amateur, I was not familiar with all of the publications in the field, and so I thought I would see where the heavy-hitters published their articles. This professor was one of the heaviest, and the computer displayed a long list. Reading the list, I saw that he had written an article about the encounter between King Saul and the witch of Endor in 1 Samuel 28. I wrote down the names of some of the journals where his articles had appeared and also the citation for his witch of Endor article.

I was eager to read the professor's explanation of this episode. We had read about the witch of Endor in the electric company Bible class, and I was unsatisfied by the teacher's discussion. As was his wont, he approached the chapter from the seamy side. That is, he pointed out the three occasions where he saw bad joins of disparate source material. I saw the incongruities he brought to our notice, but the entire event struck me as incongruous. The chapter describes a witch's conjuring and a meal she serves a (supposedly) witch-hating king. Why, in a tract that despises witches and prizes hospitality, is a witch shown to be both successful in materializing a prophetic ghost and hospitable in succoring her worst enemy? Perhaps the prominent professor I had looked up would treat this larger problem as well as encompass the troublesome details my teacher had observed, for I knew from the professor's other work that it was not his style to resort to the multiple-author rationalization.

The library had the journal containing the professor's article, and I sat right down to read it. The chapter in Samuel starts by telling us that King Saul had rid the land of mediums and wizards (1 Samuel 28:3). Now the Philistine army is threatening; the prophet Samuel is dead. King Saul gets no advice from dreams or from any supernatural source, and he is sore afraid of the Philistines. He asks his men to seek out a witch that he may inquire of her, and his men do so. Saul, in disguise, and two of his men go to the witch. Saul asks her to bring up someone that he will name, but she reminds him that King Saul has cut the witches and diviners out of the land and accuses him of laying a deathtrap for her. Saul swears by the Lord that no punishment will come to her and asks her to materialize the dead prophet, Samuel.

When the witch succeeds in calling Samuel forth from the dead, she recognizes that her customer is the king. She cries out that he is Saul and that she has been deceived. Saul commands her to tell him what she sees, and she describes an old man with a mantle. Saul knows that this apparition is Samuel, and he bows before the prophet. Samuel and Saul have a question-and-answer period that goes badly for Saul, and he falls to the ground in fear and in frailty, for he has been fasting all day and all night.

The witch comes in to Saul, sees his terror, and suggests that, as she listened to him and took her life in her hands, he should now listen to her and have a morsel of bread to strengthen him on his way. Saul at first refuses, saying, "I will not eat," but his men and the witch convince him, and he rises from the earth and sits upon the bed. The witch quickly kills a calf, takes flour, kneads and bakes unleavened bread, and brings it before Saul and his servants. They eat and leave.

Before I read very far into his article, I saw that the professor argued that the severity of the prophet was balanced by the tenderness and hospitality of the witch. "That's not right," I said to myself, disappointed that his essay was not going to contribute to my understanding. To read the text his way seemed too pro-witch to me. Given the Bible's firm anti-witch stance ("Thou shalt not suffer a witch to live," Exodus 22:17; "There must not be found among you anyone who makes his son or his daughter to pass through the fire, or that uses divination, or an observer of times, or an enchanter, or a witch," Deuteronomy 18:10), I could not believe the author intended to show the woman in so favorable a light. I finished the paper, clucking dissent as I read, and before I left the library, I looked at several more articles about the chapter. All of them lauded the benevolence of the witch.

That night in bed I thought about the witch/king rendezvous. "All right, Missy," I said to myself, "everyone's wrong, so what is right?" In order to imagine myself as the witch, I fantasized that I was the last Jewish dentist in Berlin in the waning days of the Second World War. I chose Berlin because Saul had rid the land of witches, and Hitler had rid the land of Jews. I do not know why I chose to be a dentist except that I wanted to have an occupation wherein my most hated and feared enemy, Hitler, could need my help.

In order for me to survive in Germany, my clients protect me, maintain me, and keep quiet about me—just as the witch's clientele must have had to conceal her. I never venture out on the street, and I see only my regular patients. When three strange men arrive at my hideaway, I am terrified. Like the witch, I cry: "Why have you set a trap for my life to bring about my death?" One of the men assures me that he is just there for a toothache and bids me do my job.

My mind is racing, "What to do; what to do? If I relieve the toothache, they'll need me no longer and kill me or turn me over to the Gestapo." Lest I provoke my visitors, I pretend to be calm and professional, as I try to steady myself enough to think. I seat the patient in my dental chair and examine him. It is Hitler in my chair! Just as the witch screamed when she recognized Saul, the nemesis of all her kind, I scream as I penetrate Hitler's disguise. Like Saul, he tells me to get on with my work and promises that no harm will come to me. Yeah, right.

First, as a dentist, I realize that I have the means to kill my archenemy. But then what will his two bodyguards do to me? I've survived this long; I want to go on living. I decide to tell him I'm giving him a temporary filling, and he'll have to come back. That way, he'll still need me; he won't kill me, and I'll buy a little time. Maybe I can get away, or the war will be over before he returns. Just then we hear the Russian guns very loud to the East. I realize, and from my patient's drained face I know he realizes, that the war will be over in a day. The temporary filling ruse is not going to work; he won't need me again. My fright is insuperable. Now I apprehend the jeopardy of my role model when Samuel prophesied that Saul would die on the morrow. The witch recognized that King Saul, assailant of necromancers, would need her services no longer. He had no reason to let her live, and she had been the medium of bad news—literally. Just how hospitable was she feeling at this juncture? How kind? How tender? I was right not to accept the analyses of the Bible scholars; they *were* wrong. The witch somehow saves her life with that meal, but she is no beneficent Betty Crocker.

The next day I read closely every word of the chapter in the light of my new empathy. I saw the proposition by which the woman bargains for her life and makes a covenant with Saul. I saw the contract-affirming effectiveness of the meal. I saw the blood sacrifice to the dead that was the meal itself. And I saw Saul and his men join the witch in apostasy. Perhaps because I was giddy with excitement at these revelations, I had an experience that struck me as eerie, though suitable to the subject matter. As I was poring over the chapter, translating the Hebrew word by word, I came to a word I knew without the help of the dictionary. It was the word for sacrifice. When I read it, my head reflexively jerked back as if to pull out of a fall. For that is exactly how I felt; when I saw that word, I felt as though the text were parting before me, and I was falling into it.

The witch sacrificed the calf. She did not kill it or butcher it or slaughter it as the English translations maintain. In the next verse she offers it. She does not serve it to, or set it before, the men. A woman, a sorceress, makes a sacrifice and an offering. To whom? Certainly not to the Lord; men of non-priestly lineage, to say nothing of women, do not licitly sacrifice in the Israelite ritual. Saul, his men, and the witch criminally partake in this prohibited tribute—in the unleavened bread and in the meat that, it is further indicated, is eaten raw with the blood.

The three "bad joins," pointed out by the rabbi that taught the Bible class, were no longer rough welds but fit smoothly into this new interpretation of the text. The first of these is the witch's recognition of Saul once she raises Samuel from the grave. The rabbi said that the text errs in having the witch detect and address Saul at this point. When the ghost appears, he said, it must be Samuel that she recognizes. My exegesis explains why she identifies the disguised Saul upon raising Samuel.

The rabbi's next cavil was the narrator's statement that the witch came in to Saul after he had fallen on his face in grief and terror at Samuel's pronouncement of doom. The rabbi asked, "What is the purpose of telling us the witch came in? We were never told that she went out." My analysis shows that the witch's "coming in" has nothing to do with her whereabouts and everything to do with her desperate effort to save her life. Biblically, the expression "came in" has a sexual connotation, just as the modern slang "came on to" a person implies sexual approach.

The third authorial "mistake" the teacher drew to our attention was the narrator's report that Saul sat on the bed. The rabbi could see no reason for the narrator to provide this fact and yet fail to describe where the king's men and the witch were sitting or standing. In my commentary, the position of Saul's retinue and of the witch are immaterial. As I demonstrate, however, Saul's perch on the bed links him by linguistic association to idol-worship—to his further degradation and disrepute. The author, redactor, genius of 1 Samuel made no mistakes.

Exhilarating as my exegesis was to me, it was all the more fulfilling because it permitted me to make a feminist statement in defense of the Bible's evenhandedness. It is true that men, more often than women, are the principal actors in the narrative. When women are depicted, however, Scripture refreshingly eschews stereotypes. Contemporary feminist commentators treat biblical women as victims or saints—valiant either way. Patronizing male exegetes have for centuries seen the witch of Endor as a womanly, albeit slightly ditsy, nurturer. The text, however, with gender-impartial objectivity sees her as intelligent and adept—in less admirable terms, shrewd and crafty. And her pagan will prevails over her adversary's faltering monotheism. The author neither venerates the female nor condescends to the little lady. You might say that she is portrayed like a man.

The witch of Endor has cast a spell over biblical commentators. Despite God's virulent denunciations of soothsayers, Josephus says, "It would be well . . . to imitate the example of this woman" (*Antiquities* 6.14.4); Origen writes of her as a "type of Christ"; Jerome calls her "industrious and practical."[1] Equally enchanted, the moderns extol her "pity" (Beuken), her "motherly care" (Fokkelman), her "generosity"

---

[1] Patricia Cox, "Origen and the Witch of Endor: Toward an Iconoclastic Typology," *AThR* 66 (1984): 144; *The Jerome Biblical Commentary* (ed. Raymond E. Brown, Joseph H. Fitzmyer, and Roland E. Murphy; Englewood Cliffs, N.J.: Prentice-Hall, 1968), 173.

(Ades), her "insight of an angel" (Simon).[2] According to these exegetes, the bustling domesticity of this paragon of womanly solicitude results in a beneficent meal that revives King Saul's physical strength, relieves the torpor into which he has sunk, and fortifies his determination to face, courageously, certain death in battle. The reader is also served by the witch, Alfons Schulz tells us, for the homely conclusion of Saul's encounter with her has a calming effect and relieves emotions contemporary authors would "whip up."[3] Hans Hertzberg says our sympathy for Saul is roused by the moving description of the witch's hospitality, for although the chapter depicts Saul's fate as well-deserved, we respond to the tender concern the woman shows the king and are thereby led to see the "tragic element" in Saul's punishment.[4] Saul's dignity is restored, David Gunn writes, for the "mundane incidentals" of normal sustenance turn the reader's attention from Saul's enervating fear to his ordinary, fast-induced hunger.[5] The literary device of devoting so much of the chapter to the everyday details of food preparation, John Ades says, ends the account of God's judgment on Saul on a "touching diminuendo."[6]

I too am charmed by the witch of Endor, but I find her motivation to be self-preservation, not hospitality. She is not a model of motherly protectiveness but of mother wit, professionalism, resourcefulness, and daring. Although imperiled, she does not become petrified like Saul but, controlling her fear, manages to manipulate her adversary, protect herself, and do her job. She not only raises a ghost but offers a ritual meal that assures her survival. The God of Israel is a jealous God, and the infernal worship that secures the witch's life blasts what is left of Saul's. The purpose of this chapter is to demonstrate by a close reading of the text that the meal the witch prepares for Saul has many functions other than nourishment. Firstly, it is a mantic sacrifice to the dead entailing the stringently proscribed eating of blood; secondly, it is an unholy but legally effective covenant between God's anointed and an idolatrous shaman; thirdly, it warrants Saul's consequent suicide; and lastly, it provides a contrast of

---

[2] Wim Beuken, "1 Samuel 28: The Prophet as Hammer of Witches," *JSOT* 6 (1978): 13; Jan P. Fokkelman, *The Crossing Fates* (vol. 2 of *Narrative Art and Poetry in the Books of Samuel;* Assen: van Gorcum, 1986), 620; John I. Ades, "Samuel, Whear 'Ast Tha Been Sin' I Saw Thee?" *Mappings of the Biblical Terrain: The Bible as Text* (ed. Vincent L. Tollers and John Maier; Lewisburg: Bucknell University Press, 1990), 263; Uriel Simon, "A Balanced Story: The Stern Prophet and the Kind Witch," *Prooftexts* 8 (1988): 165.

[3] Alfons Schulz, "Narrative Art in the Books of Samuel," in *Narrative and Novella in Samuel: Studies by Hugo Gressman and Other Scholars, 1906–1923* (ed. David M. Gunn; JSOTSup 116; Sheffield: Almond, 1991), 156.

[4] Hans Hertzberg, *1 and 2 Samuel* (Philadelphia: Westminster John Knox, 1964, repr. 1976), 220.

[5] David M. Gunn, *The Fate of King Saul* (JSOTSup 14; Sheffield: JSOT Press, 1980), 109.

[6] Ades, "Samuel, Whear 'Ast Tha Been," 266.

Saul's perfidious complicity with David's later faithful integrity in an analogous situation. The witch does not set before the king so dainty a dish as has been hitherto supposed.

The pericope begins by reminding us that Samuel is dead and that all Israel mourned him (1 Samuel 28:3). Samuel's prominence is reiterated for a reason as we shall see.[7] We are also told that Saul removed (הסיר) mediums and diviners (אבות and ידענים) from the land, which was his kingly duty (v. 3). In vv. 4–5 we learn the Israelites and the Philistines are massed for war, and the sight of the Philistine camp incites fear in Saul and a great trembling of the heart. He inquires of the Lord and receives no answer, neither by dreams, nor by Urim, nor by prophets. Saul feels alienated from access to God; he could seek reconciliation through prayer and repentance, but he does not attempt these avenues of grace. He is looking for the occult. The thrice repeated גם (neither, nor, nor) in v. 6 tolls God's rejection of Saul's predilection for the numinous. God is not to be coerced.

Unable to wrest instruction or assurance from God, Saul tells his servants to seek out (בקש) a witch that he might inquire of her (v. 7). In Leviticus 19:31 God commands the Israelites, "Do not seek out [בקש] a witch" because "I am the Lord."[8] Seeking witches is apostasy, unfaithfulness to God. The alacrity with which a witch is located and her convenient proximity to Saul's camp have been noted by many commentators.[9] At one time Saul may have removed witches from the land, but they have either returned or new practitioners have become established. Canaanite cultic practice is difficult to eradicate, as the Hebrew Bible tells us over and over again.

Saul disguises himself in order to visit the witch (1 Samuel 28:8). He needs to. Although Israelites were commanded, "You shall not suffer a witch to live" (Exodus 22:17), obviously there has been toleration, albeit not by the king. If the witch were to learn the identity of her regal client, she might cast a retaliatory hex or be too intimidated to perform. Some critics think Saul has to pass through Philistine lines to get to the witch and disguises himself for military reasons, but a man whose heart trembles within him at the sight of the Philistine camp would hardly venture to penetrate its defenses with so small a cohort.[10]

---

[7] First Samuel 3:20 also testifies to Samuel's renown.

[8] Though documentary theorists propose that the laws of Leviticus were written after the books of Samuel, sequence of authorship is immaterial to my literary view of the Bible. I believe the artistically consummate, received text of the MT is intended by the "author" (authors, editors, final redactor) to be read as a cohesive, consecutive, integrated whole.

[9] See, for example, Fokkelman, *Narrative Art,* 597 n. 1; Hertzberg, *1 and 2 Samuel,* 218 n. e; Ralph W. Klein, *1 Samuel* (WBC 10; Waco: Word, 1983), 271.

[10] Diana Edelman ascribes Saul's disguise to martial caution and cites others who agree (*King Saul in the Historiography of Judah* [JSOTSup 121; Sheffield: JSOT Press, 1991], 242). Klein says he intended to hide his identity from both the Philistines and the witch (*1 Samuel,* 271).

Since we are told in the first clause of 1 Samuel 28:8 that Saul disguises himself, why in the second clause of v. 8 are we further told that he puts on other clothing? As he was unlikely to possess a wig, make-up, or false beard at his military camp, he must have effected his disguise by replacing his royal robes with commonplace garments; therefore, the first clause of the verse suffices to inform us that Saul changes his apparel and renders the second clause unnecessary. The apparent redundancy invites examination. The verb used in the second clause for "put on" (לבש) is often used in a figurative sense to mean becoming clothed in a personal attribute.[11] For example, one puts on (לבש) righteousness (Isaiah 59:17), majesty (Psalm 93:1), or desolation (Ezekiel 7:27). Literally, Saul puts on clothing, but the word selected for "clothing" and the word "treachery" have the same root (בגד). The Hebrew word denotes infidelity. In seeking out a witch, Saul is being disloyal to the Lord; he is "whoring after other gods" (Judges 2:17). The needless duplication of the second clause in 1 Samuel 28:8 (ויתחפש שאול וילבש בגדים) implies that Saul clothes himself with faithless treachery. Further, the image of Saul attired specifically in בגדים (rather than in שמלת, כסות, לבושם, כתנת, מדים—synonyms for apparel) will be adduced to his disadvantage later in the chapter.

Saul uses the same root to accuse his army of treachery (בגדתם) when he discovers them sinning against the Lord by eating meat on the blood (1 Samuel 14:33). What precisely was the sin of Saul's army? Jehoshua Grintz distinguishes between the trespass of eating blood (Genesis 9:4; Leviticus 3:17; 7:26–27; 17:10, 12, 14; Deuteronomy 12:16, 23; 15:23) and that of eating "on" or "upon" (אל and על) the blood (Leviticus 19:26, 1 Samuel 14:32, 33, 34 [אל]; Ezekiel 33:25 [על]). The former offense is prohibited because "the blood is the life." The stricture against the latter sin of eating "on" or "upon" the blood is based, he believes, upon the second clause of my epigraph, Leviticus 19:26: "You shall not eat on the blood; you shall not practice divination nor witchcraft."[12] He argues that Saul's army was sacrificing to chthonic powers for the purpose of divination (84) and compares their slaughter to the act prohibited in 17:5–7: "sacrifice in the open field . . . unto satyrs they whore after."

Though, as Grintz states, "modern Jewish Biblical research has continued to understand the verse in the same way: viz. that the act of 'eating on the blood' was for purposes of divination" (80), the Talmud does not associate the law against eating blood in the first clause of 19:26 with the continuation of that verse. The sages connect it with rather more distantly

---

[11] BDB says that "very often" the verb is used with figurative clothes as in Job 7:5 (worms) and Isaiah 49:18 (inhabitants), but "more often the garment is some abstract quality" (528).

[12] Jehoshua M. Grintz, "'Do Not Eat on the Blood': Reconsiderations in Setting and Dating of the Priestly Code," *Annual of the Swedish Theological Institute* (vol. 8; ed. Hans Kosmala; Leiden: E. J. Brill, 1972), 78–105.

related restrictions against eating the flesh of a live animal and against eating the flesh of the sacrifice before the blood has been ritually sprinkled on the altar.[13] However, Jewish scholars of the Middle Ages, with the exception of Saadia Gaon, did understand eating the blood to be an element of soothsaying and sorcery (Grintz, 79). Maimonides discusses eating the blood and says:

> They thought it was the food of the spirits [the dead]; by eating it, man has something in common with the spirits, which join him and tell him future events. . . . They imagined that . . . love, brotherhood, and friendship with the spirits were established, because they dined with the latter at one place and at the same time; that the spirits would appear to them in dreams, inform them of coming events, and be favorable to them. . . . The Law [the Pentateuch], which is perfect in the eyes of those who know it, and seeks to cure mankind of these lasting diseases, forbade the eating of blood, and emphasized the prohibition in exactly the same terms as it emphasizes idolatry.[14]

In commenting on 19:26, Nachmanides says that eating on the blood is "a kind of witchcraft" and that in 1 Samuel 14, when Saul's men feared the Philistines, they were:

> eating with the blood in order to perform that craft. It is for this reason that Scripture there states, "Then they told Saul, saying: 'Behold the people sin against the Eternal, in that they eat with the blood.' And he said: 'Ye have dealt treacherously [בגדתם].'"[15]

Saul's use of בקש (seek) in 28:7 and the narrator's choice of the root בגד (clothing/treachery) in v. 8 presage Saul's imminent commission of the same deadly sin.

When Saul asks the witch to divine for him, her response is heavily weighted with her fear (vv. 8–9). She accuses Saul both of seeking her life and of causing her to die. She assumes everyone knows of the king's zeal in casting out witches and is apprehensive of any stranger who could and should denounce her to the authorities. Although we are told in v. 3 that Saul has removed (הסיר) the sorcerers, the witch says that Saul has cut them off (כרת). Unlike modern literary stylists, the biblical author does not vary vocabulary merely to avoid repetition.[16] We are meant to notice that the witch uses a more lethal verb than does the narrator. It expresses her perspective on Saul's extermination of her profession. Though it may be translated as "cut off," it is a technical term used for the death penalty;

---

[13] b. Sanhedrin 63a.

[14] Moses Maimonides, *The Guide for the Perplexed* (trans. M. Friedländer; 1904; repr., New York: Dover, 1956), 362.

[15] *Ramban (Nachmanides) Commentary on the Torah: Leviticus* (trans. C. Chavel; New York: Shilo, 1974), 307.

[16] See Robert Alter's chapter, "The Techniques of Repetition," in *The Art of Biblical Narrative* (New York: Basic, 1981), 88–113.

it is also the specific term used for agreeing to a covenant. One "cuts" a covenant just as, in contemporary English vernacular, one "cuts" a deal.[17] The author may also have used this verb to foreshadow subtly the impending covenant-cutting between Saul and the witch.

Saul reassures the woman in the name of the Lord and asks her to bring up Samuel (vv. 10–11). When she succeeds in manifesting the prophet, she realizes that her visitor is the king (v. 12). Many exegetes are troubled by her recognition of Saul upon the sight of Samuel. With no scriptural foundation, *Leviticus Rabbah* 26:7 advances the fanciful midrashic solution that spirits of the dead normally rise from the netherworld upside down, but if they rise at a king's behest, they emerge right side up. When the witch, therefore, sees Samuel emerge right side up, she pierces Saul's disguise. P. Kyle McCarter offers a source-critical explanation: the verses are confused and emended; the woman recognizes Saul from hearing his imperious tone in v. 10 and would have unmasked him earlier had the verses been in correct order.[18] Several commentators maintain that only an important person would presume to request the raising of another important person, or that only one individual, Saul, would be interested in interviewing Samuel in time of war.[19] In either of these cases, however, the witch would have identified Saul as soon as she heard whom he wanted; there would have been no need for her to see Samuel to make the connection. Wim Beuken also makes this point and offers his theory that the very presence of the prophet strips away all ambient deceit and enables the witch to see through Saul's disguise.[20] Jan Fokkelman, too, relies upon the power of the prophet to dissipate Saul's disguise. He suggests the "energy field" between the prophet and the king is so highly charged that the witch intuits Saul's identity from the "aura" Samuel's emergence generates.[21]

My reasoning is rather more prosaic. Judging from Samuel's querulous, "Why have you disturbed me, to bring me up?" (v. 15), the shades apparently prefer to preserve their posthumous rest. As an effective prophet of God and a celebrity in life, Samuel's ghost must have been frequently sought in vain by an anxious populace on the brink of war. He would allow himself to be raised only by those to whom he had strong emotional ties. Samuel's regard for Saul has been frequently underscored. When he

---

[17] BDB says that one "cuts" a covenant "because of the cutting up and distribution of the flesh of the victim for eating in the sacrifice of the covenants" (503).

[18] P. Kyle McCarter Jr., *I Samuel: A New Translation with Introduction and Commenary* (AB 8; Garden City, N.Y.: Doubleday, 1980), 423.

[19] Hertzberg, *1 and 2 Samuel*, 219. He also dismisses the notion that an anonymous ghost was replaced by Samuel in a later redactional stage, though Ades ("Samuel, Whear 'Ast Tha Been," 263), and McCarter (*I Samuel*, 423) subscribe to the idea.

[20] Beuken, "1 Samuel 28: The Prophet as Hammer of Witches," 9.

[21] Fokkelman, *Narrative Art*, 606.

anoints him (10:1), he kisses him—a gesture of affection not repeated with David. Samuel grieves for Saul and cries out to God all night in Saul's behalf after the Lord repents of having made Saul king (15:11). Even after this event, Samuel honors Saul in the eyes of the people (vv. 30–31) and mourns Saul's failure as king (v. 35) so obsessively that the Lord chides him (16:1). The witch of Endor, amazed to see Samuel actually rise to a summons, knows that her tall client is Samuel's beloved king.[22]

By her great cry of distress when she recognizes Saul (28:12), the text makes the point that the woman fears the king, not the ghost. She was frightened when three anonymous men came to her; now she discovers that one of these men is her chief enemy. Up to this time Saul has acted as an individual. His conversations with his men and with the witch have been personal; the narrator has used only Saul's name and will revert to this exclusive use after the one utterance Saul makes with the power of his position. In the only instance in this chapter in which Saul is termed "the king" and speaks in this capacity, he orders the woman not to fear and asks what she sees (v. 13). He has already invoked the Lord's majesty, but, until this moment, he has not compromised his own, and he proves reluctant to be as free with his own authority as he was with God's: in God's name he swears surety; as king, he does not promise the woman immunity from punishment. Since the reader knows Saul is speaking here with the might of the kingship, his peremptory directive to the witch may be interpreted as a mandatory royal command: "Do not be so frightened that you cannot do your job!" The witch knows the king can cut her off. Her jeopardy is now official.

Saul's self-absorbed answer to Samuel's question reveals the extent of his narcissism and of his estrangement from God (v. 15). His own state of mind is his first concern: "I am greatly troubled." He sees the Philistine threat to Israel in personal terms as well: "The Philistines are attacking me." That God's spirit no longer rests upon him takes the position of least significance in his list of woes, and this loss seems to be regretted only because, without advice, he cannot plan his military tactics.

The sequence of Samuel's response rebukes Saul and displays the proper ordering of priorities (vv. 16–19).[23] The issue of greatest importance is Saul's loss of God's support, and Samuel addresses it first, not last. Saul is then told the land of Israel will fall to the Philistines, and only after that is he informed of his own fate. He learns he and his sons—that is, the dynasty—will perish on the morrow. Of least moment is that his army, too, will succumb to the Philistines. They are soldiers, after all, and it is the common lot of soldiers to die in combat. However, the loss of land,

---

[22] Saul's unusual height is mentioned in 1 Samuel 9:2 and 10:23.

[23] Peter Miscall notes without discussion that Samuel's first point is Saul's third (*1 Samuel: A Literary Reading* [Bloomington: Indiana University Press, 1986], 169).

the holy land God promised to Israel, is an uncommon calamity. No Philistines had dwelt within Israel's borders since Samuel's prayerful intercession had resulted in the recovery of previously lost territory (7:13–14). Though there were brief incursions during Saul's reign, the integrity of the boundaries had endured. The coming battle will leave part of the holy land under Philistine occupation (31:7).

Saul was told in 15:23, 26, 28 that his kingdom would be torn from him and from his heirs for his failure to execute Agag, the king of Amalek. From Samuel's denunciation he now learns not only the precise day of his death but also of further punishments and disasters.[24] Land will be lost, he and his sons will die violently, and his army will be vanquished. Throughout the Hebrew Bible there is a strong sense of appropriate justice, of measure for measure. If the failure of the dynasty is the consequence of sparing Agag and the best of the Amalekite spoil, what offenses led to the additional penalties?

In 1 Chronicles 10:13 we are told Saul died for failing to kill Agag and for consulting a ghost. The extended retribution, then, is a result of the divination. *Leviticus Rabbah* 26:7 adds Saul's slaughter of the priests of Nob (1 Samuel 22:16–19) to the list of sins justifying punishment. Pseudo-Philo (*Biblical Antiquities* 58.63.3) blames the army of Israel for not interceding on behalf of the priests and rescuing them as they had Jonathan (1 Samuel 14:45). No source I have found hazards a reason why land is lost to the Philistines (or even acknowledges the loss), but I believe the immediate discovery and proximate location of a witch in 28:7 teaches that under Saul, and in spite of his witch-hunting, the land has become polluted with death cults and their attendant mediums.

In his response to Saul, Samuel repeats the sacred tetragrammaton, יהוה, seven times.[25] The extraordinary power and influence of the mystical number seven is evoked over and over in the Bible. The seven fat cows and seven lean cows in Pharaoh's dream (Genesis 41:18–19) and the seven priests with seven horns circling Jericho seven times on the seventh day (Joshua 6:4) are but two examples among hundreds. Samuel makes one last formidable attempt to turn Saul back to God and away from the pagan conjuring to which he has resorted. By the sevenfold repetition of the name of God, Samuel tries but fails to turn Saul to God and to prevent the desecration of God's name (Leviticus 20:6) that is to come. The

---

[24] Against Miscall, who says, "The dead have nothing new to say" (*1 Samuel*, 171) and Fokkelman, who asserts that the message is "in no way new" (*Narrative Art,* 605). McCarter says that clauses a and c [of v. 19] are the conflated versions of one original clause (*I Samuel,* 419). Samuel R. Driver says, "Clauses a and c are almost identical; and the verse is decidedly improved by the omission of one of them" (*Notes on the Hebrew Text and the Topography of the Books of Samuel* [London: Oxford University Press, 1913; repr. 1966], 218).

[25] Verses 16, 17 (twice), 18 (twice), 19 (twice).

prophet delivers his necessarily harsh message with a potent formula that testifies to his love for Saul and to his abhorrence of the grievous sin Saul is poised to commit.[26]

Saul's interview with Samuel is over. As unwilling to listen to Samuel as he was to hearken to the voice of God, Saul falls crushed to earth by the weight of the divine retribution foretold for his sins (1 Samuel 28:20). Emotionally, he suffers from great fear and, physically, he is weakened by a twenty-four hour fast.[27] The witch's fear of Saul, already great, must also have intensified with Samuel's prophesy. Her arch nemesis may have been willing to let her live as long as he might need her services, but now he will require her powers no longer. He might even, in an attempt to mollify God, order her immediate execution. She has literally been the medium of bad news to Saul; that alone is sufficient ground for the king to put her to death.[28]

Unlike Saul, the woman does not collapse under her fear but takes the first desperate action that occurs to her, and, hoping to buy her life with her body, she approaches Saul sexually: "And the woman came in to Saul" (v. 21).[29] Although "coming in to" (בוא) is often a sex-neutral expression, a woman coming in to a man, particularly a specific man—as here where the woman comes in expressly "to Saul"—may bear a sexual insinuation.[30] In current English slang, one might say the woman "comes on" to Saul. The Hebrew expression need not convey this interpretation, but I see no other reason for the narrator to tell us the woman came in. We were never told she went out; nor are the goings and comings of Saul's

---

[26] Samuel's formulaic repetition of God's name fails to influence Saul, but, when Abigail employs the sevenfold reiteration in 1 Samuel 25, mentioning the name of God in v. 26 (twice), v. 28 (twice), and vv. 29, 30, 31, she successfully deters David from bloodshed. See Chapter Ten, p. 185, and Chapter Four, p. 73.

[27] Both Miscall (*1 Samuel,* 170) and Simon ("A Balanced Story," 163) differentiate between conscious fasting and failure to eat. Simon asserts that Saul does not fast but loses his appetite in nervous apprehension of the coming battle. Klein (*1 Samuel,* 272) offers that Saul may not have eaten due to the rigors of the trip to Endor and also joins McCarter (*I Samuel,* 421 n. 20) in suggesting that Saul engaged in a ritual fast to purify himself for the witch's conjuration. Saul may have fasted on the eve of battle to engage God's support, according to Edelman, but "His reasons for not eating seem to have been deliberately shielded from the audience to raise the question of his intentions"(*King Saul,* 249).

[28] See 2 Samuel 18:21–22 in which Joab dispatches an expendable Cushite to convey bad news to David and tries to dissuade Ahimaaz from being the messenger.

[29] The interweaving of sexual and death cult imagery is ubiquitous throughout the Bible. See Theodore J. Lewis, *Cults of the Dead in Ancient Israel and Ugarit* (HSM 39; Atlanta: Scholars Press, 1989), 149–50, 158.

[30] See Genesis 19:33–34 in which Lot's daughters, in turn, come in to (בוא, that is, have sexual relations with) their father; 2 Samuel 11:4 in which Bathsheba comes in to (בוא) David; and Ruth 3:7 in which Ruth comes into (בוא) Boaz for what is an arguably chaste but undeniably sexually-charged encounter.

men recorded. They are present in v. 23, but we do not know whether or not they attended the seance. This extraneous information is not important to the narrative; neither is the woman's coming in unless it bears an erotic allusion.[31]

She makes carnal overtures to Saul but then sees that he is paralyzed by terror and changes her tack. She tenders him a proposition in the form of an equation, a formal statement of equality: "Behold your handmaid hearkened to your voice and set my life in my hand, and I hearkened to your words that you spoke to me. And now you please hearken also to the voice of your handmaid and I will set a morsel of bread before you" (vv. 21–22). It is not appropriate for a woman, and especially a woman so low in the social order, to set the terms for a king. The witch expresses her proposition with intelligence, delicacy, and tact. The terms she sets are obviously unequal. It is up to the king to correct the equation; he must make the mental computation and understand her to be actually saying: "I hearkened to you and set my life in your hand; now you hearken to me and set your life in my hand."

The witch tells the king that she listened both to his voice and to the words he spoke to her, but she pointedly asks him to hearken only to her voice. Shrewdly, she directs Saul's attention away from her exact words. She wants him to apprehend her vital message from her tone and from her syntax but not to heed the disingenuous "morsel of bread" words of her equation. Her contract is not about bread; it equates a life with a life. Since she leaves it open-ended, Saul may also understand the bargain to be, "As you save my life, so will I save your life." She is offering to perform her augury, to make an idolatrous sacrifice to the spirits of the dead in order that Saul will not die as Samuel foretold. The advantage of the covenant to her, of course, is that Saul will spare her life. Beuken says the witch "unwittingly" proposes a covenant to Saul, for "by listening to others and acting accordingly, people enter into covenant with each other and God with them."[32] I believe the witch to be neither so unwitting nor so winsome as male exegetes seem to find her.

Fokkelman finds "reciprocity" in the witch's compact and a "natural and efficient tit for tat."[33] I do not consider a human life, even a witch's life, in exchange for a morsel of bread to be reciprocal tit for tat. Simon observes the "marked lack of both symmetry and proportion" in the

---

[31] Edelman sees echoes of Abigail's exchange with David and says that both women attempt "to steer [the men] toward a correct course of action [!]. . . . Whether the woman of Endor is making sexual overtures toward the king as Abigail seems to have been doing to David is open to the imagination." Edelman further argues that the witch's knowledge or ignorance of Saul's fate is "irrelevant to the plot line" (*King Saul*, 250–51).

[32] Beuken, "1 Samuel 28: The Prophet as Hammer of Witches," 13.

[33] Fokkelman, *Narrative Art*, 620.

witch's proposal and finds the "logical weakness" part of her "delightful charm." The behavior Simon interprets as generous hospitality to Saul and as innocence of any grudge toward him for cutting the spiritualists from the land seems to him to exhibit "marvelous faithfulness to the truth of life."[34] I think it far from realistic to suppose that a menaced and evidently terrified woman overlooks the mortal danger her worst enemy inflicts upon her and becomes his gracious hostess. Indeed, in such a predicament, a response of eager hospitality would be bizarre. It is more true to life for a frightened, hunted, and condemned person to try to outwit and outmaneuver her adversary to save her own life than to try to feed him to save and fortify his.

Saul understands and initially refuses the witch's offer. He may want to make a pact with the woman that might save his life and the lives of his sons, but God's laws and Samuel's words against rebellion, witchcraft, and *teraphim* (15:23) restrain him.[35] Eventually, however, Saul-like, he cannot withstand the urging of the witch and of his courtiers, and he gives in to the force of their persuasion and to his own inclination as three times previously he has given in to pressure. At Gilgal in 13:8–12 he disobeys God's command and performs an untimely sacrifice to keep his men from scattering; in 14:45, abandoning the oath he made in God's name, he spares Jonathan's life at the people's insistence, and in 15:24 he transgresses the commandment of the Lord because, he says, "I feared the people and listened to their voice." Though Saul hearkens neither to the voice of God nor to the voice of Samuel, he does, in the end, hearken to the voice of the witch and of his men (28:23).

Saul rises from the earth, but not to his feet; he sits upon the bed (v. 23). Contrary to Gunn (see note 5), the Bible does not record "mundane incidentals." Why then are we told that Saul sits upon the bed? We are not informed of the position of the witch and of the courtiers. I believe only Saul's posture is important to the story because of the identity of the phrase אל־המטה (on the bed, upon the bed) with the same phrase in 19:13, 16, describing the placement of the *teraphim* Michal, Saul's daughter, uses to save David's life.[36] In all of Scripture the expression אל־המטה is used only of Saul, of Michal, and of Jacob at his death (Genesis 49:33).

---

[34] Simon, "A Balanced Story," 164–67.

[35] *Teraphim* are defined as ancestor figurines used for divination and cultic inquiry directed to the dead. See Harry Hoffner Jr., "Hittite *Tarpiš* and Hebrew *Terāphîm*," *JNES* 27 (1968): 66; Ktziah Spanier, "Rachel's Theft of the Teraphim: Her Struggle for Family Primacy," *VT* 42 (1992): 405, 410; Karel van der Toorn, "The Nature of the Biblical Teraphim in the Light of the Cuneiform Evidence," *CBQ* 52 (1990): 204, 213, 215, and 222. Spanier says, "Saul was rebuked by Samuel for resorting to teraphim for the purpose of divination (1 Samuel 15:23)," 406.

[36] Note that only the *teraphim* are אל־המטה, "on the bed"; David, in the same passage, is said to be במטה, "in bed" (19:15).

The last may also be mentioned to remind us of *teraphim*, for in v. 27 Jacob's son, Benjamin (Saul's progenitor), is designated as the divider of the spoil; on Jacob's death he may have taken possession of the *teraphim* stolen by his mother, Rachel, from her father (31:19). The Bible may be intimating that the *teraphim* were handed down from mother to son to Saul, the distant heir. Samuel's pointed scolding of Saul (1 Samuel 15:23), mentioning *teraphim*, plus Saul's identification with *teraphim* established by אל־המטה disparage the king by associating him with idolatrous practice.

The nexus between 1 Samuel 28 and 19:11–17 is illustrated by a number of other correspondences: David is told, "If you do not save your life tonight, tomorrow you will be slain" (v. 11); Saul also knows that he has only this one night in which to save his life, for tomorrow, Samuel tells him, he will die (28:19). Michal disguises the *teraphim* with a cloth, בגד (19:13); Saul, as we have seen, is disguised with בגדים—having the same root word (28:8). Saul asks Michal, "Why thus have you deceived me?" (19:17); the witch asks Saul, "Why have you deceived me?" (28:12). The word "why," למה, a *Leitwort* in chapter 28, is used there four times (vv. 9, 12, 15, 16). It is accentuated in chapter 19 by being enunciated by two different speakers in the same verse (v. 17). Its first use is echoed by the witch as quoted above; its second use, "Let me go; why should I kill you?" attracts notice because of the idiosyncratic phraseology. One would hardly suppose that a desperate, fleeing man had time for questions. It seems a more natural lie for Michal to claim David had said, "Let me go, or I will kill you."

In a general discussion of biblical literary devices, Meir Sternberg writes of the "rhetorical power [of] implicit intertextual and interepisodic relations" and of the "intertextual analogy-by-allusion."[37] Robert Alter observes, "The biblical writers like to lead their readers to inferences through oblique hints rather than insisting on explicit statements."[38] The analogous portrayals of Saul and of *teraphim*—both אל־המטה, both covered with בגד—may hint at what the once majestic Saul has become: a hollow man, a fake, an abomination. The allusion to *teraphim* in relation to Saul may also be a portent of the forbidden ancestor worship to come.

The witch sacrifices (זבח) a calf (28:24). She does not "kill" it (KJV and RSV), "slaughter" it (AB and NJPS), or "butcher" it (WBC); she sacrifices it. The word for sacrifice (זבח) is used 129 times in the Hebrew Bible, and, according to Jacob Milgrom, it refers to cultic ritual slaughter and sacrifice in 127 of those instances.[39] If the word, זבח, is used twice to mean

---

[37] Meir Sternberg, *The Poetics of Biblical Narrative* (Bloomington: Indiana University Press, 1987), 497.

[38] Alter, *The Art of Biblical Narrative*, 183.

[39] Jacob Milgrom ("Profane Slaughter and a Formulaic Key to the Composition of Deuteronomy," *HUCA* 47 [1976]: 1–2) excepts only Deuteronomy 12:15, 21. In these two cases alone he believes the word refers to secular slaughter for food. In 1 Samuel 28 he believes זבח indicates some undefined but permissible ritual slaughter and sacrifice, for he finds it unlikely "that the witch of Endor would

secular slaughter, I could believe it refers to secular slaughter in our passage too were there not several other indications in the text, discussed below, that also point to ritual sacrifice.

Along with the meat, the witch provides unleavened bread (מצה). Unleavened bread is a constituent of a sacrificial offering; it is the meal-offering and is a sign and symbol of sacrifice. In Leviticus 2:4 the MT specifies מצה for the meal-offering, and in 2:11 we are told that no leaven may be brought to the altar for this purpose. Of course one cannot prepare quickly any bread other than unleavened bread, for leavened bread needs time to rise. However, the unleavened nature of the bread the witch serves need not have been specifically emphasized. In Genesis 18:5–6, to use a particularly apt parallel, when Abraham rushes to provide a "morsel of bread" for three strange men who unexpectedly arrive at his dwelling, his wife hastily makes "cakes of bread" (עגות).[40] Unlike מצה, this word may refer to bread that is leavened or unleavened. The cakes, or loaves, Sarah bakes are of necessity unleavened, but the word, מצה, is avoided. There is no hint of ritual sacrifice.

After the witch sacrifices the calf, we are not told how she prepares it. The absence of detail in this regard is especially noticeable because we are given so many particulars to describe the preparation of the מצה; she takes flour, kneads, and bakes—three verbs. If we look again at the paradigmatic hospitality scene of Abraham and the three strangers in Genesis 18:6–7, we see that an equal number of operations is itemized for the bread and for the meat. The bread is prepared-quickly (one word in Hebrew), kneaded, and made; the meat is fetched, given to the servant, and dressed. No commentator has remarked upon this deficiency in regard to the meat in 1 Samuel 28, but Fokkelman at least has sensed it; he fills the lacuna for us by stating that the witch "applies herself to baking and roasting."[41] What roasting? We do not know if the meat was roasted, boiled, or barbecued, and I submit it was not cooked at all but eaten raw with the blood.

In discussing the "depth and sophistication" of biblical narrative, Adele Berlin says the narrator may "leave gaps in the story to be filled in by the reader."[42] The yawning gap in this story is one more indication that God's

---

have prepared a profane [secular] meal before the very king who troubled himself to improvise an altar on the battlefield so that his troops would not be guilty of profane or illicit slaughter (I Sam 14:32–35)." Though Milgrom thus agrees with me that the witch proffers a ceremonial oblation rather than a domestic repast, he considers the witch's sacrifice lawful.

[40] The comparison of Genesis 18:1–8 and 1 Samuel 28:22–25 is singularly pertinent, for in both passages a "morsel of bread" is prepared for three unexpected, unknown, male visitors.

[41] Fokkelman, *Narrative Art*, 621.

[42] Adele Berlin, "Point of View in Biblical Narrative," in *A Sense of the Text* (JQRSup; Winona Lake, Ind.: Eisenbrauns, 1982), 112. See also Sternberg's chapter on "Gaps, Ambiguity, and the Reading Process," in *The Poetics of Biblical Narrative*, 186–229.

chosen, anointed, first king of Israel ate meat with the blood as part of the abominable rite of divination. The narrator stresses the preparation of the bread and leaves a void concerning the meat so that, by means of the disparity, this degrading and treacherous (בגד) act of Saul's may be inferred.

The witch takes the raw meat, the blood, and the sacred bread and offers them in the presence of Saul and his men (v. 25). The KJV translates "offers" (נגש) as "brought." The RSV says "put." WBC and the NJPS have "set." The word שׂום (put or set) is the word one is led to expect here from the two precedents established by its use in v. 21, "I have set (שׂים) my life in my hand" and in v. 22, "Let me set (שׂים) a morsel of bread before you." Any variation in a rhetoric that stresses repetition confers added significance on the variant. The change of verb alerts the careful reader that, though the woman asked permission to "set" (שׂים), in the actual event she "offers" (נגש).[43] שׂום is a neutral verb that denotes "place" or "put"; נגש, however, is a loaded verb that connotes both the priestly approach to the altar and sexual intercourse.[44] This verb choice confirms that the witch sacrifices, not butchers, the calf. Here, instead of setting (שׂום) food before Saul, she is offering (נגש) gifts to the dead.

For Saul the forbidden food propitiates the spirits. For the witch the communal meal seals a covenant—that is, it performs the legal function of a treaty, eliminating enmity and establishing peace between the participants. Åke Viberg lists all the biblical covenantal meals that satisfy his criteria for the symbolic, yet legal, act.[45] He does not include the meal shared by the witch, Saul, and the courtiers. Nevertheless, this meal fulfills the four indications of legality he stipulates:

> These indications are, firstly, the pivotal position of the meal in the literary structure, followed by a geographical dislocation, secondly, the use of terminology within the context otherwise well known from covenant-making, thirdly, the lack of any other explicit means of satisfying the covenant, and fourthly, the mere fact that the meal is mentioned.[46]

The pivotal position of the meal in our text is marked; we are told that Saul and his men rise up and leave (geographical dislocation) in the same verse in which we are told that they eat (v. 25). Covenantal terminology is first implied by the witch's use of the technical word for cutting a

---

[43] Alter says, "Where the narration so abundantly encourages us to expect . . . repetition, on occasion the avoidance of repetition, whether through substitution of a synonym or of a wholly divergent word or phrase for the anticipated reoccurrence, may also be particularly revealing" (*The Art of Biblical Narrative*, 180).

[44] The verb choice hints that the witch offers food to the dead and offers herself sexually to Saul and his men (see note 29 above).

[45] Åke Viberg defines a legal symbolic act as "a non-verbal act which fulfills a legal function when it is performed under the proper circumstances" (*Symbols of Law* [Stockholm: Almqvist & Wiksell, 1992], 9).

[46] Viberg, *Symbols of Law*, 75.

covenant, כרת, and then realized by Saul's acceptance of her obliquely equilateral proposition. The presence of two witnesses (Saul's men) is another technical indication of the legal context.[47] Viberg's third criterion is achieved, for, other than the shared meal, no means of satisfying the covenant is explicitly specified. The fourth criterion is extensively fulfilled, for the meal is not only mentioned but dwelt upon. In our pericope of twenty-three verses (vv. 3–25), talk of the meal, preparation of the meal, and consumption of the meal occupies five verses.

The witch of Endor intends to survive. She instigates this meal because, as a covenant, it safeguards her life. She does not promote it in order to nurture her enemy by bolstering his declining strength. Nor does the author provide a calming breather for the reader; on the contrary, Saul's apostasy intensifies our apprehension. The loathsome conviviality of this prohibited sacrifice does not arouse our sympathy for Saul; rather, our contempt for him is increased. And it does not suggest that the witch is a ministering angel; it establishes that she is a clever, capable, determined woman.[48]

The witch's sorcery may have saved her life, but it fails Saul. The next morning he goes into battle—heroically, according to the commentators.[49] They believe him gallant because, they think, he braves the battlefield in the certain knowledge of death. Stoically, he submits to God's sentence for himself and for his sons rather than leave them behind to an uncertain future. However, Saul, unlike David (16:18), is never identified as a "mighty man of valor" or a "man of war." Saul's father is distinguished as a "mighty man of valor" in 9:1, whereas Saul is introduced in the very next verse as "a young man and handsome." Perhaps the comparison is indirectly derisive. Certainly, the reader notes Saul "hiding among the baggage" in 10:22, sees him afraid to engage Goliath himself but willing to let David, as a sort of proxy, fight the giant dressed in the king's armor in 17:38, and observes his self-abasement before David on being spared death at the latter's hands in chapters 24 and 26. Is the reader then to accept that Saul is suddenly, uncharacteristically, totally unafraid of death and willing to consign not only himself but also his sons to certain oblivion? In my exegesis, Saul risks battle only because he believes he has enlisted the protection of the infernal deities. He is not courageous but is encouraged by the witch's conjuring to trust that the friendly ghosts, the spirits with whom he shared blood, will save him and his heirs.

---

[47] Viberg, *Symbols of Law,* 10.

[48] Lewis says, "Little can be said about the woman's feast. It may be enticing to look for some type of cultic ritual here uniting Saul with a meal for the dead, but the text, with its emphasis on the woman's compassion, does not seem to support such a notion" (*Cults of the Dead,* 117). Contrary to Lewis, I find no emphasis on compassion in our text, but ample accent on appropriately responsive, survival-oriented intelligence which does, indeed, support this notion.

[49] *Leviticus Rabbah* 26:7; Josephus (*Antiquities* 6.14.4); Simon praises Saul's heroism (169) and cites others who glorify it ("A Balanced Story," 171 n. 15).

With the death of his sons, Saul realizes the witch's necromancy has not been a shield. Writhing (יחל, "writhe" or "whirl"—not "wounded" as it is frequently translated) in mental anguish, contorting with fright, cowering, or perhaps dodging the archers, he ends his life by suicide, lest the Philistines torture him to death (31:2–4).[50] This denouement provides the reader with a sense of equity. After Samuel's pronouncement, it seemed no further punishment could possibly be given Saul, yet the retribution he receives for eating the blood is fitting. The horror that spurs his suicide goes beyond Samuel's prophecy and fulfills the measure-for-measure standard of judgment. It is as though God had said: "You feared death; now you will fear to live. You wanted to escape your fate; now you will run toward it."

The meal Saul shares with the witch has yet another function beyond sacrifice and covenant. It provides a means of comparing Saul and David directly, to Saul's decided disadvantage. In 2 Samuel 12:16–23, David beseeches God for the life of his ill son, the fruit of his adulterous union with Bathsheba. The prophet, Nathan, has already foretold that the child will die because of David's sin. The thematic parallels between this scene and the witch of Endor scene are striking. Both kings are shown by prophets to be sinners, both hear a forecast of doom, both are threatened with the death of progeny, both fast, lie on the ground, refuse food, change clothes, rise from the earth, and finally accept food.[51] For seven days David resists the exhortations of his servants, never accedes to them, but insists upon doing what he knows to be right; Saul gives in to far less coaxing, though he knows he is acquiescing to the ultimate iniquity.

The lexical correlations between the two scenes are also remarkable. In both scenes, and nowhere else in the Hebrew Bible, mention is made of joining the dead: Samuel tells Saul that tomorrow Saul and his sons "will be with me" (1 Samuel 28:19), and David, speaking of his dead son, tells his servants, "I shall go to him" (2 Samuel 12:23).[52] In both scenes, and nowhere else in the Hebrew Bible, there is the locution "and he rose from the earth," ויקם מהארץ (1 Samuel 28:23 and 2 Samuel 12:20). The reader is guided to compare the supplicatory behavior of the two kings by similarity of incident, of issue, and of expression.[53]

---

[50] Those who believe that after Saul stabbed himself the Amalekite killed him see Saul's end as (a more acceptable) euthanasia rather than suicide (2 Samuel 1:6–10). By either the Amalekite's or the narrator's account, however, Saul committed suicide or tried and failed to commit suicide.

[51] David's changing of clothes is expressed by the matter-of-fact ויחלף שמלתו rather than by the metaphorically significant וילבש בגדים used for Saul.

[52] In Genesis 37:35 Jacob says that he will go to his son in Sheol; however, the reader knows that Jacob is deceived; his son is alive.

[53] That David's behavior is not normative Israelite ritual is shown by the consternation of his servants (2 Samuel 12:21). Lewis makes the, to me rather dubious, case that David's seven-day fasting and lying on the ground constitute a

Both David and Saul are disappointed in their appeals. David washes himself after his polluting association with death, faithfully worships the Lord despite the severe chastisement he has received, and eats an appropriately secular meal in his own house. Saul does not wash after the defilement of his contact with the ghost of Samuel, sits on a bed in the house of a witch, worships his ancestors instead of the Lord, and eats a detestable witch's stew of raw meat, blood, and unleavened bread.

I have presented arguments that expose the witch's motivation and King Saul's defection from monotheism. The charge against Saul is grave, but the text demands it. His record of yielding to entreaty, his proclivity for magic, and his fear-numbed stupor constitute the background for his penultimate act of desperation. Among the evidence in the foreground is the pointed use of the root בגד tying Saul to treachery, to the eating of blood by his army, and to *teraphim*. The phrase אל־המטה (on the bed) used in the Bible only of Saul and of *teraphim*, again links Saul to ancestor worship. The witch's use of distinctly covenantal terminology—the technical term, כרת, plus her equation in the form of: as I did x, now you do y—delineates the heretical bargain. The absence of detail in the meat preparation (made noticeable by juxtaposition of fuller detail in the preparation of the bread) becomes substantive evidence of the bloody rite when coupled with the use of the word זבח (sacrifice, rather than a verb meaning, simply, slaughter) and the needlessly explicit mention of the unleavened, and thus sacrificial, character of the bread. That the witch's meal is a blasphemous ritual is further indicated by the surprising use of the allusive word נגש (offer, approach) where we are led by double precedent to expect שום (set). Saul's end, his final terror—not of death but of life—shows the playing out of an inexorable justice. It is the unforetold penalty for his treacherous blood worship of false gods.

My exegesis of 1 Samuel 28 contradicts all preceding analyses. History may be written by the victors (the Davidic faction), but it is interpreted by partisans of a particular point of view. Analysts, blinkered by their religious theologies, have been averse to allowing Saul the autonomy that God permits him. Although Samuel predicts the certain end of Saul's disobedience (15:23), and we are twice told that God repents of his selection of Saul (vv. 11, 35), prior commentators cannot let themselves perceive apostasy in God's choice for king. Saul is portrayed as a tragic, yet valiant, figure because to recognize him as the craven idolater he becomes would, in their philosophies, be tantamount to declaring that God errs.

---

ceremonial descent to Sheol. He states, "It seems quite likely that David was ritually acting out a descent into the underworld to try to bring his son back from the clutches of death" (*Cults of the Dead,* 43). Those who agree with Lewis's assertion will find yet another correspondence between Saul and David, for Saul briefly brings Samuel back from the clutch of death.

Correspondingly, in previous explications, the witch cannot have seduced Saul to heterodox worship. Her role had to be that of care-giver. The interpreter's image of a selfless and compassionate nurturer also fits an idealized standard of femininity. Even today, the biblical author's depiction of the medium as self-interested and resourceful is not a representation of woman that is readily embraced. The witch is not seen as an adroit strategist but as a generous, solicitous, and adorably illogical hostess. God's vehement condemnations of witchcraft are discounted; the human drive for self-preservation is depreciated, and the witch of Endor basks in approval, continuing to entrance exegetes down the centuries.

CHAPTER TEN

Cupidity and Stupidity: Woman's Agency and the "Rape" of Tamar

In the the electric company Bible class we read about the incestuous rape of King David's daughter, Tamar, by her half-brother, Amnon. Amnon is guilty as sin. His story begins in 2 Samuel 13, when we are told that he loves Tamar so much that he wastes away for love of her. She is a virgin, and it seems hard (or in some translations, impossible) "for him to do anything to her." His cousin, Jonadab, a subtle/shrewd/crafty (depending on the translation) fellow, learns the cause of Amnon's weight loss and advises him to pretend to greater illness than he feels. Jonadab counsels Amnon to ask his father, King David, if Tamar may come and cook food before him that he might eat it from her hand.

When David visits his bedridden son, Amnon asks that Tamar come and prepare a couple of cakes in his sight that he might eat at her hand. David dispatches his daughter, Tamar, to Amnon to prepare him food. Tamar goes to her brother's house where he lies in bed. She takes dough, kneads it, and bakes cakes in his sight. She pours them out before him, but he refuses to eat and says: "Everyone go out from me." Everyone goes out from him.

When they are alone, Amnon asks Tamar to bring the food into the chamber so that he can eat from her hand. Tamar brings him the cakes, and when she is near enough, he takes hold of her and asks her to lie with him. She refuses, saying: "No, my brother, do not force/violate/rape me." Amnon, however, will not listen to her voice, but being stronger than she, forces/violates/rapes her and lies with her.

Then, we are told, he hates her with a great hatred—a hatred greater than the love with which he had loved her. Amnon tells her to get up and go away, but she protests that there is no cause and that the wrong in sending her away is worse than the other that he did to her. He calls his servants to put Tamar out and bolt the door after her. Tamar puts ashes of mourning on her head, rends her coat of many colors, and laying her hand on her head, weeps loudly as she goes.

Absalom, another brother, sees her and asks if she has been with Amnon. He says, "Hold now thy peace/ Now keep silent/ Be quiet for now, my sister: he is your brother; do not take this thing to heart." Tamar remains desolate in Absalom's household, and Absalom hates Amnon because he forced/violated/raped his sister, Tamar.

Nothing could be more clear. I had just two minor questions when we read this chapter in class: why did Tamar want to remain with her rapist so ardently that the door had to be bolted behind her, and why did Absalom tell her to be quiet because Amnon was her brother? To me, the relationship exacerbated the crime; it did not alleviate it. In answer to the first question, the rabbi who taught our class suggested that Tamar had been rendered unmarriageable, and she knew that unless she became the bride of Amnon, she would live a spinster. In response to the second, he explained that Absalom wants to punish Amnon personally rather than legally.

The teacher's answer did not address the consanguinity aspect of Absalom's injunction, but since, a few verses later, David hears about the rape and does nothing but get angry, I thought perhaps Absalom believes the incest so scandalous it would be useless for Tamar to appeal to her father for justice. The king would hush the matter up, and Amnon would go unpunished unless Absalom, himself, avenges his sister.

A couple of years after this class, I read a book about various women in the Bible. It was a feminist appraisal that dealt only with victims. When I started the book, I believed that Tamar was a victim, but by the time I finished the chapter about her, I was almost ready to defend Amnon. She was lauded as so pure and wise and noble, so deserving of pity, so perfect in every respect, that she seemed far too good to be true. Amnon, on the other hand, could not catch a break from this feminist author. Every word used in her retelling of the chapter put him in the worst possible light. I knew, for example, that in Hebrew the chapter says Amnon loved Tamar; in this writer's exegesis, however, Amnon lusted for Tamar. I wondered if the author were taking liberties in her description of Amnon to make him sound even more of a beast than he was, and so I looked up the Hebrew word for love in the authoritative *Hebrew and English Lexicon of the Old Testament* (known to Bible scholars as BDB, after its editors: Brown, Driver, and Briggs) to see if possibly this word also means lust. I found that the dictionary translates the word as love in all of the hundreds of times it is used in the Bible, except for the Amnon and Tamar chapter, where it is translated as carnal desire. The feminist author was supported in labeling Amnon's emotion as lust.

On the treadmill, there is plenty of time to think, and one day at the gym I was musing about the lexicographer's task of definition. I could not fault his judgment in defining Amnon's passion as carnal desire because shades of meaning are established by context. Perhaps it is in this chapter that we learn the Hebrew word for love can also mean desire. The standard authority for the English language, the *Oxford English Dictionary,* quotes paradigmatic sentences for each word in order to show nuances determined by context. In the *Oxford English Dictionary,* of course,

English words are in English sentences. With the *Hebrew and English Lexicon of the Old Testament* there is the added problem of translation. But since Amnon raped Tamar, lust does seem a more appropriate translation than love.

On the other hand, I thought, it is a truism that every translation is an interpretation. What if Amnon had not raped his sister after all? Relying on the translation, the chapter explicitly says he forced or violated or raped her. But what if all the English translators whose work I had seen were, like the dictionary, so sure of Amnon's guilt that they translated accordingly? Perhaps there were a more literal, but less contemptible, Hebrew word for sexual intercourse that would have been more accurate than forced or violated or raped.

As soon as I got home from the gym, I consulted my Hebrew concordance. A concordance is a necessity in Bible study. It lists alphabetically each use of every biblical word, quotes the phrase in which the word appears to show the context, and gives chapter and verse for each usage. I wanted to look up the actual Hebrew verb or verbs the chapter used to describe Amnon's act to see how they were utilized and how they were translated in the rest of the Bible.

Two verbs were used to describe Amnon's actions. The first was שכב, or "lie," as when he says: "Come lie with me, my sister." It is used again in the chapter when it says he "laid" her. It does not sound romantic, but it is not rape in either English or Hebrew. The other verb used in this chapter, translated as "forced/violated/raped," is ענה. This verb can mean "to afflict," but it can also mean "to answer," which implies reciprocity. As a carnal expression, the Bible does not use it for rape but rather to indicate sexual intercourse of which it disapproves—as when Lot's daughters sleep with their father. Naturally, the Bible would also deprecate the union of Amnon and Tamar as they are half-siblings; theirs is an act of incest.

The proof text that convinced me the Bible does not use ענה for rape is Deuteronomy 22:24. It says that when a man lies with a betrothed virgin in the city, they are both to be stoned, the man because he had intercourse, ענה, with another's fiancée and the woman because she did not cry out. The assumption is that had she cried out in the city, a populated area, she would have been heard and rescued. The woman's failure to cry out evidences her consent. Here again, the Bible deplores the immorality with the word ענה, but the felony is not rape.

English readers must accept that Amnon was a rapist, but why were the translators of the Bible, experts in Hebrew, so sure that Tamar did not consent that they selected loaded and inaccurate words to describe the sexual act? They must have thought they were being true to the story, but whatever happened to Tamar, happened in the city, and we are not told that she cried out. She cried loudly after Amnon threw her out and barred the door behind her but not when he was about to have sex with her. Well, well, well. Let's have a closer look at Miss Goody Two Shoes.

I took piano lessons as a child, and if my practice pieces had lyrics, I sang as I played. One of my pieces had a line that always got a laugh out of my mother: "You can tempt the upper classes with your villainous demitasses, but heaven will protect the working girl." My mother explained to me that demitasses were little elegant cups of after-dinner coffee, but that the working girl, unfamiliar with upper-class culture, thought they were some kind of naughty food. I did not understand the concept of naughty food then, and I do not believe in aphrodisiacs now. Such comestibles, however, are popular today in many cultures and have been throughout history. For example, the Bible attests to the desirability of mandrakes as an erotic edible in Genesis 30:14–16.

The biblical author hints that there is something erogenous about the cakes Tamar bakes for her brother. Jonadab suggests to Amnon that he ask his father for food from Tamar's hand. Amnon, however, asks for cakes from her hand. The term for these cakes contains the word heart; I, as well as many other exegetes, call them heart-cakes. David censors both the cakes and the propinquity necessary for hand-feeding and instructs Tamar only to prepare food. Tamar, on her own initiative, and against her father's directive, enterprisingly makes cakes. What is the reason for all this menu interplay, if not to show us both youngsters' preoccupation with concupiscent cupcakes?

Many hours of my college career were spent discussing with other girls the issue of whether we would, or whether we would not, or under what circumstances we might go alone to a boy's apartment. College boys are men now, and girls are women, but we were boys and girls in the fifties, and we had rules. No boys were allowed above the first floor in girls' dormitories; no girls were allowed above the first floor in boys' dorms, and if you knew a boy old enough to have his own apartment, your reputation was in jeopardy if you visited him alone. I own a 1926 edition of Emily Post's *Etiquette* that says: "Every young woman must be protected by a chaperon, because otherwise she will be misjudged." In view of the puritanical rigor of relatively recent years in the sexually-emancipated United States, what do you suppose the rules of rendezvous were for single young people thousands of years ago in the Middle East?

Amnon had to ask his father for permission to be visited by a sister. Obviously, brothers and sisters were kept apart. Even among family, young people of opposite sexes did not socialize. David, understandably, permitted a visit since Amnon was on his sickbed and chaperoning servants were in attendance. But, when Amnon ordered that everyone leave him, and those servants left the room, Tamar was defying formidable convention by remaining alone with a boy. What was she thinking?

This chapter proposes what the coquette was thinking. She was thinking of marrying Amnon, the king's oldest son. I believe she wanted to win his heart for a subsequent marriage rather than to sleep with him right then, but she was willing if he insisted, as matrimony could be effected by sexual intercourse according to their law. Now I saw the answers to the two questions that had occurred to me years earlier in the Bible class—why Tamar wants to stay with her alleged abuser, and why Absalom tells her to be quiet because Amnon is her brother. In Israelite law, a man who believes he is marrying a virgin may divorce his bride after consummation if she proved not to be virginal. When Amnon tries to get rid of Tamar after coitus, she clings to him and says: "There is no cause." She knows she was a virgin and considers herself legally married. She must have explained her case to Absalom to prompt the response (an emphatic one, I later saw) "Silence, he is your brother!" What an exasperating girl! Absalom knows that the sibling relationship is an insuperable impediment to any such marriage; why does she not know it?

The closer I looked at the chapter, the more evidence I found in defense of consensual intercourse. I also found an intertextual comparison between Tamar and a woman who is mentioned earlier in the Bible, Abigail. By mirrored circumstances and locutions, Tamar's foolish and counter-productive handling of her passionate brother is contrasted to Abigail's astute and beneficial management of an equally fiery David in 1 Samuel 25. The parallels between the two scenes are marked. The disparity between Abigail, introduced as intelligent and beautiful, and Tamar, introduced only as beautiful, is equally noticeable—to Tamar's detriment. She is not so wise as the feminist author had supposed.

I believe that the first readers, or listeners, understood exactly what happened in Amnon's apartment. They either knew about the titillating attributes of heart-cakes, or they were sensitive to the repeated verbal exchange over diet, culminating in Tamar's choice of cakes rather than in the more therapeutic food her father had ordered. They were shocked when she remained alone with her brother after the servants' departure; their own daughters, they were probably sure, were better behaved. When Tamar did not call out in opposition to her brother's amorous advance, the first readers understood that she consented to the lovemaking. As Hebrew speakers, they also knew that the verb עִנָּה meant sexual intercourse not forced/violated/raped. They noticed the many other evidences of Tamar's pursuit of matrimony, and their reading of the chapter was unambiguous: Tamar yielded willingly to her brother's entreaties.

If ancient readers had this understanding of the chapter, why do later readers see rape? For one reason, I think they have a less keen appreciation for subtleties than did the first readers. Later interpreters see a woman enter the house of a man who fervently loves her. He pleads for intimacy; she argues against seduction. Sexual intercourse occurs, and the woman leaves in tears. These are the basic facts; what are they to think?

Once the decision characterizing the scenario and the actors is made, it is not easy to change one's mind. Commentators either do not observe, or brush past, or make excuses for the details that do not fit their analyses. In my note 24, one exegete makes the circular argument that heart-cakes cannot have a sensual implication since they are made by the virtuous Tamar. Note 61 cites another interpreter who acknowledges that Tamar's failure to cry out exposes her to stoning; the interpreter, nevertheless, does not for a moment entertain the idea that Tamar fails to cry out because she consents.

I think gender shapes another reason later readers do not recognize Tamar's purpose and complicity in her tryst with Amnon. Male commentators do not give biblical women credit for having purpose. To them, a woman is not an actor; she is acted upon. Tamar's aspiration to marry her half-brother, the heir-apparent, is harebrained and, indeed, as Absalom curtly points out to her, impossible. It is a foolish plan, but it is a plan nevertheless. The Bible portrays women as motivated, but male analysts frequently perceive them as passive to the point of stupor.

Feminist commentators often view women as prey. Before this article was published, I presented an abbreviated version at an American Academy of Religion/Society of Biblical Literature Conference. After my talk, a young woman in the audience sprang up and denounced me for blaming the victim. She said that I had an anti-feminist agenda and, boiling over with tears of rage and sympathy for Tamar, she ran from the auditorium. I was sorry she left because I wanted to explain to her that, on the contrary, I have an ultra-feminist agenda. I believe that biblical women can have aims and agency. They can be powers for good like Abigail who stops David from committing violence; they can be powers for malevolence like Tamar who provides Absalom with an excuse for murder. They can not only be smart; they can also be stupid. Just like men.

"You have ravished my heart, my sister, my bride (לבבתני אחתי כלה)." (Song of Songs 4:9)

Everybody knows Amnon raped his half-sister, Tamar.[1] English speakers know because English translations make a different interpretation untenable. Bible scholars know because it has been the received reading for well over 1,000 years, because it fits neatly into the larger story, and because Absalom seems to believe it. They cling to their knowledge, though it requires them to ignore or to misconstrue copious contradictory evidence. The purpose of this chapter is to present this exculpatory evidence. By a close reading of 2 Samuel 13, its sister-text, 1 Samuel 25, and related

---

[1] "The rapist is guilty. In the reception of the text, so far as I can ascertain, this has never been disputed" (Fokkelien van Dijk-Hemmes, "Tamar and the Limits of Patriarchy: Between Rape and Seduction [2 Samuel 13 and Genesis 38]," in *Anti-Covenant: Counter-Reading Women's Lives in the Hebrew Bible* [ed. Mieke Bal; Sheffield: Almond, 1989], 145).

passages, I shall prove that the sexual intimacy of Amnon and Tamar is consensual, and that their incestuous union is encouraged by Tamar's flirtatiousness and supported by her easy virtue, persistent ambition, and implacable stupidity.

Although there is unanimity on the rape verdict, opinion is divided on the question of incest. The majority of commentators believe Amnon is not also guilty of incest because marriage between the half-brother and sister was permissible at that time.[2] According to source critics, parts of the books of Samuel predate the Pentateuch, and so at the time of the monarchy, the incest laws of Leviticus 18:9, 11; 20:17; and Deuteronomy 27:22 were unknown.[3] These critics find proof of their theory in Tamar's plea that Amnon ask their father, David, for her hand (2 Samuel 13:13). They reason that she would not have suggested an impossible marriage, for such a notion would have been too preposterous for Amnon to entertain and would not have restrained rape. Therefore the marriage of half-siblings must have been acceptable in those days.[4]

The rabbis of the talmudic period also thought Tamar's suggestion decisive and infer from it that Tamar was somehow permitted to marry Amnon by Jewish law. As a plausible though legalistic explanation for the acceptability of the union, they propose her mother was an unconverted war captive when Tamar was conceived, and so Tamar was not the daughter of a legitimate marriage.[5] Mindful of David's honor and reputation as beloved of God and hero of the Jewish people, traditionalists do not believe he would have condoned incest, and therefore they follow the talmudic teaching.

Between these camps is a middle ground. Jan Fokkelman, for example, finds approval of brother/half-sister marriage in Genesis 20:12. Even though the union of Amnon and Tamar antedates the giving of the law at Sinai, he maintains the prohibitions listed in Leviticus and Deuteronomy cannot be applied, as the "extratextual facts" conflict, and the incest question must be decided wholly within the text of 2 Samuel 13. He decides it by pointing out that Amnon's impasse in v. 2 is caused by Tamar's virginity, not by her consanguinity. He also agrees with both the source critics

---

[2] Shimon Bar-Efrat, *Narrative Art in the Bible* (Sheffield: Almond, 1989), 240. Charles Conroy lists scholars on both sides of the question (*Absalom, Absalom!* [Rome: Biblical Institute Press, 1978], 17–18 nn. 3, 4).

[3] On the other hand, some scholars date the Pentateuch to the tenth century B.C.E., in which case the books of the Pentateuch, the writing of Samuel, and the early monarchy would all be contemporary. See, for example, Gary Rendsburg, "David and His Circle in Genesis 38," *VT* 36 (1986): 438; "Reading David in Genesis," *Bible Review* 17, no. 1 (February 2001): 20–33, 46. Susan Rattray considers the possibility that the rules of Leviticus were known, but the royal family was exempt ("Marriage Rules, Kinship Terms and Family Structure in the Bible" [*SBLSP* 26, 1987], 538 n. 4).

[4] For example, William Propp, "Kinship in 2 Samuel 13," *CBQ* 55 (1993): 45 n. 22.

[5] *b. Sanhedrin* 21a.

and the traditionalists that Tamar's appeal for marriage is a "genuine alternative" that proves the legality of such an affiliation.[6]

From my perspective, the order in which the books of the Hebrew Bible were composed is immaterial. My bias is toward a text that has, at the least, been heavily edited by a master of literary sophistication for an audience of acute sensibility. I believe the inspired "author" (authors, editors, final redactor) intended it to be read as an integrated, consecutive, coherent document. Accounting for what others have explained away as misplaced verses, grammatical anomalies, and other errors, this chapter will show that incest can be established within the text but that rape cannot. Although to other feminist exegetes the so-called rape of Tamar is a proof text of male domination, my analysis will demonstrate that it is a story of woman's opportunity to be an agent for peace and of Tamar's failure in that agency.

In 2 Samuel 13:1 we are unnecessarily, redundantly informed that Absalom and Amnon are sons of David. Their patrimony was established in 3:2–3 and need not be repeated.[7] Tamar, who is introduced for the first time in 13:1, is not identified as a daughter of David.[8] The reticence about her parentage admits the possibility that she is not a daughter of David and that she and her brother, Absalom, are half-siblings through their mother. She and Amnon (half-brother to Absalom on the father's side) would therefore have no common parent, and the love Amnon bears for Tamar would be appropriate.[9]

This possibility is obviated in v. 2 when Tamar is delineated further as Amnon's sister also. Why are readers given the opportunity for confusion in v. 1? It might be to lead them on a short trip down the garden path, complacent in the contemplation of Tamar's beauty and Amnon's love, only to confront them with an uncomfortable fact in the next verse. With a shock, their sentimental image of licit romance is superseded by an incest problem. Had this been the author's sole aim, he could have achieved it more economically by omitting both "son of David" phrases. Instead, by the inclusion of these phrases, he both jolts the reader and dissociates

---

[6] Jan P. Fokkelman, *King David* (vol. 1; *Narrative Art and Poetry in the Books of Samuel;* Assen: van Gorcum, 1981), 103.

[7] Jenny Smith says the repetition serves the "very practical function of reminding the hearers that David has two sons called Absalom and Amnon" ("The Discourse Structure of the Rape of Tamar," *VE* 20 [1990]: 24). This would then be an exceptional case; the biblical audience seemed to enjoy genealogies (hence those long series of "begats") and to be able to remember them.

[8] Van Dijk-Hemmes notes this omission with no comment ("Tamar and the Limits," 139). Bar-Efrat says that Tamar is defined as Absalom's sister to indicate that she is his full sister (*Narrative Art*, 241).

[9] Against Bar-Efrat, who says, "From v. 1 where we read that Tamar is Absalom's sister and that both Absalom and Amnon are David's sons, it is clear that Tamar is Amnon's sister by his father" (*Narrative Art*, 244).

Tamar from David. Absalom is a true son of David in his propensity for revenge; Amnon is a true son of David in his desire for a woman forbidden to him, but Tamar, so dense and tactless (as we shall see), is completely unlike her father in this regard (1 Samuel 16:18).

We learn that Amnon loves Tamar from the omniscient narrator in 2 Samuel 13:1 and from Amnon's direct speech in v. 4. He expresses his love vigorously by placing the verb in the emphatic final position of the sentence.[10] Indeed, he loves Tamar so much he becomes ill for love of her. If he *could* marry her, as most commentators posit, why does he not do so? Men were allowed multiple wives; what difference would one more make? Such a marriage would serve his interest politically, for it would solidify his position as putative heir to the throne; David's firstborn son legally married to a daughter of David's would have a formidable claim.[11]

If most analysts are correct and Amnon could gratify his desire by marrying Tamar, the fact that Amnon loves his sister raises no dramatic tension. In order to provide a conflict, they must assume Amnon is a scoundrel. They need to paint him as a villain of so deep a dye that he prefers rape to the easily attained fulfillment of his love in a politically advantageous marriage. With their understanding of the law, they must postulate Amnon's caddishness, for, without it, there is no reason for the story to develop along any lines other than simply "boy meets girl, boy loves girl, boy marries girl." Though the reader has not been given a textual basis to suppose Amnon's love any less honorable than the love of Jacob for Rachel, Phyllis Trible, certain of his "brutality" and "cruelty," translates "love" as "desire" throughout. In speaking of Amnon's illness, she coins a new word, "lust-sickness."[12]

In v. 2 we learn that in Amnon's eyes it is hard/difficult or wonderful/marvelous to do anything regarding Tamar. The word פלא has both meanings and both are simultaneously descriptive here. It is impossible for him to do anything regarding her because she "is a virgin," but in his love-sick fantasies, doing something to or for Tamar would be extraordinarily wondrous. The expression לה is always translated here as "to her," bolstering the universal rape interpretation, but "for her" is equally correct.[13] For all

---

[10] Phyllis Trible, *Texts of Terror* (Philadelphia: Fortress, 1984), 40; Conroy, *Absalom, Absalom!*, 29.

[11] That marriage to the king's daughter is an advantage to the succession is shown by Saul's retraction of Michal (1 Samuel 25:44) and by David's insistence on regaining her (2 Samuel 3:13).

[12] Trible, *Texts of Terror*, 38–40, 46. Trible's translation is adopted by Alice Keefe ("Rapes of Women/Wars of Men," *Semeia* 61 [1993]: 87). Even BDB, which as a dictionary should be neutral, has made up its collective mind about Amnon and defines the verb, אהב, as "love" in every case except in our chapter's citation where it is defined as "of carnal desire" (12–13).

[13] The preposition ל after the infinitive construct לעשות, to do, is used to mean "for," in 2 Samuel 12:4; 2 Kings 4:13–14; Isaiah 63:12, 14; Ezekiel 16:5; 36:37;

we know he may dream of doing something for Tamar, rescuing her from drowning or dragons; we do not know what he wants to do, and neither, I think, does he. The narrator admits us into the privacy of Amnon's thoughts where circumlocutions are unnecessary.[14] If Amnon pines to consummate his love for Tamar, I would think him able to admit his amorous design to himself. Charles Conroy says the reader is "alienated from Amnon . . . from the start, for the euphemism of v. 2 hints fairly clearly at the merely lustful nature of his love."[15] To me, especially in connection with the double meaning of פלא, it hints of Amnon's ambivalence.

To his cousin, Jonadab, Amnon confesses love for Tamar, whom he identifies as Absalom's sister (v. 4). He prefers to gloss over the fact that she is his own half-sister by mentioning only her full relationship with Absalom. Thus he shows his awareness of, and his uneasiness with, the incest problem. Jonadab advises Amnon to feign illness and, when his father visits, to ask that Tamar give him bread, לחם, and prepare food, בריה, in his sight that he might see it and eat at her hand (v. 5). Amnon repeats to his father the elements of seeing and of eating at Tamar's hand, but asks for two heart-cakes, לבבות, instead of bread and food (v. 6). The word, לבבות, that I, along with many others, have translated as "heart-cakes" (because of לבב, heart, embedded in it) may have aphrodisiacal implications.[16] It is frequently associated with the word לבבתני in my epigraph, which is said to mean "sexually aroused me" rather than the familiar rendering, "ravished my heart."[17]

Why does Amnon use this loaded word rather than Jonadab's "bread" or "food" and so expose his libido to his father? Fokkelien van Dijk-Hemmes says it is a slip of the tongue by which Amnon might unconsciously be asking permission for sexual access to his sister.[18] I think Amnon may, equivocally, be seeking both permission and prohibition. The ambiguity in v. 2 shows us he was ambivalent in his intentions toward Tamar, and he has not lost his inhibition.

Job 28:25; Nehemiah 13:7; and 2 Chronicles 25:9. Joel Rosenberg maintains the translation "to" but recognizes the dual sense of פלא as "was wonderful/ was unthinkable" (*King and Kin* [Bloomington: Indiana University Press, 1986], 140).

[14] Smith says these words are a euphemism denoting lustful thoughts; they are used by Amnon to disguise the truth from himself ("The Discourse Structure," 26–27).

[15] Conroy, *Absalom, Absalom!*, 23.

[16] Fokkelman, *King David*, 105–6; van Dijk-Hemmes, "Tamar and the Limits," 140.

[17] P. Kyle McCarter Jr., *II Samuel: A New Translation with Introduction and Commenary* (AB 9; Garden City, N.Y.: Doubleday, 1980), 322 n. 6; Michael Fox, *The Song of Songs and the Ancient Egyptian Love Songs* (Madison: University of Wisconsin Press, 1985), 135; Nahum Waldman, "A Note on Canticles 4:9," *JBL* 89 (1970): 215.

[18] Van Dijk-Hemmes, "Tamar and the Limits of Patriarchy," 140.

It is difficult to imagine David's thoughts upon hearing Amnon's request. If he believes Amnon fears poison, Amnon's mother, if she were alive, or his full sisters, if he had any, would be safer food preparers than the full sister of Absalom, a rival for the throne.[19] Amnon must seem gravely ill. His appearance was sufficiently haggard to cause concern in v. 4, and now he is pretending to be even sicker than he looks. If David, who just lost a son in the preceding chapter (12:19), fears Amnon is dying, he would want to indulge any craving that might comfort or cure him. And, yet, in repeating Amnon's request to Tamar, David rejects the intimacy stipulated by both Jonadab and Amnon in the phrase "from her hand," מידה. He tells his daughter to make her brother food; he does not tell her to serve him. He also censors out the erotic "heart-cakes" and replaces them with בריה (13:7).[20] The word David uses is not a generic word for edibles but the rare noun form of a verb used in 3:35 and 12:17 to signify food appropriate for breaking a fast. This is surely more suitable fare for an emaciated patient than heart-cakes.

Numerous exegetes have said that David is "unwitting" or sends Tamar to Amnon "unwittingly,"[21] but these variations on Amnon's request show that David has his wits about him. He may have made the changes because he thought בריה more curative than heart-cakes, or he may have been conscious of Amnon's secret thoughts and unwilling to encourage his suit by authorizing a tête-à-tête between the siblings. Supposing the latter case, why does he, nevertheless, dispatch Tamar? I think he believes Amnon far too ill to be a threat, knows there will be chaperoning servants about, and trusts his hitherto virtuous daughter to call out in the case of a sexual advance.[22] Mindful of one dead son and apprehensive of losing another, David makes a mistake with Amnon and a mistake with his daughter.[23]

---

[19] Smith says the references to watching Tamar cook and eating at her hand might allude to poison, and, if so, they cast an indirect aspersion on David's court ("The Discourse Structure of the Rape of Tamar," 29).

[20] Against Bar-Efrat who says that to David "it is immaterial what food Tamar prepares for Amnon," (Narrative Art, 255), and Fokkelman who says, "The unsuspecting monarch indeed hears 'a few cakes'" (King David, 105).

[21] David Gunn, The Story of King David (JSOTSup 6, Sheffield: Almond, 1978), 9; George Rideout, "The Rape of Tamar," in Rhetorical Criticism, Essays in Honor of James Muilenburg (ed. Jared J. Jackson and Martin Kessler; Pittsburgh: Pickwick, 1974), 77; Rosenberg, King and Kin, 146; Conroy, Absalom, Absalom!, 18; Trible, Texts of Terror, 42; Keefe, "Rapes of Women," 93.

[22] "If there is a young woman, betrothed to a man, and a man finds her in the city and lies with her, then you shall bring out both of them to the gates of the city and you shall stone them with stones that they die: she, because she did not cry out, being in the city, and the man because he had intercourse with the wife of his neighbor" (Deuteronomy 22:23–24). Though these verses refer to one betrothed, the principle—that the cries of a woman in the city will be overheard—is clear.

[23] Against Gerald Hammond who says that in sending her to Amnon, David plays a "shady part" ("Michal, Tamar, Abigail and What Bathsheba Said: Notes

Obediently, Tamar goes to her half-brother's house and sets about her cooking. Disobediently, she makes heart-cakes (v. 8).[24] The author's use of the minor character, Jonadab, while also indicating that Amnon is not so sly as to originate his stratagem, deftly permits the fourfold repetition of the patient's menu—accenting the psychologically revealing appearance, disappearance, and reappearance of the heart-cakes. The text is careful to tell us that Amnon can observe all Tamar's actions.[25] With what joy the love-sick swain must have watched her work! Either his father relayed the heart-cake request, thus giving his tacit permission for sex, or the heart-cakes are Tamar's flirtatious idea; his love is reciprocated.

As the reader knows, the heart-cakes are indeed Tamar's independent idea. She has another idea; she wants to marry the heir apparent and one day be queen. If she can arouse Amnon's desire with heart-cakes, she is sure her father will not stand in the way of their union (v. 13). After all, theirs would be a liaison no more proscribed than David's with Bathsheba or David's with Michal.[26] It is a foolish aspiration, for it is one thing for David to gratify his own illegal longings and quite another for him to advance someone else's. But Tamar is not a clever woman.

Amnon, doubtless delighting in the sight, watches Tamar until her work is done and then refuses to eat. In direct speech, he orders all men/everyone (כל־איש) out.[27] The narrator, reiterating the point, tells us that everyone leaves. Is Amnon a peevish patient or a vacillating lover? Is he too sick to continue, or has he recognized the impropriety of his incestuous attraction and abandoned his ruse? Is Tamar, her father's assignment accomplished, among those who heed Amnon's directive? We are led to suppose that she is, for, had the author intended simply to record the departure of the servants, he could have said, "Amnon sent his servants away." There would have been no need to introduce the possibility that everyone is commanded to leave nor to repeat the nonspecific phrase in stating that all men/everyone indeed left (v. 9). By the astutely

---

Toward a Really Inclusive Translation of the Bible," in *Women in the Biblical Tradition* [ed. George J. Brooke; Lewiston, N.Y.: E. Mellen, 1992], 62).

[24] Smith is so sympathetic to Tamar, and so determined to believe the rape hypothesis, she challenges the etymology of "heart-cakes" for the reason that, as Tamar made them, they cannot have had an erotic connotation ("The Discourse Structure," 31).

[25] Against Rideout who says, "At this point the narrative becomes even more expansive, introducing details of no particular importance to the basic plot" ("The Rape of Tamar," 79).

[26] David committed adultery with Bathsheba, and, according to Deuteronomy 24:1–4, his first wife, Michal, was forbidden to him after her interim marriage to Palti (1 Samuel 25:44).

[27] Just as in English, the Hebrew for "all men," כל־איש, can refer literally to males or idiomatically to all humankind. See 1 Chronicles 16:3 for a conclusive illustration of the latter usage.

crafted double employment of the ambiguous expression, all men/everyone (כל־איש), the reader is steered to presume Tamar's withdrawal.

As previously noted, Fokkelman assumes Amnon has scruples about violating Tamar's virginity. Amnon's longing, however, is not frustrated by her virginity, for this condition still obtains in vv. 11 and 14 when he finds it quite possible to lay her (a literal, though vulgar, translation). Tamar's maidenhood thwarts Amnon only because it makes her physically inaccessible to him. The necessity for application to David in order to be visited by his sister supports this analysis (v. 6).[28] Virgins, obviously, were not free to visit even sick male siblings.[29] When everyone is ordered from the room, an alarm should go off in the brain of such a sequestered, strictly-raised virgin.

Tamar's work is finished; her father's instructions are fulfilled. Instead of choosing to leave the room with the servants, however, as her upbringing dictates and as the reader expects, Tamar startles us by boldly venturing beyond David's mandate. Remaining alone with Amnon, she accepts the summons to his inner chamber. She joins him with the heart-cakes "that she had made." Both Jenny Smith and Shimon Bar-Efrat find the words "that she had made" in v. 10 redundant. We already know who made the cakes, they argue (they do not specify "heart-cakes," so inconsequential do they find this detail); why stress the fact? Smith believes the repetition slows the narrative and increases suspense. Bar-Efrat says the words convey a hint of irony in that Amnon does not eat the food that has been prepared.[30] I contend the words are repeated here to show Tamar's complicity in the coming denouement.

The words ויחזק בה in v. 11, usually translated as "And he took her," need convey no physical menace. A better translation for these same words (allowing for the gender difference בו/בה, him/her) is that employed in Judges 19:4, "And he urged [her]."[31] This rendering respects both the high regard in which Amnon still holds Tamar and his tender appeal which follows, "Come lie with me, my sister."

If Amnon were committing rape, why need he importune Tamar at all? He could take her and ravish her without a word, as Shechem takes Dinah in Genesis 34:2. Amnon's invitation shows he is not heartlessly indifferent to resistance, but is an ardent lover seeking concession and even reciprocity. The words "come" and "with" imply mutuality. The phrase "my sister," while it underscores the incest, is a term of affection as in my epigraph.[32]

---

[28] Thus, contra Fokkelman (see my note 6), the incest factor cannot be dismissed by Amnon's use of "virgin" rather than "sister" in v. 2.

[29] With McCarter who says "most commentators" agree virginity was vigilantly safeguarded (*II Samuel*, 321 n. 2).

[30] Smith, "The Discourse Structure of the Rape of Tamar," 33; Bar-Efrat, *Narrative Art*, 256.

[31] See also 2 Kings 4:8.

[32] Bar-Efrat says, "He speaks to her gently, in a tone designed to win her heart," *Narrative Art*, 259.

So entrenched, however, is the conviction that Amnon is a ruthless rapist, that P. Kyle McCarter, in the AB, liberally translates the request as a demand—"'Come on, sister!' He said to her. 'Lie with me!'"—making Amnon sound like a gangster.[33] Even so sensitive and meticulous an exegete as Robert Alter omits the persuasive "come" in his analysis and says, "Amnon addresses to his half-sister exactly the same words with which Potiphar's wife accosts Joseph—'lie with me'—adding to them only one word [sic], the thematically loaded 'sister' (2 Samuel 13:11)."[34] He includes all Amnon's words in a later work but still labels his supplication a "brutally direct imperative."[35] On the contrary, linguistically Amnon's entreaty is affectionate, and phonetically it is mellifluous and poetic, for in Hebrew all four of his words rhyme.

Sexual intercourse between an unbetrothed virgin and a man to whom she is not related constitutes marriage, but, even though Tamar wants matrimony and considers the half-sibling relationship no impediment, this impetuous disregard of marital protocol is unseemly. There ought to be a betrothal, a bride-price, whatever court etiquette dictates for the nuptials of a king's daughter, whatever is usually done in Israel (יעשה כן בישראל, v. 12). Were she to submit to an indecorous and hasty tryst, she would not only miss out on the betrothal amenities, but she might also suffer derision and bear reproach (אוליך את־חרפתי, v. 13) as a loose woman for having been alone with a man in a position to be seduced. And what if word of those heart-cakes circulated?

Tamar is willing to flirt, to arouse Amnon's desire with libidinous confections, and to be alone with him after the servants depart, but this quick coupling without parental permission or preparation is not what she wants. Her assurance to Amnon in v. 13 that the king will not refuse him her hand tells us her objective. Many commentators, as noted above, maintain Tamar's exhortation proves that half-sibling marriage is legal; if it were not, her suggestion is nonsensical as a deterrent. In fact her suggestion does not deter Amnon and proves only that, in her ignorance, her foolishness, or her ambition, *she* believes she and Amnon can marry in propriety and with David's blessing.

In Scripture, calling out is the efficacious response to sexual assault, but Tamar is not being attacked, and she does not call out.[36] She attempts to curb Amnon's impetuosity with argument. Her first words to him in vv. 12–13 contain four negatives. (The italics are, of course, mine.) "*No,*

---

[33] McCarter, *II Samuel*, 314.

[34] Robert Alter, *Art of Biblical Narrative* (New York: Basic, 1981), 73.

[35] Robert Alter, "Putting Together Biblical Narrative," in *Cabinet of the Muses: Essays on Classical and Comparative Literature in Honor of Thomas G. Rosenmayer* (ed. Mark Griffith and Donald Mastronarde; Atlanta: Scholars Press, 1990), 120.

[36] See my note 22.

my brother. Do *not* subdue me, for it is *not* done thus in Israel. Do *not* do this foolish thing." She then speaks first of herself and asks rhetorically where she will go with the reproach she will receive. Speaking next of him, she predicts that he will be "like one of the fools in Israel," and, finally, she asks that Amnon go to the king, "for he will not withhold me from you."[37] It would have been simpler and more direct for her to have said: "for he will give me to you," and so her phraseology catches our attention—of which more later.

Tamar's words are ineffective. Not only does Amnon go on to have his way with her, but he also comes to hate her. What should she have said? The Bible answers this question in advance by providing an example of a woman's skillful deterrence in the sister-text to this pericope, 1 Samuel 25. I call the scene between David and Abigail a sister-text because of the duplication of theme and language in the two chapters. Although the physical settings of the two scenes differ, both women are faced with passionate men bent on wrongdoing. Both offer food in the preface to the confrontation. Both attempt to control the behavior of the men and assuage their intensity by force of argument. Abigail succeeds and averts bloodshed at a sheep-shearing party; Tamar fails and fratricide at a sheep-shearing party results. Abigail engenders admiration in her initially hostile adversary and, finally, marries him. Tamar provokes hatred in her initially loving pursuer and seems to live forever single.

The use of identical language in the two chapters, especially terminology exclusive to these passages, adds rhetorical emphasis to the thematic intertextuality. The word for sheep-shearers, גוזזים, is used in Scripture only in these two chapters. The expression "withheld me," that we noticed in 2 Samuel 13:13, occurs only there and in the Abigail scene (1 Samuel 25:34). The locution "from her hand"—a *Leitwort* in 2 Samuel 13 (vv. 5, 6, and in v. 10: "from your hand") —also occurs only there and in the Abigail scene (1 Samuel 25:35).

Additional evidence of the thematic nexus between the chapters is the summary of David's treatment of Abigail in 1 Samuel 25:35. David's acts are not recited in order of their performance, as one would expect, but instead are named in the order in which Amnon performs the opposite of these same acts in 2 Samuel 13. The tension created by the otherwise inexplicable progression in 1 Samuel 25:35 is resolved by the sequence of events in 2 Samuel 13.[38] David is said to accept what she brings him from

---

[37] BDB defines נבל as foolish, senseless, or churlish with the collateral idea of ignobility and disgrace—especially with sins of unchastity (614).

[38] Because the inventory of David's actions is not listed in the order in which they occur in 1 Samuel 25, Fokkelman says the last three clauses of 1 Samuel 25:35 are inverted as a *hysteron proteron* (*The Crossing Fates* [vol. 2; *Narrative Art and Poetry*; Assen: van Gorcum, 1986], 519). Such reordering is uncharacteristic of Fokkelman, who sternly calls McCarter a "bull in a china shop" for placing v. 31 after v. 26 (513).

Abigail's hand; Amnon does not seem to take what she brings him from the hand of Tamar. David says עלי, "go up," to Abigail; in his lover's petition to Tamar, Amnon says בואי, "come"—the reader may supply the implied moral and physical direction, i.e., down (to his bed). Abigail is sent by David in peace (שלם, wholeness, completeness) to her own house; Tamar is callously dismissed by Amnon, hymen and garment torn, and she dwells in the house of her brother. David says he heard Abigail's voice; Amnon would not hearken to Tamar (v. 16). Finally, David says he lifted Abigail's countenance (made her happy and smiling); whereas we see that Amnon's conduct casts down Tamar's countenance, leaving her wailing, with ashes of mourning on her head. David's words in 1 Samuel 25:35 gain increased resonance because "your house," "your voice," and "your countenance," the final words of his three clauses, rhyme in Hebrew (just as Amnon's sexual invitation to Tamar rhymed) and will ring in the reader's memory when compared to 2 Samuel 13.

Oblique allusion to the analogy between these texts is insinuated further by less striking (because not restricted to these two chapters) verbal correspondences. The word חרף, reproach, occurs in 2 Samuel 13:13; 1 Samuel 25:39, and five other places in the Bible. The curious name of Abigail's husband, נבל, fool, villain, is the root of Tamar's words, "foolish thing" and "fools in Israel."[39] In Abigail's peroration to David, she predicts that he will be bound in the bundle of life with God (v. 29). "Bound" and "bundle" share the root צרר, straits, distress. Her figure of speech is unique and is the only distinctly amiable application of this root in the Bible.[40] The doubling of the root may be employed to secure the reader's attention. In 2 Samuel 13:2 the narrator uses the same root to tell us of Amnon's distress. The atypical positive use of צרר applied to David contrasts with its negative denotation when applied to Amnon. Scripture suggests; it does not insist. The reader may be led as early as the second verse in our chapter to compare Amnon to David and one scene to the other.

The inference made by the signal thematic and verbal parallels of these two chapters is that had she followed the example of Abigail, whose words are a paradigm of artful persuasion, Tamar would have halted Amnon's lust and kept his love. Abigail does not say "no" to David, put consideration of herself first, predict an evil name for him, or omit men-

---

[39] Robert Polzin finds similarities between 2 Samuel 13 and Judges 19–21 (especially in the use of the word נבלה, foolishness) and draws parallels between the tragedies in David's immediate family and the history of Israel (*David and the Deuteronomist: 2 Samuel* [Bloomington: University of Indiana Press, 1992], 137–38); Rendsburg finds seven correspondences between the story of Amnon and Tamar and the Genesis story of Judah and Tamar and concludes the latter was written during David's monarchy as a political satire ("David and His Circle," 445).

[40] The root is, of course, frequently used with neutral coloration.

tion of God. She abases herself, calling him "my lord" and herself "your handmaid," takes blame upon herself instead of casting it on David, and flatteringly predicts God will reward him by slinging out his enemies and making him a prince over Israel (as opposed to Tamar's "fool in Israel").[41] Her speech is also quite long, giving David time to calm down (1 Samuel 25:24–31). In the course of her monologue she repeats the sacred tetragrammaton seven times (vv. 26 [twice], 28 [twice], 29, 30, 31). Seven is a mystical number in Scripture used to influence events by divine power.[42] Abigail uses the potent formula here to gain the aid of God in diverting David from violence.

Abigail is introduced as intelligent and, secondly, as beautiful (v. 3).[43] Tamar is only beautiful (2 Samuel 13:1). The Bible teaches physical beauty in a woman or in a man is not enough.[44] The narrative's original audience, primed by Abigail's brilliant rhetorical ability, and prompted to make a comparison, must have writhed at Tamar's gaucherie and stupidity.[45] To approach the skill of Abigail's oratory, and to effect an equally salutary outcome, Tamar needed to say something similar to the words improvised below (but at a length sufficient to allow Amnon's fervor to subside):

> Upon your handmaid, my lord; upon your handmaid is the blame. Your handmaid should not have tempted my lord with heart-cakes, for, as God lives and as thy soul lives, my lord is beloved of the king and is stainless in his sight. Surely, as my lord has not offended him in any way, he will make thee his successor over all thy brothers, and thou shall have a sure house in Israel. Blessed be God who has kept thee from transgression. And when the king shall have dealt well with my lord, remember your handmaid.

Here is persuasion—not a negative word, no mention of fools or foolishness, just reminders of God, of the king's regard, and of the likelihood of Amnon's succession to the throne. Could Amnon have hated the speaker of such honeyed words? Hardly. But Tamar is no Abigail, and her speech is quite different from the one synthesized above.

---

[41] In "Characterization in Biblical Narrative: David's Wives," *JSOT* 23 (1982): 77, Adele Berlin says Abigail's prophesy of David's eventual authority "is hardly relevant to the events of the Abigail story"; Alice Bach denigrates Abigail's "cloying humility" in "The Pleasure of Her Text," *USQR* 43 (1989): 43.

[42] Seven priests bearing seven ram's horns circling Jericho seven times on the seventh day in Joshua 6:4 is but one example of the use of this number. In 1 Samuel 28, Samuel uses the same sevenfold repetition of God's name in a futile attempt to turn Saul from his treacherous course. See Chapter Nine, p. 157.

[43] Hammond prefers the REB translation which reverses the order of these adjectives because, he says, David values beauty over intelligence ("Michal, Tamar, Abigail and What Bathsheba Said," 66).

[44] Absalom, who commits fratricide and goes to war against his father, is praised for beauty over all others in Israel (2 Samuel 14:25).

[45] Trible says Tamar is "the wise woman"; she "replied with wisdom" and "continues to speak wise words" (*Texts of Terror*, 56).

Crucial to the interpretation of v. 14 is the translation of the verb ענה, which I have construed above as "subdued." Although the verb censures the incestuous act, it specifies only heterosexual intercourse.[46] Usually translated here as "forced," "ravished," "defiled," or "humbled," it may, with equal correctness, be translated as "subdued" or "seduced"—in the sense that the woman acquiesced, submitted, accepted the man as her husband.[47] Amnon, more adamant, חזק, than Tamar,[48] first subdues or seduces her, ענה, and then lays her, שכב אֹתָהּ. Because שכב is accompanied by the impersonal definite direct object indicator, אֹתָהּ, the coarse expression is a more literal translation than "lays *with* her."[49] This is not to suggest that two separate sex acts took place; the use of these two verbs, in this order, with their respective suffix or direct object indicator connotes a change in Amnon's feelings.[50] His regard for Tamar undergoes development. Once she surrenders to him, he no longer sees her as an ideal of virtue; she becomes an object of lust in his eyes.

Amnon had admired Tamar's virginity. It was not a stumbling block to him; it was proof of her virtue. We may assume the moral tone of the court is low, for the king sets the standard for his people and the model for his children. If the father stoops to adultery, attempts passing off his child as another's, and conspires to accomplish manslaughter, we are not surprised when his children commit incest and fratricide. Virginity may have been a rare attribute at David's court.

Amnon adored Tamar's chastity, but now he sees that the woman once thought so pure not only flirts, but submits to intercourse without attempting to call out (we learn in v. 17 that her call would have been heard),[51] has inane ideas about sibling marriage, and, additionally, has

---

[46] Moshe Weinfeld says, "When used in connection with women the verb ענה appears, then, to connote sexual intercourse in general rather than rape, and it is to be rendered accordingly" (*Deuteronomy and the Deuteronomic School* [Oxford: Clarendon, 1972], 286).

[47] Note that in v. 12 Tamar is resisting seduction not rape. The current convention is that the reluctance of one partner precludes further suit, but it is not so very long (1924) since a popular song lyric said, "Your lips tell me 'No, no,' but there is 'Yes, yes' in your eyes." In the Bible, genuine protest is signified by calling out (see note 22).

[48] Though חזק is often rendered here as "stronger," implying physical strength, it may be translated as "resolute" or "unyielding" as in Deuteronomy 12:23.

[49] Fokkelman, *King David*, 105, and Trible, *Texts of Terror*, 47, agree with me that the use of the direct object indicator here serves to objectify Tamar. According to Conroy its use is pejorative, *Absalom, Absalom!*, 32.

[50] Alter says the narrator gives us "a string of three verbs where one would suffice" ("Putting Together," 121). However, חזק (firm, determined) is not used as a verb, and the two verbs are necessary to express Amnon's transition from love to hate.

[51] Amnon's servants hear and respond to his summons. Though it might be argued that Tamar does not call out because she believes Amnon's attendants will not come to her aid, she can be certain neither of their reaction nor of the range of

more or less called him a scoundrel. In the course of v. 14 Amnon's love turns to hate. Tamar is the archetype of the virgin who gives in to immoral suasion and is not respected in the morning. Analysts who consider Tamar's speech eloquent, and do not even conceive of her consent, explain Amnon's revulsion of feeling as a sort of heightened post-coital *tristesse* or as projection: rather than acknowledge his own guilt, Amnon hates the object of his lechery.[52] In my exegesis, Amnon may well recognize their mutual guilt in the crime of incest, making him all the more resentful of Tamar's apparent insensibility to the transgression.

The verb treatment of the rape scene in Genesis 34:2, which reverses that of 2 Samuel 13:14, corroborates my reading above. In this verse, Shechem ceases to objectify Dinah and falls in love with her. At the beginning of the verse, he sees, not Dinah, but a direct object with a feminine suffix, וַיַּרְא אֹתָהּ. He takes this object, וַיִּקַּח אֹתָהּ, and lays it, וַיִּשְׁכַּב אֹתָהּ. (Amnon, by contrast, takes or urges an individual, a "her," בָהּ.) After laying the object, Shechem then seduces "her" וַיְעַנֶּהָ—no direct object indicator; she transforms from an object to a person to him. In the next verse we are told his soul cleaves to Dinah, he loves her (and, to her, he becomes a lover). Here, in Genesis as in 2 Samuel, two verbs are necessary to describe emotional development during the sexual act. A pivotal metamorphism is conveyed by the verbs, by their order, and by the use of either the dehumanizing direct object indicator or the personalizing suffix "her."[53] The second verb and choice of particle or suffix reveal a change of heart: a rapist becomes a lover in Genesis 34, and a lover becomes a hater in 2 Samuel 13. In each instance this lexical representation of growing affection or disaffection is affirmed by the text: "And his soul clung to Dinah, daughter of Jacob, and he loved the girl, and he spoke to the heart of the girl" (Genesis 34:3); "Then Amnon hated her with a very great hatred, so

---

her voice. By the Bible's unequivocal acceptance that the cry of a woman in the city will be heard (Deuteronomy 22:24), the reader understands that, in urban situations, a shout will invariably achieve succor. Failure to call out is legally valid proof of consent according to Deuteronomy. That the Bible records no outcry from Tamar (a woman in the city, within earshot of help) conclusively compromises her virtue, confirming complicity. Contrariwise, report of Dinah's cries is unnecessary. The silence of Scripture in this regard does not incriminate Dinah (Genesis 34:2), as futile screams are always assumed of a woman taken in the field ("But if, in the field, a man finds a betrothed woman and the man seizes her and lies with her, only the man who lay with her dies. Do nothing to her . . . for he found her in the field; she cried out, but there was none to save her" [Deuteronomy 22:25–27]).

[52] Rideout, "The Rape of Tamar," 82; McCarter, *II Samuel*, 324; van Dijk-Hemmes, "Tamar and the Limits of Patriarchy," 142.

[53] Against David Freedman, who says, "As the two verbs seem to be synonymous, it is difficult to imagine that the meaning could be affected by reversing the order" ("Dinah and Shechem, Tamar and Amnon," *Austin Seminary Bulletin* 105 [1990]: 54).

that the hatred with which he hated her was greater than the love with which he had loved her" (2 Samuel 13:15).

The Talmud says the penultimate verb in Genesis 34:2 refers to natural intercourse and the final verb to unnatural intercourse.[54] Meir Sternberg finds the use of the direct object indicator, אֹתָהּ with שכב, "reduces the victim to a mere object" in Genesis, but he continues that the employment of more than one verb "quashes the idea of seduction" and "calls for an integration of the verbs in some ascending order of violence."[55] Nahum Sarna also says the verb order implies that Shechem intensifies his ferocity toward Dinah.[56] Shechem does accost Dinah as a rapist, but it is counterintuitive and inconsistent with the text to conclude that a man falling in love increases the viciousness of his attack. The Bible, furthermore, indicates intensity by a doubled use of the same verbal root rather than by the use of two different verbs.[57]

As the sequence of verbs in Genesis 34:2 leads Sternberg and Sarna to claim Shechem rapes Dinah with progressively greater savagery, the logical extension of their position is that in 2 Samuel 13:14, where the verb order is reversed, the obverse is indicated: Amnon addresses Tamar with progressively greater tenderness. Here again, it offends common sense and opposes the text to presume that a man who has come to hate his partner treats her with escalating sensitivity. In contradiction to the opinions above, I submit the use of two verbs in each passage, coupled with their personalizing or depersonalizing suffix or particle, demonstrates evolving affective attitudes. The transposed order of these terms in 2 Samuel 13 relative to Genesis 34 accords with the narrator's statements that Amnon comes to hate his partner and that Shechem comes to love his.

Amnon brutally expels Tamar after sex. She protests ejection in anguish: "[There is] no cause! This is a greater wrong than the other that you did with me, to send me away" (2 Samuel 13:16). Notice she says "with me." Though the Hebrew clearly says "with" (עם), translators, tenacious of the rape hypothesis, unwarrantedly say "to."[58] Tamar's use of "with" is another indication of her consent.

---

[54] b. Yoma 77b.

[55] Meir Sternberg, *The Poetics of Biblical Narrative* (Bloomington: University of Indiana Press, 1985), 446.

[56] Nahum Sarna, "The Ravishing of Dinah: A Commentary on Genesis, Chapter 34," in *Studies in Jewish Education and Judaica in Honor of Louis Newman* (ed. Alexander M. Shapiro and Burton I. Cohen; New York: Ktav, 1984), 145.

[57] This stylistic device is ubiquitous throughout the Bible; see Genesis 2:17; 18:10; and Exodus 17:14 for just three examples among hundreds.

[58] BDB translates עם as "with" when used with the verb, עשה, in the sense of "do," "work" (794). For examples of conjoint action using this verb/preposition combination, see Exodus 34:10; 1 Samuel 14:45; and Ruth 2:19. Even in combinatorial phrases often translated as "do kindness to," BDB translates: "do kindly with" (see Genesis 24:12; 2 Samuel 2:5; 10:2).

Followers of the rape theory struggle to explain why a savaged woman is so determined to remain in the presence of her attacker; they also wrestle with the question of why she considers being ousted worse than rape. McCarter and Bar-Efrat quote Exodus 22:15–16 (that a virgin's seducer shall pay a bride-price for her to be his wife), and Deuteronomy 22:28–29 (that rules if a man lies with a virgin, he must make her his wife and never send her away). They assume Tamar's objection is based on these verses.[59] Bar-Efrat further states that Tamar may be concerned with her future social status. Fokkelman, as well as George Rideout, say that Amnon's rejection sentences Tamar to a bleak future for he renders her unmarriageable.[60] Although he holds her guiltless, William Propp says her failure to cry out might expose her to criminal conviction (see Deuteronomy 22:24).[61]

My view is that, as she believes sibling marriage legal, Tamar is convinced she and Amnon are husband and wife by virtue of intercourse. Dismissing her is divorcing her; the verb she uses, שלח, also means "divorce."[62] To Tamar, the only conceivable ground for divorce immediately after intercourse is contested virginity. Deuteronomy 22:13–21 says if a man marries and then brings wanton charges and an evil name against his bride, saying he did not find the tokens of virginity in her, her parents are to display the tokens of her virginity: "And they shall spread this garment before the elders of the city" (v. 17). The elders fine the man and require him to stay married to the woman for life. If, however, the tokens of virginity are not found, the woman is stoned to death because she "played

---

[59] McCarter, *II Samuel*, 324; Bar-Efrat, *Narrative Art*, 267.

[60] Fokkelman, *King David*, 108; Rideout, "The Rape of Tamar," 76. I do not agree that lack of virginity precludes marriage, nor do I concur with McCarter and Bar-Efrat (see preceding note) that Deuteronomy 22:28–29 reflects on the future marriageability of the maiden. These verses discourage rape by imposing a stricture on the rapist. Without the law prohibiting divorce in such cases, affluent men could pay the virgin's father the bride-price, satisfy the obligation to marry, and institute divorce when desire subsided—thus relinquishing responsibility and perhaps abandoning an already pregnant woman. That the verses do not imply the unmarriageability of rape victims is shown by the absence of any law regulating the remarriage of such a woman should her enforced marriage end in widowhood. Exodus 22:15–16, which sets the fine a seducer must pay if the virgin's father absolutely refuses such a son-in-law, is further verification that a deflowered maiden remains marriageable, for it is implausible that a father would spurn his daughter's only possible mate.

[61] Propp, "Kinship in 2 Samuel 13," 47 n. 31.

[62] BDB, 1019 (see Deuteronomy 24:1). Tamar uses the *piel* form of שלח (divorce, dismiss). Amnon, in the very next verse, 2 Samuel 13:17, uses the *qal* form (send). The variation reveals to the Hebrew reader a delicate (and untranslated) disparity in the couple's assessment of the situation. Tamar, under the impression that a marriage has been consummated, perceives divorce; whereas Amnon, from his bachelor perspective, sees dispatch.

the harlot in her father's house" (v. 17). Tamar's cry: "[There is] no cause!" affirms her previously virginal state. In her fixed opinion she is wed to Amnon. His divorcing her, bringing an evil name against her, shaming her father, and exposing her to possible stoning is far worse than marriage without parental permission. Amnon's humiliating expulsion of Tamar is boorish, but the reader can understand his wish to put a barred door between himself and such a relentlessly marriage-minded woman.

The Bible now alludes to the distinctive garment Tamar wears (2 Samuel 13:18). McCarter considers this reference a mere "antiquarian notice" describing the fashion of the time. He asserts it is out of place here and better located where her robe is again mentioned—after the servant puts her out and bolts the door.[63] This is not an observation of couture, however, nor a literary infelicity that needs revision; this is evidence. Upon this robe is Tamar's hymeneal blood, the token of her virginity. The possibility that her blood-stained robe is seen by witnesses *before* she leaves Amnon's room is established by this opportune report. Without such testimony, she has no case. If her robe were referred to only after the door were bolted behind her, she might be suspected of purposely bloodying it herself when alone.

At least two witnesses are required by Hebrew law in capital cases (Deuteronomy 17:6), and only one servant seems to have expelled Tamar. Yet in 2 Samuel 13:17, the text hints at the presence of the necessary second witness when Amnon, ordering "this female" sent away, uses the imperative plural form of the verb "send," as though he were talking to more than one servant.[64] Further support for this reading is the superfluous "on her" in v. 19, repeating the "on her" in v. 18; the Bible emphasizes that the robe was on Tamar throughout. Those who have read ahead know that an inquiry never takes place. Amnon is not married to Tamar and is not required to keep her. Such a potential exists only in her ambitious dreams, but the first reader is in suspense at this point: is it possible King David will abrogate even the incest prohibition?

Most commentators note the expression describing Tamar's robe is used for Joseph's famous "coat of many colors" (Genesis 37:3) and nowhere else in Scripture. They account for the identity by recalling Joseph's fraternal strife and his attempted seduction by Potiphar's wife. Referring to the evidence of Joseph's death concocted by his brothers, Alter adds: "[Her] fine garment, like his, may well be blood-stained, if one considers that she has just lost her virginity by rape."[65] I propose that just as Joseph's brothers produced evidence of Joseph's blood-stained robe for their father, so does Tamar intend to exhibit her bloody evidence to

---

[63] McCarter, *II Samuel*, 325. In his translation, he relocates this phrase after v. 18b (315).

[64] McCarter says the use of this plural verb is "a simple error" (*II Samuel*, 318).

[65] Alter, "Putting Together Biblical Narrative," 120.

her father and to the community. The Bible uses the same words to denote the two robes so that the reader does not overlook the significance of a blood-stained garment as validating proof.

Rape victims often hide their shame. If Tamar had been raped by her brother and was concerned that the loss of virginity would spoil her marriage prospects, it would be in her self-interest to cover up the event. Amnon would be unlikely to brag of such degeneracy. But Tamar makes a public outcry: "And she went her way and she cried" (2 Samuel 13:19). Bar-Efrat, among others, says the word used for "cried," זעק, has a "legal connotation, being sometimes used with regard to lodging a complaint with the authorities."[66] I suggest the reason for Tamar's open display is her expectation that her prior virginity will be officially acknowledged, forcing Amnon to accept the marriage and keep her all his days (Deuteronomy 22:19).

Fortunately, before Tamar reaches her father, her brother Absalom intercepts her. It is not likely that she purposely goes to Absalom for protection or vengeance.[67] She seeks her father because she still desires a match with the crown prince. Nevertheless, her wail and her hand-to-head posture make a sufficient spectacle to attract attention, and Absalom may have been skulking about his brother's apartments. Jonadab, David's nephew, is cousin to both Amnon and Absalom. That he is privy to the confidence of both brothers is shown by Amnon's revelation of his love to his cousin and by Jonadab's inside knowledge of Absalom's long held secret resentment in v. 32. Jonadab may have told Absalom about Amnon's scheme simply because he was a busybody, stirring his spoon in every pot. The Bible hints at this trait by his questioning of Amnon, by his offering of unsolicited advice in v. 5, and by his answer, ענה, in v. 32 to David before any question is asked.

Absalom cautiously interrogates Tamar (v. 20). As he asks only if Amnon has been with her, his question can be interpreted as comprehending either consensual sex or rape. Advocates of the rape theory have varying explanations for the vagueness of Absalom's inquiry. Smith, for example, says Absalom's euphemism has "a hollow, cynical ring."[68] Bar-Efrat's more popular explanation is that the euphemism is employed to spare Tamar's feelings and discreetly blur the reality of the outrage.[69] Glossing over such a traumatic event, however, would deny the legitimacy of her grief and would hardly be a therapeutically sound way to calm her if that were indeed Absalom's intention. The woeful sight of Tamar is sufficient to convince Absalom of the reason for her cry. His question is

---

[66] Bar-Efrat, *Narrative Art,* 267.

[67] Against J. Jacob Hoftijzer, "Absalom and Tamar: A Case of Fratriarchy?" in *Schrift en Uitleg* (ed. D. S. Attema et al.; Kampen: J. H. Kok, 1970), 60.

[68] Smith, "The Discourse Structure of the Rape of Tamar," 40.

[69] Bar-Efrat, *Narrative Art,* 270.

equivocal, and he silences her before she can answer because he does not wish to hear that answer; he chooses to view the coitus as rape (vv. 22 and 32). Envious, perhaps, of Amnon's primogeniture and encouraged by dynastic aspirations, he prefers to believe the worst of his brother.

Absalom's deliberately erroneous assessment will rationalize murder. The duplicate theme in Genesis 34 and 2 Samuel 13 of penetrated virgin, parental immobility, and sibling revenge fosters intertextual analogy, enriching both texts. Justifying their homicides, Dinah's brothers say, "Should he treat our sister as a whore?" (Genesis 34:31). Commerce with a prostitute, however, involves neither rape nor marriage. Their distorted appraisal of Shechem corresponds to Absalom's purposeful misreading of Tamar's grief. Just as Dinah's brothers employ a false sanction for their reprisal, so will Absalom nurse and avenge a spurious grievance.

Absalom's brusque silencing of Tamar, "Silence! He is your brother" (2 Samuel 13:20), poses a problem for some adherents of the rape hypothesis. Conroy characterizes the imperative "be silent," חרש, as gentle and comforting, although he does admit: "This is the only text where the imperative of חרש is used in a comforting function."[70] This is exegesis by fiat. The sole reason for him to suppose that in this text, and only in this text, "Silence!" is an imperative expression of comfort is that, if construed in the usual way, it will not fit into his theory.

Fokkelman terms the imperative "a very curt command" and says that, although Absalom wishes to soothe Tamar, he is even more interested in preventing her from (unspecified) legal action. He wants to avenge the rape himself. According to Fokkelman, Absalom adds "He is your brother" to point out that a scandal in the reigning family would be injurious to the monarchy.[71] Fokkelman's reasoning here seems flawed: surely Absalom's premeditated (13:32) murder of his brother is no less a scandal to the monarchy. If Absalom had wanted to preserve the regime from calumny, he would not have committed fratricide.

I believe Absalom grasps the juridical nature of Tamar's cry. He knows the procedure outlined in Deuteronomy 22:13–21 will not be imposed because the king, contrary to Tamar's expectation, will not condone incest. Her absurd conviction of the permissibility of half-sibling marriage annoys him, and thus his gruff, "Silence! He is your brother," both quiets and disabuses her. Her obstinate attachment to a ridiculous marital delusion serves to provoke hatred in one brother and exasperation in the other. Absalom's irritation notwithstanding, he tells Tamar not to take the matter to heart and gives her the protection of his home where a confrontation with her father may be avoided. Mired in the never-never land of her matrimonial fantasy, Tamar does not realize that such an interview would be unpleasant. Awkward questions might be asked about heart-

---

[70] Conroy, *Absalom, Absalom!*, 34 n. 68.
[71] Fokkelman, *King David*, 110–11.

cakes, about remaining alone with Amnon after her cooking was completed, and about failure to call out for help.

In 2 Samuel 13:20, speaking to Tamar, Absalom identifies Amnon as "your brother." The exaggerated repetition of the terms "brother" and "sister" in our pericope is repeatedly remarked upon by commentators. Those who deny that incest was proscribed at this time claim the reiteration indicates merely that Amnon's ardor was unbrotherly and unfamilial.[72] Those who embrace the conviction that incest at the time of the monarchy was a criminal act think, as I do, that the undeniable overemphasis of these terms supports their position.[73] Absalom appends "your brother" to clarify the unreasonableness of Tamar's plan and to underscore the repugnance and gravity of Amnon's offense.

We are told Tamar remains desolate, שממה, in her brother's house. The Hebrew word implies barrenness (Isaiah 54:1), a connotation of interest to the reader who thus learns the succession will not be complicated by the birth of a son to Amnon, nor will David's line be disgraced by the existence of a ממזר (though often translated as "bastard," it designates a child born of incest or adultery). Tamar seems to remain unmarried, and analysts, in exacerbation of Amnon's guilt, proffer that the loss of virginity has rendered her unmarriageable. Yet, nowhere in Scripture is it implied that non-virgins are unmarriageable. On the contrary, we learn in Leviticus 21:14 the only Israelite who must marry a virgin is the high priest. Lack of virginity lowers a woman's bride-price, but history and literature have taught that king's daughters are relatively easy to marry off.[74]

It is David's responsibility, or perhaps Absalom's, since she is living under his protection, to see to Tamar's prospects. David does not do so, I think, because he is angry with her. Absalom does not do so in order to sustain his resentment of Amnon. Were Tamar married and the happy mother of children, it would be more difficult to justify the murder of Amnon when the opportunity for fratricide arose.

David's anger when he hears "these things" (2 Samuel 13:21) is undifferentiated. Many critics accept the LXX addition that, though angry with Amnon, David does not chastise him because he is the beloved firstborn. With Gerald Hammond, I find this gloss "banal"; it impoverishes the text to expound that David's ire is confined to Amnon.[75] David's wrath is undifferentiated in the MT because he is not furious only at Amnon; he is angry at Jonadab, at Tamar, and, most deeply perhaps, at himself. After all, he heard Amnon's request for heart-cakes, he appreciated that such a craving was inappropriate, and he nevertheless sent Tamar to her seducer.

---

[72] For example, Bar-Efrat, *Narrative Art,* 245.
[73] For example, Keefe, "Rapes of Woman," 87.
[74] See my note 60.
[75] Hammond, "Michal, Tamar, Abigail and What Bathsheba Said," 61.

The unusual recurrences of the terms "brother" and "sister" in this chapter not only serve to accent the incestuous fornication, but also make obvious the lack of one particular kinship term: father. David exists as a father only in the imagination of Jonadab (v. 5). Nowhere do his children refer to him as a father, nor does the narrator so refer to him.[76] Throughout the pericope, he is David, the king, or King David. The reader may infer that had he been a good example to his children, their transgressions would not have occurred—not the incest, not the fratricide. As a father (and certainly as ruler and judge) he might be expected to punish Amnon and Tamar, but, just as Nabal turned to stone when Abigail told him "these things," so David becomes immobilized. If punishment were to start, where would it end? How would he punish himself? David's heart, like Nabal's, may have died within him when he learned what his children had done.

The tell-tale heart-cakes, Tamar's willingness to be alone with a man, and her failure to call out all refute a rape verdict. The use of two verbs for intercourse in v. 14 when juxtaposed with the same two verbs in the rape of Dinah passage also testifies against sexual assault. In Genesis the verbs, their order, and their associated particle or suffix signify Shechem's progression from rapist to lover. The syntactical inversion of these same terms in 2 Samuel reveals Amnon's reversed emotional transformation from one who tenderly loves Tamar and desires her reciprocity to one who hates her and demands her removal.

These arguments are compelling evidence for consensual sex, but they are not the only confirmations of Tamar's ability to act independently. As early in chapter 13 as v. 2, readers sensitive to biblical style prick up their ears upon hearing that Amnon is in narrow straits, in distress—that is, bound, as David was twice said by Abigail to be bound. This initial impression of possible association between 1 Samuel 25 and 2 Samuel 13 is strengthened and ratified by word echoes that reverberate throughout these two chapters and nowhere else in the Bible and by corroborating behavioral motifs. Guided by these identities, the reading audience is led to consider the similarities between David's rage and Amnon's passion and the contrasts between Abigail's diplomacy and Tamar's tactlessness. Both David and Amnon are depicted as impulsive, miscreant, initiators of the action; Abigail and Tamar are portrayed as independent agents of possible redemption. The women are not passive receptors but are shown to have the autonomy to conceive and to execute their own plans, shaping the consequences of the men's initiative.

Nabal's only provocation is refusing to yield to David's "protection racket."[77] David is wrong to expect a reward for refraining from harming

---

[76] Contra Danna Fewell and David Gunn who state, "As the story progresses we see David pulled into its purview, as father, and especially as king" (*Narrative in the Hebrew Bible* [Oxford: Oxford University Press, 1993], 150).

[77] Rosenberg, *King and Kin*, 49.

Nabal's shepherds or stealing his sheep (1 Samuel 25:7). Amnon is also wrong to seduce his sister, but these chapters do not focus on the deplorable faults of the men. Their concentration is on the influence, for good or for ill, of the women. There is no doubt that Scripture is androcentric, but in our sister-texts the crux of the narratives center on the disparate attributes of Abigail and Tamar. David's summation in 1 Samuel 25:35 of the happy outcome of the crisis at Carmel, giving full credit to Abigail, prepares us in every mirrored detail for the unhappy outcome in the royal palace and the murder at Baal-hazor—with the implied blame falling on Tamar as the blundering precipitator of disaster, not on Amnon. Quick-witted Abigail cools and curbs David's threatening recklessness. Tamar feeds Amnon's forbidden passion, fails to deter him, falls to his persuasion and her own ambition, allows Absalom's tragic misapprehension, and ensures future bloodshed.

My analysis of the erroneously termed rape of Tamar may be inimical to those who find her cruelly exploited by an oppressive patriarchal society. Partisans of the rape theory may accuse me of blaming the victim, but Tamar is not the victim of male domination; like her eponymous forebear in Genesis 38, she engages willingly in incest. Not only does this interpretation have the advantage of accounting for and integrating what others have termed mistakes or unimportant details, but the culpability of Tamar is more compatible to the larger story than is the blamelessness upheld by previous exegetes. The sins of Amnon and Absalom are the fruit of David's crimes with Bathsheba and Uriah. Those who believe Tamar's innocence is violated consider her undeserved suffering a regrettable concomitant of the retribution meted David. There are, however, no innocents among David's progeny. Tamar's acquiescence to Amnon's immoral entreaty dishonors her father, and the pair of illicit lovers requites David appropriately for his own prohibited carnality.

CHAPTER ELEVEN

Vindicating God: Another Look at 1 Kings 13

When I was a child I decided to be a courtesan when I grew up. I had read about courtesans but did not fully understand the job description. It seemed to me that this occupation consisted of being maintained to the tune of exquisite clothes, jewelry, and dinners at fancy restaurants in return for the pleasure of scintillating conversation. I thought I could handle the scintillating conversation because I also planned to spend my time (whenever I was not actually on the job, talking) attending salons. Nothing seemed to me more enjoyable than going to the homes of cultured, informed, and voluble intellectuals and dining each evening on art, literature, politics, law, science, and philosophy—all seasoned with delicious gossip and witty repartee. I was not sure if any of this happened in America, but it did not matter, as I also intended to know French by the time I was grown.

I never did learn French or become a courtesan, but I did discover that there were salons in America, right in the neighboring town. The cultured, informed, and voluble intellectuals at these salons deliberated all of the above except for gossip, as they were almost all observant Jews who met at one another's houses late Saturday afternoons, from a half-hour before sunset to an hour or so after the Sabbath was over, to read and discuss the Bible. I was already attending the Bible class at the electric company, but that one-hour session had a formal teacher/student format. I liked the idea of sitting around a dining table heaped with salads, fruit, and sweets, drinking soft drinks, coffee, and tea, while issues I wanted to talk about were addressed for longer than an hour by thoughtful, intelligent people I admired and respected.

One of the members of this Shabbos Group sometimes came to my Monday lunch-hour Bible class, and one day I nerved myself to ask her if I could attend their sessions. She was warmly welcoming and told me that, as it happened, the coming Saturday's session was to be at her house. The members took it in turns to lead the group, and that first Saturday the leader was a professor of comparative literature. In expounding the chapter that had fallen to him, he referred to Dante and to some French philosopher I had never heard of. He used Hebrew words without bothering to translate them and literary terms like "protasis" and "apodosis" that everyone else around the dining table seemed to know. I could not follow the discussion and felt far out of my depth.

That night when I described my inadequacy to my husband, I told him that I liked the people I met; I enjoyed the conversations that briefly preceded and followed the study session, but I was too much of a novice to comprehend such a high level of exposition and would not go back. My husband said, "Nonsense. That's the way you always feel about the first day at anything. Go for a few weeks and then decide." He was right. After a very short while, I felt comfortable asking whoever was leading, "What does that word mean?" And it was not much longer before I was taking my own turn leading.

It is probably fifteen years now that I have been attending the group, and though my turn to lead comes up a couple of times each year, I have not become nonchalant. Instead I am nervous each time. The majority of the members are college professors—history, literature, classics, languages—or have Ph.D.s and do not teach. The remainder are predominately doctors and lawyers, and so I am the only one without a graduate degree and almost the only one who is not fluent in Hebrew and has not had a thorough grounding in the Bible. I think to myself, "How can I tell this crowd anything?" Consequently, I prepare for weeks before my turn so that, if I know nothing else, I feel that I know an hour and a half's worth of interesting opinion about the chapter allotted to me.

First Kings 13, the subject of "Vindicating God," was one of the chapters I drew. It is full of incident and rich with dialogue. It tells of an unnamed prophet, the man of God, who prophesies against King Jeroboam's idolatrous altar in Bethel. The man of God says that one day a descendant of David, Josiah, will come and burn men's bones on this altar. As the ruler orders his men to seize the man of God, the king's hand is paralyzed. The king pleads, the man of God prays for him, and the king recovers. Jeroboam invites the man of God to his house for refreshment and reward, but the man of God refuses, saying that he would not accept the invitation for half of Jeroboam's kingdom, as God has commanded him to neither eat, drink, nor return to his home city by the route he took to Bethel.

As the man of God makes his way home, an individual called the old prophet is told by his sons what the man of God did and said to the king. The old prophet bids his sons to saddle his ass, and he rides to meet the man of God. The old prophet invites the man of God home with him to eat and drink, but the man of God refuses and repeats God's injunction. The old prophet lies to the man of God, saying that an angel has instructed him to be his host. The man of God then accompanies the old prophet and eats and drinks at his house. While still at the table, the old prophet is visited by a true revelation from God. This prophecy proclaims that as the man of God has not obeyed the Lord's commandment, which is now repeated for the third time in the story, his carcass will not be interred in the grave of his ancestors.

The old prophet saddles his ass for his guest (the narrator no longer designates the man of God by his previous prestigious title, although the old prophet continues to refer to him this way), and the duped prophet resumes his journey and is torn and killed, but not eaten, by a lion. When the old prophet hears of this unusual death, he knows that it has been visited on the man of God by the Lord. He has his sons saddle his ass, and he goes to where the lion stands near the uneaten carcass. The old prophet, unmolested by the lion, takes the carcass, buries it in his own grave, makes lamentation for his brother prophet, and tells his sons to bury him in that same grave when he dies. He prophesies that the words of the man of God against Jeroboam's altar will be fulfilled, and he extends the malediction to all the places of prohibited worship in the cities of Samaria. In the epilogue to this chapter, 2 Kings 23:16–18, Josiah burns the bones of past idolaters on the altar in Bethel but orders that the bones of the man of God, and therefore also those of the old prophet, laid together in one grave, remain undisturbed.

To me, it seemed unfair and excessive that God punishes the man of God with violent death and, by denying him rest in his family plot, penalizes him even beyond death. After all, the man of God obediently refused two invitations of hospitality and only acquiesced because he was deceived. And why, to compound the inequity, should God twice reward the lying old prophet with the gift of true prophecy and also spare *his* bones? I knew that it would be against the author's theodicy to depict God as unreasonable and unjust. Therefore, I must have read the chapter with twentieth-century inattention, and so I went carefully back over it.

I had two indications of where to concentrate my close reading. One was the triple repetition of God's command to the man of God not to eat, drink, or retrace his steps. Why did the author need to thrice repeat that directive? The Bible is always so terse; yet here the author says the same thing three times over. But is it always the same thing, or are there subtle, character-revealing differences in each recurrence? On closer inspection, I saw that there are indeed variations in each retelling—variations that, coupled with a better understanding of the man of God's response to Jeroboam's invitation, led me to recognize that prophet's venality. His undoing by the old prophet testifies to W. C. Fields's maxim: "You can't cheat an honest man."

My other hint was all the saddling of the ass that takes place. Usually the author does not bother to inform us of the mundane details of everyday life. When the man of God comes to Bethel, we are not first told that he saddles an ass; he just comes. We do not learn how he gets there; for all we know he could have come on foot. Yet, three times in this chapter we are told about ass-saddling, and I did not feel that I needed to hear about it even once. Or did I need to hear? The biblical author is not fulsome; he charily dispenses information on a need-to-know basis. The saddling must be important to the narrative, but why?

When I noticed who was doing the saddling for whom, I had the key to the old prophet's transformation from liar to God-graced visionary. After God gives him the gift of true prophecy, the old prophet is riven by remorse. His sorrow and shame is shown by his servile attention to the man of God, saddling his ass for him when it was his own habit never to saddle his ass but rather to have his sons perform this labor. Once I recognized this, I could see further evidences of his repentance. The man of God is reduced to a carcass in God's sight; the lying old prophet, by virtue of his atonement, becomes God's messenger. Josiah, in protecting the contents of the man of God and the old prophet's mutual grave, is the Lord's unwitting instrument. It is the conscience-stricken old prophet, not the fallen man of God, in whose honor the bones are spared desecration.

Although I felt now that I understood the chapter, I was still uneasy about my presentation and not sure that my exegesis would occupy an hour and a half. I went to the library to read what scholars had said about it; perhaps there were other nuances that I had missed. Although this chapter is much analyzed, I found, to my amazement, that professional Bible scholars had noticed none of the subtleties—one, for example, says that the man of God refuses Jeroboam and the old prophet "in identical terms" (see below). Another's comments are illogical to the point of absurdity (see notes 21 and 24). I was up in arms; besides these deficiencies, how could academics, versed in biblical theology, suppose that the author would depict God as "demonic." Such a portrait would be antithetic to every other biblical representation of God and would not fit into the narrative. I felt I had to counterpose their conclusions with mine.

A rabbi, in disagreeing with one of my articles, once said to me: "The Bible doesn't mince words; if the author wanted to say what you think he wanted to say, why didn't he just say it, without hinting?" I stood blinking at him. I had no ready response. He was right; the Bible neither minces words nor glosses over sex, violence, or scatological details. When I thought about it, however, I realized that to expect a simplistic level of communication from so consummate an artist was like asking a mystery writer: "When you said the baronet was found murdered in the library, why didn't you just tell us that the butler did it and spare us having to read two hundred pages of hints and clues?" The biblical author, like the mystery writer, seemed to want to excite our consideration, to engage us in participation, to involve us in the pleasure of discovery, and thus to knit us to the text. If that was his plan, it appears to have been successful, as readers return to the Bible again and again, perceiving new insights and penetrating deeper meaning.

[T]he story seems to express a doubtful moral level.[1]

[God] behaves in a manner which violates our sense of justice to the core.[2]

---

[1] Alexander Rofé, *The Prophetical Stories* (Jerusalem: Magnes, 1988), 173.
[2] K. Schwarzwäller, quoted in Walter Gross, "Lying Prophet and Disobedient Man of God in 1 Kings 13: Role Analysis as an Instrument of Theological Interpretation of an OT Narrative Text," *Semeia* 15 (1979): 109.

We must frankly say that the view of God's nature underlying this chapter is crude and insensitive.[3]

Opinion as to the date, form, genre, theme, structure, and provenance of 1 Kings 13 is frequently published and contentiously divided.[4] There is, however, one aspect of this widely discussed text upon which scholars agree. In reviews of the ethical value of the story, God receives bad press. A few of his notices are quoted above; I could have included many more. Disapproval of the representation of God seen in this chapter is a common hermeneutical ground of literary and theological analysts, from Uriel Simon's respectful, though negative, appraisal of God's punishment as harsh and stringent, to James Crenshaw's vehement assessment of God's behavior, which in his view "approaches the demonic."[5]

Sympathetic exegetes describe the man of God as a duped innocent, a gullible, or at least an unwary victim of the old prophet's duplicity. Consequently, they judge the sentence God imposes upon him as disproportionate to his ingenuousness. My purpose is to propose a reading of 1 Kings 13 antithetic to this commiserative evaluation. I argue that, far from innocent, the man of God is a guileful, acquisitive schemer. His avarice, and his open aversion to the return to Judah God demands, incites the old prophet's stratagem and assures its accomplishment. The capital punishment God's faithless messenger receives for his ready capitulation is deserved. Through a close reading of this chapter and analogous texts, I will demonstrate that the author of the narrative confirms rather than violates the reader's sense of God's justice.

When King Jeroboam invites the man of God to his house for refreshment and reward, the man of God responds (vv. 8–9):

> "Even if you give me half your wealth, I will not go in with you, nor will I eat bread or drink water in this place; for so I was commanded by the word of the Lord: You shall eat no bread and drink no water, nor shall you go back by the road by which you came." (NJPS)

Commentators think this rejoinder constitutes a refusal. I contend that it is the second stage of a mutually desired commercial transaction. Jeroboam

---

[3] James M. Robinson, *The First Book of Kings* (CBC 17: Cambridge University Press, 1972), 162.

[4] Histories of interpretation may be found in Werner E. Lemke, "The Way of Obedience: 1 Kings 13 and the Structure of Deuteronomistic History," in *Magnalia Dei, the Mighty Acts of God: Essays on the Bible and Archeology in Memory of G. Ernest Wright* (ed. Frank Moore Cross, Werner E. Lemke, Patrick D. Miller Jr.; Garden City, N. Y.: Doubleday, 1976), 301–4; Uriel Simon, "1 Kings 13: A Prophetic Sign—Denial and Persistence," *HUCA* 47 (1976): 81–85; and Dwight W. Van Winkle, "1 Kings 13: True and False Prophecy," *VT* 29 (1989): 32–33.

[5] Simon, "1 Kings 13," 93, 96; James L. Crenshaw, *Prophetic Conflict: Its Effect upon Israelite Religion* (BZAW 124; Berlin: de Gruyter, 1971), 48.

offers a reward, and the man of God suggests the amount of that reward. For half of Jeroboam's kingdom, he will transgress God's express command and go to work for the king of Bethel. A talented prophet from Judah—who might seem to the populace to confer a southern seal of approval upon the northern king's idolatrous practices, who can readily effect the restoration of withered hands, and who is willing to disobey God in order to enter Jeroboam's employ—is an expensive commodity. The man of God starts the haggling at a high figure, but he may expect to take less than half the kingdom for his services; this is the beginning of the bargaining.

The manner in which the man of God's proposition is expressed is typical of the "no means yes" style of face-saving monetary negotiation we see elsewhere in the Bible. The terms of a deal are formulated negatively so that either party may withdraw without loss of dignity or prestige. In Genesis 23:4–16 Abraham wishes to buy a burying-place. The seller first affects to refuse the sale and offers the field to Abraham as a gift. Then, in v. 15, though still maintaining that the field is as nothing between friends, he names his price, four hundred shekels. In v. 16 we are told that Abraham gives the seller his announced price, and the four hundred shekel amount is reiterated. The Bible does not unnecessarily and verbosely record the common practice of the day; surely, the price is twice mentioned here because it is unusual for a buyer to pay the full stipulated price with no further bargaining.

In 2 Samuel 24:21–24 we see another instance of this conventional negotiating custom of feigned reluctance. King David wants to buy Araunah's threshing-floor. Araunah disdains to name a price, but in vv. 22–23 offers the king whatever seems good to him as a gift. Correctly performing his part, David disregards Araunah's politely assumed antipathy to commerce and pays him fifty shekels for his threshing-floor and oxen.

The most apposite example of a "no" answer that actually signifies "yes, at the stated price" is the pagan prophet Balaam's response to King Balak in Numbers 22:18: "Though Balak were to give me his house full of silver and gold, I could not do anything, big or little, contrary to the command of the Lord my God." Here Balaam starts the haggling at an even higher level than does the man of God. Rashi, the great medieval exegete, sensitive to the biblical social institution of the face-saving business deal, says:

> This tells us that he [Balaam] was avaricious and covetous of other people's wealth. He said: He ought to give me all his silver and gold, for behold, he would have to hire many armies. It is doubtful whether he would conquer or not conquer, but "I" would certainly conquer.[6]

Rashi says nothing about the man of God's similar entrepreneurship. Perhaps he was disinclined to ascribe venality to a man of God. We learn,

---

[6] Abraham M. Silbermann, *Chumash with Rashi's Commentary* (Jerusalem: Silbermann Family, 1934), 109.

however, from God's denunciation in 1 Kings 13:21–22 that the man of God is not above sin. Moses and David, each called "man of God," sin and are punished for their sins.[7] The title does not guarantee innocence.[8]

Had the man of God sincerely despised Jeroboam's wealth, he could have refused his offer in unambiguous words that left no opening for further negotiation. In Genesis 14:23 Abraham (then Abram) firmly refuses to accept so much as a "thread or a sandal-strap" from the king of Sodom. Instead of naming his price, Abraham names items of trivial value. In 2 Kings 5:16 the prophet Elisha, despite urging, unequivocally rejects the proffered gift of the idol-worshiping king of Aram with the statement, "As the Lord lives, whom I serve, I will not accept anything."

Even without these examples of conventional commercial exchange and of genuinely disinterested refusal, it becomes evident that employment was the delicately couched message of the king's overture and of the man of God's response when the offer of reward is abandoned. Most interpreters posit that gratitude is the king's motivation for the invitation and offer of reward.[9] If so, he would still want to reward the man of God even after his hospitality had been declined. Jeroboam may not have brought gold and silver with him to the altar, but certainly a king would possess some token with which to reward the restorer of his hand—a robe, a ring, a horse. Ostensibly, the man of God has refused only to go home with Jeroboam and to eat and drink in Bethel.[10] He reports that God's charge forbids him to do these things, but he does not say that he is forbidden to accept a gift; the king could still reward him.

No further mention is made of reward because Jeroboam recognizes the man of God's greedy ploy and withdraws from the transaction. He may have been willing to pay the prophet by the job, or even to hire him at a more modest wage, but so hefty a retainer is out of the question.[11] Jeroboam retreats from the deal with no loss of face as, to all appearances,

---

[7] For references to Moses as "man of God": Deuteronomy 33:1; Joshua 14:6; Psalm 90:1; Ezra 3:2; 1 Chronicles 23:14; 2 Chronicles 30:16. For references to David as "man of God": Nehemiah 12:24, 36; 2 Chronicles 8:14.

[8] Compare Rofé, *The Prophetical Stories,* 177: "By the use of these terms the author apparently wished to underline his conviction that the man belongs to God, much as an angel belongs to his sender."

[9] Though gratitude is the stimulus most frequently mentioned, scholars have suggested several different incentives. These opinions are documented in Gross, "Lying Prophet," 120; Thomas Dozeman, "The Way of the Man of God from Judah: True and False Prophecy in the Pre-Deuteronomic Legend of 1 Kings 13," *CBQ* 44 (1992): 384 n. 23; and Jerome Walsh, "The Contents of 1 Kings 13," *VT* 39 (1989): 358 n. 6.

[10] Against Robert Cohn who states that the man of God refused the king's reward ("Literary Technique in the Jeroboam Narrative," *ZAW* 97 [1985]: 32).

[11] References to piece-work payment for prophecy are made in 1 Samuel 9:7–8; 1 Kings 14:3; and 2 Kings 5:15. Nathan and Abiathar, however, seem to have been salaried members of David's court.

obedience to God required the man of God's refusal. Since his terms were set forth in the negative, the man of God too preserves his self-esteem when his conditions are not met. Bystanders have heard him refuse the king; they have not heard the king refuse him.

There are parties, however, who understand the implicit significance of the veiled conversation. In 1 Kings 13:11 we are told that a son of an old prophet of Bethel tells his father all the works the man of God did that day. The old prophet's other sons, perhaps older and more worldly, tell him all the words the man of God spoke to the king. Some commentators maintain that the differentiation between a singular "son" reporting the man of God's works and plural "sons" reporting his words is an error.[12] I think a sentence may contain one scribal error, but hardly six. In referring to the report of the works, the Hebrew words for "came" and "told" are singular in agreement with "son," and in referring to the report of the words offered by the *sons*, the verb "told" is plural and the suffix to "father" (i.e., "their" father) is plural. I conclude that the distinction is purposefully intended to indicate that the issue of overriding interest to the old prophet is the man of God's willingness to remain in Bethel in defiance of God's command, not his ability to heal a withered hand.

This intention is further underlined by the duplicate use of the verb for "tell" (ספר rather than the much more common נגד). The verb ספר is typically used to recount a dream, a genealogy, the Passover story, or the words of God—that is, when the transmission of every detail is important. This verb is used to describe the man of God's acts, and it is needlessly repeated in the last clause of v. 11 solely in reference to the man of God's words, stressing their importance. The son (or sons) could have told about both the works and the words with just one use of the verb. Nowhere else in the Bible is the relating of the words of an episode given prominence by distinguishing them from the relating of the action.[13]

The old prophet pursues the wonder-worker, and, on finding him, asks if he is the man of God (v. 14). As Thomas Dozeman points out, this question has a double meaning.[14] It may be used both to identify the man and to query his adherence to his commission. The man of God responds affirmatively, but, possibly realizing the imprecision of his question, the old prophet probes with greater specificity. He invites the man of God to his home for bread (v. 15). With this invitation he can discern if the Lord truly

---

[12] For example, "The text of vv. 11–12 is either corrupt or simply confused in speaking first of a single son and then of several" (Simon De Vries, *1 Kings* [WBC 12; Waco, Tex.: Word, 1985], 171).

[13] See Joshua 2:23, in which Joshua's spies return from their adventures and conversations with the harlot and tell (ספר) him "all that had befallen them" (literally, "all they had found, come upon") and Esther 6:13 in which Haman, after his interview with the king and his arraying of Mordecai, recounts (ספר) to his wife and his friends, "everything that had befallen him."

[14] Dozeman, "The Way of the Man of God," 388.

prohibited the man of God from eating, drinking, and retracing his steps in Bethel and if the man of God is still faithful to this command.[15]

The threefold enunciation of God's prohibition in vv. 8–9, 16–17, and 22 has been much discussed by interpreters. The majority state that the re-iteration serves to emphasize the primacy of God's word.[16] In a general analysis of the biblical uses of repetition, however, Robert Alter says:

> [E]ntire statements are repeated . . . with small but important changes intro-duced in what usually looks at first glance like verbatim repetition.

> Broadly, when repetitions with significant variations occur in biblical narra-tive, the changes introduced can point . . . to some unexpected, perhaps unset-tling, new revelation of character or plot.[17]

God's word is certainly important in our pericope, but I believe the pri-mary function of the triple repetition is the introduction of slight, but pregnant, variations that enhance the characterization of the man of God and clarify any ambiguity for the old prophet and for the reader.

In v. 8, responding to Jeroboam, the man of God said לא אבא ("I will not go"). In v. 16 he answers the old prophet's invitation with the words לא אוכל ("I may not," "I am not able"). The contrast thus made between volition and compulsion is obvious; he would go with the old prophet and accept his hospitality if only he could.[18] If he were ever resolved to obey God's command, he is resolved no longer.

Another revealing disparity between the man of God's answer to Jeroboam and his answer to the old prophet lies in the use of the Hebrew locution "with you." Although את and עם are synonyms for "with," their connotations differ. According to BDB (87), את "expresses closer asso-ciation" than עם. The preposition את is used to suggest fraternity, ideo-logical union, and even close spiritual communion as in "Noah walked with God" (Genesis 6:9). In his reply to Jeroboam, the man of God said "with you" only once and used the impersonal עם (1 Kings 13:8). In replying to the old prophet, the man of God repeats "with you" three times and uses the intimate את term each time. The insistent tap, tap, tap of the comradely "with you," thrice repeated, sounds a counter mes-sage to the plain sense of v. 16. Subtly, and without explicit exposition, the old prophet is made conscious of the man of God's intense longing to join him.

---

[15] Abarbanel suggests that the man of God may have dissembled in his reply to the king's invitation because he did not wish to accept his hospitality (cited in Adolph J. Rosenberg, *1 Kings, A New English Translation of the Text, Rashi and Commentary Digest* [New York: Judaica, 1980], 148).

[16] Compare Rofé, *The Prophetical Stories*, 174; Van Winkle, "1 Kings 13," 36.

[17] Robert Alter, *The Art of Biblical Narrative* (New York: Basic, 1981), 97–98.

[18] See 1 Kings 20:9 for another example of the expressive contrast between "will" and "may."

That this longing is not impelled by simple hunger or thirst is indicated by the man of God's retention of a firm "I will not" for eating and drinking with the old prophet as well as by his use of the supplementary, seemingly unnecessary, verb שוב ("turn back," "return," "apostatize"). He told the king he would not בוא ("go"); he informs the old prophet both that he is unable to שוב and to בוא. Alerted by novelty and redundancy in this variant, the reader notices that the word בוא is used only after the evocative שוב. Precedence, and thus consequence, is given to a verb that is frequently used to denote apostasy (BDB, 997). Clearly, the man of God is contemplating something other than refreshment.

There is one more telling discrepancy between his original assertion to Jeroboam and his restatement to the old prophet. In the restatement, the man of God diminishes the very gravity of God's command with a subtle change of verb; צוה ("commanded") in v. 9 is downgraded in v. 17 to merely דבר ("said"). It is as though the prohibition were no longer a strict commandment but just a casual remark spoken in passing—as one cautions a prospective traveler to some parts of the world not to drink the water.

From the evidence advanced above, I infer that the man of God is anxious to return with the old prophet because he prefers to defect to Bethel and unite with its inhabitants in apostasy. After all, conditions in Judah are not so pleasant. The previous chapter describes the king of Judah's tyranny, the onerous corvée, and the civil strife. Life is hard in Judah; perhaps it will be easier in Bethel. Simon observes that by the rejection of the old prophet's invitation "in identical terms," the second refusal serves to stress that "the resistance of the man of God to temptation had not weakened."[19] On the contrary, I argue that the man of God was tempted by the king's reward, and the variance in the terms of his second response imparts that he is further tempted by the old prophet's invitation despite the absence of a gift offer.

The divergence between the man of God's answer to the king and his answer to the old prophet supports the latter's suspicion of corruption. Relieved of uncertainty, he confidently proclaims (and forewarns), "I am also a prophet, like you" (v. 18, my translation). He uses both גם ("also") and כמוך ("like you") to affirm not only that he is also a prophet but that he is just such a prophet as the man of God—a prophet with his back to God and his eye on material advantage.[20]

The old prophet tells the man of God that he was instructed by God's word to be his host (v. 18). The old prophet lies, but he can excuse his lie with the rationalization that the man of God is ready to be enticed, desires it, and certainly, by his cupidity, deserves it. Perhaps the old prophet would not have attempted deceit had the man of God shown constancy.

---

[19] Simon, "1 Kings 13," 108.
[20] Against Rofé who says that the old prophet "compares himself to the Man of God almost by chance" (*The Prophetical Stories,* 181).

And, had the man of God been steadfast, he would not have been swayed by a falsehood from a functionary of an idolatrous city. The faltering dedication of the man of God provides the old prophet with his opportunity, his justification, and his success.

The old prophet's motivation in waylaying the man of God and bringing him home has been disputed. Hospitality is often proposed.[21] Simon writes that the old prophet wishes to cast doubt on the word of the Lord by tricking the man of God into contravening the sign representing that word.[22] According to my analysis, upon hearing of his words to King Jeroboam, the old prophet suspects that the man of God is covetous and willing to establish a prophetic practice in Bethel. After his own conversation with the man of God validates this supposition, he wants him for a business partner. Who could be a more desirable addition to a visionary firm than one who has so spectacularly established his powers before king and subjects?

God condemns the man of God before any partnership proposition is made. A variation in this third repetition of the prohibition in vv. 21–22 serves as an added reproof to the man of God for his substitution of "said" for "commanded." God's censure of the man of God uses צוה, the root for "command," twice ("commandment," "commanded"). There is no question that the prohibition had the solemn status of a commandment, for God's forceful rhetoric makes it doubly clear.

The word "commandment" used in the singular to signify other than the Ten Commandments or the entire Mosaic law is rare in the Hebrew Bible.[23] Its only other such use in the MT is in 1 Samuel 13:13. Here King Saul breaches God's instruction to refrain from making a burnt-offering until joined by Samuel in Gilgal. Saul's punishment is that his kingdom is torn from him.[24] The man of God's punishment is more severe—a fate

---

[21] Lists of possible motives may be found in Gross, "Lying Prophet," 121 and Simon, "1 Kings 13," 92 n. 30. Erik Eynikel published a problematic hypothesis subsequent to these lists. He states that the old prophet's motivation was to shield his own bones from desecration by having them buried in a common grave with the "pious Judean." The old prophet lied in order to provoke the man of God's transgression. Eynikel does not explain how the old prophet was so prescient as to know that the man of God's punishment would be death, that it would occur before the old prophet's demise, that it would take place sufficiently near Bethel for the old prophet to hear of it, that its manner would be such as to preserve the bones for burial, that the corpse would be recoverable, and that the joint sepulcher of the two sinners would not be violated ("Prophecy and Fulfillment in the Deuteronomistic History," in *Pentateuchal and Deuteronomistic Studies: Papers read at the 13th IOSOT Congress, Leuven, 1989* (ed. Christianus Brekelmans and Johan Lust; Leuven: Leuven University Press, 1990, 234).

[22] Simon, "1 Kings 13," 92.

[23] For a fuller discussion of the use of this term, see Gross, "Lying Prophet," 104.

[24] Eynikel's theory (see note 21 above), depends upon the old prophet's conviction that transgression of God's unusual command will result in the man of God's premature death. The precedent set here of non-capital punishment for the

even worse than violent and untimely death: his body is never to lie in the grave of his fathers (1 Kings 13:22).[25] In the Hebrew Bible men are not chastened for lust in the heart, secret thoughts, furtive avidity; they are penalized solely for their acts. The man of God is punished explicitly for violating God's word, but, in pronouncing sentence, God may take motive into account. The author intimates the man of God's hidden agenda in his first words to Jeroboam; succeeding narration and dialogue corroborate the initial insinuation of the miracle-worker's rapacity. The narrator's art reveals the man's inner inclination and discloses that he is not an unwitting target of chicanery but a predisposed participant in disobedience. Is God unfair to castigate one who so eagerly renounces his commandment and traduces his lofty mission? The punishment is stern because it extends beyond death, but it is not unjust.

In the epilogue to our chapter, 2 Kings 23:17–18, Josiah forbids degradation of the man of God's ossuary, and, consequently, the old prophet's bones are also rescued. The proscription is evidently based on the man of God's earlier standing and the fulfillment of his prophesy. Scholars therefore assume that the man of God's status secures the integrity of the prophets' tomb, for the passage of years has somehow brought God to forgive his emissary's transgression and to reward his bones with continued rest.[26] In opposition to this conclusion, I propose that it is the old prophet who finds favor with God and whose merits safeguard the joint sepulcher.

In 1 Kings 13:21 the old prophet transmits God's denunciation of the disobedient messenger; in v. 32 he endorses the man of God's prophesy and extends the malediction to "all the cult places in the towns of Samaria." His appointment as bearer of God's word and his ability to amplify the man of God's revelation attest that he has now become God's agent in Bethel. The culmination of his forecast in the man of God's supernatural death and the destruction of the altars in Samaria (2 Kings 23:19) confirms his divine assignment.[27]

Almost a third of 1 Kings 13 is devoted to demonstration of the old prophet's profound contrition—as exemplified by his self-abasement in saddling an ass for the man of God,[28] by his courage in braving the lion to

---

infraction of the only similar special ordinance would have weakened, if not precluded, such certainty.

[25] We learn the importance of being buried with, or sleeping with, one's fathers from the frequent repetition of these phrases throughout the Bible; they are repeated thirty-five times in 1 and 2 Kings alone.

[26] For example, an analysis of the reversal in the man of God's destiny and his final revelation as a "salvific figure" may be found in Walsh, "The Contents of 1 Kings 13," 360–61.

[27] Commentators agree that it would have been natural for a lion to devour his kill.

[28] Verses 13 and 27, in which he bids his sons to saddle his ass, evidence that it is not the old prophet's custom to perform this subservient office.

recover the corpse (scornfully labeled נבלה, "carcass," ten times in six verses by the word of the Lord and by the narrator), by his remorse in lamenting the death, and by his charity in interring the deceased in his own burial place.[29] The specific causal dependency of his burial instructions upon his confidence in the inevitable outcome of the man of God's prediction, "Lay my bones beside his, for (כי) what he announced . . . will surely come true" (vv. 31–32), points to prophetic foreknowledge of his own body's sanctity. Posthumously sheltering the man of God's bones is the last reparation he can render the man to whom he lied. If there is to be enduring stability of the grave, it is the old prophet's responsibility to provide it; he has heard God's rigorous admonition and demeaning invective and knows that the "carcass" cannot be depended upon for asylum. Even had the old prophet no prevision of the eventual preservation of their shared resting-place, his request to be laid humbly beside his "brother" sinner evinces a heart changed from that of the selfish liar of v. 18.

Despite Josiah's intention in sparing the bones, the considerations adduced above testify that immunity for the common reliquary is not achieved by virtue of the man of God. Unknown to Josiah, but known to God and to the reader, the old prophet's penitence justifies the conservation of the combined relics and results in undisturbed peace for the remains of both men. Though Josiah issues the command preventing disruption of the tomb, he is but the human intermediary for God's judgment. This ironic denouement advances the tenets that only repentance earns forgiveness and that God's will, not man's, prevails in history.

---

[29] According to BDB (615), נבלה (vv. 22, 24–25, and 28–30) is used to designate the bodies of animals, idols, and sinners. The translation, "corpse," given in *Tanakh* is insufficiently denigrative.

Afterword

In grade school and high school I was taught that the correct way to write an essay was to start with an outline. This doctrine was reiterated in my college English class too, but constructing outlines is tedious and difficult, and I always felt I could organize my thoughts well enough without one. The students in the university class, however, were required to show their rough drafts to the professor to be vetted before they typed their fair copies. When I brought in my first rough draft, the professor asked to see my outline. I told him, "I never bother with an outline."

"The trouble with you, Miss Tamarkin," he said, "is that you think you're 'too bright and good for human nature's daily food.'"

The accuracy of my professor's assessment dumbfounded me; I could make no response. I recognized the quotation from Wordsworth's "She Was a Phantom of Delight." The poem was anthologized in Francis Palgrave's *Golden Treasury,* a book I had grown up with, but I could not remember—in the embarrassment of the rebuke and the novelty of being addressed as "Miss Tamarkin"—whether Wordsworth thought being too bright and good for human nature's daily food was a plus or a minus. From my teacher's tone and his preamble: "The trouble with you is," I knew *he* thought it was a minus. But I could not help thinking: "Of course, I think I'm too bright and good for human nature's daily food. How can you, of all people, not think so too?" Though all the freshman in the university were required to take English, this professor's class was limited to the twenty or so students who had passed a qualifying examination for "Advanced Composition." As far as I was concerned, this achievement alone should have set me above human nature's daily food in his estimation. Besides, my parents' fond affirmation of all five of their children's brightness and goodness had convinced me long ago of my status vis-à-vis everyday edibles.

I had the sense to confine my self-esteem to myself and made appropriately apologetic and acquiescent murmurs as my professor expanded on the absolute necessity of an outline. For the next essay, I tried hard to compose one, but as the deadline for providing the rough draft neared, I gave up, wrote my draft, and extracted an outline from it afterwards. My professor was happy, and I was happy. I furnished a post hoc outline for each subsequent assignment as well. Advanced Composition taught me that no one can tell anyone else how to write; what worked for my professor did not work for me.

Nowadays, I delay starting essays for fear I will not find the words to express my meaning and will not present my hypothesis well enough to convince others. To force myself to write, I reserve my thoughts, holding them in, until I can keep them in no longer. If I talk at all about my ideas, if I confide the juicy gossip, the startling revelation, the case for the prosecution or the evidence for the defense, all the air seems to go out of my reasoning. Once I decrease the mental pressure by verbalizing my thoughts, I am no longer driven to write them.

When I am pumped full of inspiration and feeling ready to burst, I plan my first sentence. Just one sentence is not too scary. I try to think of one that will initiate my argument and will also make the reader wonder what could be coming next. Before I type it, I place *Merriam-Webster's Collegiate Dictionary* next to my computer with the reassuring, "All the words you're going to need are right here." The prepared first sentence dictates the second, and each statement leads to the next until I get stuck. I push down my rising fear by saying, "Think what you want to say, and then say it; you don't have to make it good." This is my writing mantra. If I thought I had to make my writing good, I would dither forever over how to go about it. Whenever I get stuck, I think what I want to say, and then I say it. That is all.

It is only after I have written my rough draft and my fair copy that I look for help. And I look first to my husband, Ronnie. I know what I meant to prove, but did I made my case clear to someone who has not been brooding over my argument night and day for months, someone unfamiliar with the biblical passage in question, someone who knows nothing of the conventional interpretation my essay contests? Is my discussion as exciting and compelling as it seems to me, or are there boring stretches, sentences that must be read two or three times before their meaning is apprehended, repetitive patches of exposition? I want Ronnie to catch these lapses for me, and mostly he does, and mostly his comments irritate me. "What does *he* know about it," I ask myself.

Ronnie's critical pencil unerringly crosses out just those parts of my essay I like the best—the apt word, the amusing phrase, the antagonistic footnote designed to mortify rival biblical scholars. "Too fancy," "too cute," "too mean," he writes in the margin. How much gratitude do I owe to one who abandons whatever he is doing, reads every article the minute I finish it, and is rewarded for his thoughtful analysis by opposition each and every time? I explain to him, coldly, that the word I used is a perfectly common (and even, household) word, that my wit may elude him but plenty of other people think I am a riot, and that footnote warfare is the standard in academe. And then I go back to the computer, go over my essay again, and find that Ronnie is not so wrong. In fact, he's right.

My next readers are my brother, Maurry Tamarkin, and my daughter, Elizabeth Reis. I am not so defensive about their criticism. Perhaps they proffer their remarks more cautiously. Maurry is my younger brother, and I have not hit him in decades, nor grounded my daughter, but they may nevertheless regard me with more deference than obtains in a marriage.

Although they live 3,000 miles apart and do not confer on their recommendations, they always tell me the same thing, and I always need to be told: get your thesis up front. My natural inclination is to try to surprise and astonish the reader by describing all the other commentators' analyses, pointing out the problems attendant upon their solutions of biblical cruxes, and whipping out my resolution with a flourish and a great "Tada." "Boring," my brother and daughter say. "Tell your audience what you want to prove, and then, in proving it, take them with you." I am grateful for the good advice Lizzie and Maurry give me, for the perceptive insights that improve my text, and for the enthusiastic attention they give to my work.

On the day of Lizzie's wedding to Matthew Dennis, I said to her, "Lizzie, you're doing the right thing." I was thinking only of Matt's personal qualities; I did not know then that he was a line-editor par excellence. After I wrote my first article and sent it to Lizzie for her critique, Matt asked her if she thought her mother would mind if he looked it over. Would I mind? I was happy if anyone wanted to read it. When I got it back from Matt, all polka dot with red ink and with his sensitive and astute suggestions in teeny, tiny script in the margins, I knew just how the spider felt when the fly ventured into her parlor. The Lord has delivered him into my hands, I thought, and approved of my daughter's choice even more emphatically.

It has become part of Matt's duty as a son-in-law to edit my articles. Once or twice I have brought an article with me to Oregon (Lizzie and Matt are professors of history at the University of Oregon) and felt guilty when I saw how much the editing job imposed on his crowded schedule—but not so guilty that I did not want him to do it. No dangling clause or errant comma is safe from him, and he knows all the rules, however arcane, for punctuating citations, but it is not his command of grammar and punctuation that endears him to me as an editor, it is the seriousness that he brings to the task. Far from defending my writing from him, I trust his taste and judgment because I know that he gives my every sentence his earnest consideration and because he catches infelicities that others do not. My appreciation for his deft editing and for his painstaking diligence cannot be overstated.

My son, David, told me that he wanted to be mentioned in this book, and I have already referred to him a couple of times. He is my darling boy, but he is useless to me as a critic because his comments invariably match his dad's. Obviously he was not switched in the maternity ward, because, exactly like Ronnie, he objects to recondite words, to any attempt at humor, and to vicious footnotes. I am grateful, despite the duplication, for his interest in my work.

My other regular readers are Donna Dalnekoff, a friend from the Shabbos Group, and Alvin Wainhaus, the rabbi who taught me the *aleph-bet*. I can get pretty much any breezy biblical, talmudic, or midrashic generalization past my family, but Donna and Alvin are too knowledgeable to accept as gospel whatever I assert about these sources. Not only have they prevented stupid mistakes, but they have also suggested verses, corroborative of my hypothesis, that I missed. This is not to claim that either of them agrees with my analyses. Often, they do not. With each article, I am convinced that I have discerned the author's intent. I never think that I am advancing one possible reading; I am always certain that, given the textual evidence, mine is the only possible reading. It is difficult for me to understand how anyone can maintain an opinion contrary to mine, but Donna and Alvin are more generous than I. They both help willingly despite their disagreement, and I am indebted to them for their encouragement and expertise.

P. T. R.
Branford, Connecticut

Index of Names and Subjects

documentary hypothesis. *See* source criticism

Doeg, 133, 135–37, 136n7, 138–39, 140–45

Dozeman, Thomas, 73n52, 74n52, 81n78, 203n9, 204, 204n14

Driver, Samuel R., 157n24

drunkenness, 75–76, 75n61, 76n63, 79

Edelman, Diana, 136n7, 138, 138n14, 152n10, 158n27, 159n31

Eliot, T.S., 6

Elisha, 203

Elohim, 5, 8, 18, 26, 71, 73, 73n51

Enoch, 80

Ephraim, 74n57

Esau, 47, 49, 51, 102

Eve, 24, 28, 35, 115

exodus parallels, 41–2, 57–58, 81–86, 100

Exum, J. Cheryl: female victimhood, 58n2, 67n29, 117n27, 119n30, 121n37, 124n42, 125n47; Jephthah, 110nn3–4; Jephthah's daughter, 118n29; nature of sacrifice, 112n12, 124, 124n45

Eynikel, Erik, 207nn21, 24

Fagen, Ruth, 27–29, 35, 54, 105, 126n52

Fensham, Frank C., 77, 77n66

fertility strategies, 56–57, 60–62, 60n8, 61nn8–9, 13, 66n27

Fewell, Danna, 118n27, 127n56, 194n76

Fields, W.C., 199

The First Hebrew Primer for Adults (Stahl), 3

Fokkelman, Jan: Absalom, 192, 192n71; Ahimelech, 137n12, 143, 143n39, 144, 144nn40, 42; David with Abigail, 183n38; David's flight from Saul, 135–36, 135nn2, 4, 136n6, 140, 140nn21, 23, 142, 142n31; direct object indicator, 186n49; Doeg's loyalties, 136n7; Goliath's sword, 142; half-sibling marriage, 175, 175n6; heart-cakes, 178, 178n16, 179n20; marriageability of non-virgins, 189, 189n60; Saul, 155, 155n21, 157n24; Tamar and Amnon, 181, 181n28, 192; the witch of Endor,

150–52, 151n2, 152n9, 159, 159n33, 162, 162n41

food details: feast definitions, 75, 75n60, 162; five loaves of bread, 139–41; heart-cakes, 169, 172–74, 178–82, 179n20, 180n24, 185, 193–94; "morsel of bread," 159, 162–63, 162n40; shewbread, 135–36, 140–41, 141nn25, 27; unleavened bread, 148–49, 162, 166; witch of Endor's menu, 159–60, 161–66. *See also* ritual meals

Fox, Everett, 31n1, 75n60

Fox, Michael, 178n17

Freedman, David, 187n53

Gaon, Saadia, 154

Garfinkel, Stephen, 114n17

Gershom, 82

Gerstein, Beth, 120n35, 127n53

Ginott, Haim, 117n27

Goliath, 140, 164

Goliath's sword, 131, 133, 136, 140–43, 142n30, 145

Gordon, Cynthia, 64n22, 68nn33–34

graves, 198, 202, 208–9

Grintz, Jehoshua M., 153, 153n12

Gruber, Mayer, 34, 35n16

Gunkel, Hermann: adoption, 61n9; Hagar, 72, 72nn44, 47; Ishmael, 78n70; Sarah, 65n23, 78n70, 80, 80n77; scribal error, 66n28

Gunn, David, 118n27, 127n56, 151, 151n5, 160, 179n21, 194n76

Habermann, Abraham M., 31–32, 32n4

Hackett, Jo Ann, 64n22, 67n30, 74n56, 75, 75n59

Hagar: Abraham's indifference to, 48, 53, 68–69, 68n33, 76–79, 81, 83; character of, 65–68, 69–73, 71n42, 79–80; memorialized in Sabbath law, 83–86; and Moses parallels, 57–58, 81–86; nationality, 48, 74n57, 84–86; offenses against Sarah, 48, 64–68, 79–80; as pagan, 73, 73nn51–52, 80; Sarah's abuse of, 48–49, 51, 68–69, 82–84; status, 60, 62–63, 87

Hagelia, Hallvard, 82n80

Haman, 204n13

Hamilton, Victor, 74n56, 78, 78n72

Index of Ancient Sources